# HOW TO BECOME A COMPLETE GOLFER

## Revised Edition

By **BOB TOSKI** and **JIM FLICK**
with Larry Dennis

Illustrations by Jim McQueen
Photographs by Leonard Kamsler
and Steve Szurlej

A GOLF DIGEST BOOK

# CONTENTS

Published by Golf Digest/Tennis, Inc.
A New York Times Company
495 Westport Avenue
P.O. Box 5350
Norwalk, Connecticut 06856

Trade book distribution by
Simon and Schuster, A Division
of Simon and Schuster, Inc.
Simon and Schuster Building
Rockefeller Center
1230 Avenue of the Americas
New York, New York 10020

Revised edition, 1984
ISBN: 0-914178-65-2
Library of Congress: 83-83247
Manufactured in the
    United States of America

# PROLOGUE

This revised edition of *How to Become a Complete Golfer* is necessary and important because it reflects our desire—and the sincere desire of all the teachers in the Golf Digest Instruction Schools program —to constantly better our methodology and ways of communication in helping all types of students improve their golf games.

Playing is a skill and teaching is an art. The instructors in the Golf Digest program have learned to do both very well. We live by a simple credo—*we who teach must never cease to learn.* We constantly try to live up to those words and have accepted, with dedication and determination, the challenge of improving the playing ability of the masses of golfers all over the world. Because of this attitude, and because of the ceaseless interchange of ideas in the teacher-pupil relationship from week to week in our schools, a new and better way of teaching every facet of the game has evolved. We feel it is important to share with you this knowledge and improvement in our school system through the revisions in our book.

We sincerely hope you will find the revised edition of *How to Become a Complete Golfer* exciting and beneficial in learning and playing the game of golf. All the answers, of course, are not in the book. There is no substitute for intelligent supervised instruction, and we hope that after reading this book

you will be motivated to further improve your game by seeking out a qualified teacher. We hoped that you will accept the need for change and give it a chance, because change takes time. With time, coupled with correct change, you can cure most problems.

Perfection, in golf as in life, is unattainable. But with the new knowledge imparted herein, we are trying to get just a little closer to the end of that rainbow of perfection.

*—Bob Toski and Jim Flick*

# FOREWORD

Bob Toski and Jim Flick met in 1956, when Flick was a first-year professional. The relationship did not exactly get off to a rousing start. Flick had invited Toski to give an exhibition at his Connersville (Ind.) club, but because he had failed to send a follow-up letter, Toski never showed before the crowd of 3,000—much to Flick's embarrassment.

Fortunately for all of us, Toski and Flick have since established a remarkable relationship. Over the years, they have worked together in seminars for the Professional Golfers' Association and the National Golf Foundation, to which they devote much time.

Since 1973, they have teamed together in the Golf Digest Instruction Schools, a partnership that has been beneficial not only to thousands of students, but to the two teachers themselves. In these laboratories, working with men and women of all ages, sizes, shapes and handicap levels, Toski and Flick have tested and refined their instructional philosophies. Their methodology is an evolving one, changing as they learn more about the golf swing and what makes it work most effectively for most players. Their ideas have grown remarkably alike, not so much because they agree on theory, but because they have seen those theories succeed in helping golfers learn.

It was in 1973, too, that I met Toski and Flick. In the 11 years since, it has been my privilege to work with them on articles for Golf Digest, to listen to them discuss golf and how to play it better, and to watch them work their magic in the schools and individual lessons.

Seeing them teach is an education in itself. It would be hard to find two more dissimilar styles and personalities. Toski is the more flamboyant, an emotionally involved showman who searches intensely for a way to get through to each student—a word picture, a physical sensation, an analogy that will drive his point across. Once, trying to help a strong, muscular man develop sensitivity and feeling, Toski bit him on the arm. He has since resisted such carnivorous tendencies, but he remains the most innovative teacher I have ever seen.

To my knowledge, Jim Flick has never bitten anyone. Quiet and patient, he uses a soft sense of humor and impeccable logic to communicate with his students. The show is less spectacular, but the results are as impressive.

*Communication* is the byword for both these men, as it is for any good teacher. While they have considerable knowledge of the game, it is their talent for imparting that knowledge that is the secret to their success. They would be effective college physics professors, if that were their field, because they are teachers first, golf professionals second.

Typical of the scholars they are, Toski and Flick never cease their research into how golf can be played better and taught better. Perhaps the most significant attribute each has is an open mind. They will listen to ideas from virtually anyone —doctors, engineers, other teachers and players—evaluating and testing to see if they are valid. To them, the one way to play golf is the way that works best, and they are constant seekers.

One person Toski and Flick listen to a lot is Peter Kostis. A member of Golf Digest's Professional Teaching Panel and a head instructor in the magazine's schools, the 37-year-old Kostis is a graduate engineer and possesses one of the game's most inquisitive intellects. He is also a tour-caliber player who has chosen to devote his life to teaching.

Says Toski: "In a few years, Peter Kostis will be the best teacher in the world."

Kostis was asked to help with this book, and his input adds immeasurable value. It is typical of Toski and Flick that they would seek this kind of help. Their goal is always to deliver a better product, whether it be to a student on the lesson tee or a reader, and Kostis' contribution has made this book an infinitely better product.

Why this book? For that matter, why any written instruction at all, when it is apparent that face-to-face lessons are the more productive

way to go? Toski answers: "Written instruction material serves an important purpose for the millions of people who play golf. It is a complement to personal instruction if it enhances their understanding of the movements they must make in the swing and the knowledge they must have to improve their skills as golfers.

"The average golfer will read far more instructional material than he will get from a professional on the lesson tee. If he studies that material thoughtfully, he has a better chance of relating to the professional instruction he receives on the lesson tee—providing, of course, that the instruction comes from a competent teacher."

This volume offers between two covers the complete knowledge of, in my opinion, the two finest teachers in the game today. For Toski and Flick, it is their *magnum opus*.

This is not a book to be skimmed, to be read in an evening. It is to be studied carefully and absorbed, to be read and re-read. If you do this, you will acquire a knowledge of how to play golf, to do with that knowledge what you will. If you are willing to follow the precepts offered, you can, as the title suggests, become a "complete" golfer.

The original book was well more than a year in the making, and the revision has required several additional months. Writing it has been the most difficult task of my professional career and assembling this body of knowledge in logical, readable form a mind-boggling ordeal. Yet at the same time, it has been an enriching experience. What I thought I knew about the game pales in comparison to what I have learned by writing this book.

If you, the reader, can learn half as much by reading it, we all will have taken a giant step down the road toward our goal—playing golf a better way.

*Larry Dennis*
*Huntington, Connecticut*
*March, 1984*

## BOB TOSKI

Golf has been in my blood since I was a small child. My mother passed away in childbirth when I was 6 and my two older brothers, Jack and Ben, often took me to spend the day at Northampton Country Club in Leeds, Mass., where they were assistant professionals. They still are pros, as is my older brother, Tom, which may make us the largest group of brother professionals around.

I had a nine-hole course around my house—over an apple tree, across the street, between two lilac bushes . . . The longest hole was about 30 yards and I believe a lot of

## JIM FLICK

I grew up in Bedford, Indiana. My father was a fine golfer who won the Bedford city championship many times, so I was exposed to the game early.

I played on the high school golf team for four years with some success, and continued to enjoy golf at Wake Forest University, playing No. 3 or 4 man my last two years. The teams included a number of fine players, one of whom was Arnold Palmer, my roommate for a while.

After a stint in service, I took my first professional teaching job as an assistant to Don Fischesser in Evansville, Ind. I spent one year the touch I possess today came from pitching balls over trees, bouncing them across the road, chipping them off grass, dirt and concrete.

In high school I won the interscholastic golf championship of western Massachusetts, which gave me the idea I might have a future in golf. After I graduated from Williamsburg (Mass.) High in 1944, I was drafted into the army. The following year I was stationed in the China-Burma-India theater, where I won the CBI army championship.

After the war I worked for my brother Jack, who was still at Northampton. We had a number of local tournaments in the area and touring pros like Doug Ford, Milon Marusic, and Ted Kroll played in them. Because of their encouragement, I joined the tour in 1949.

Toney Penna, who taught me a lot about the game and eventually signed me with the MacGregor Company, was a great inspiration to my career in those days. As I continued to play on tour, I received additional advice and encouragement from people like Jimmy Demaret, Sam Snead, Lawson Little and Ed "Porky" Oliver.

It wasn't easy. I went broke twice
(continued on page 12)

there and then became head professional at a nine-hole course in Connersville, from 1956 to 1960. From there I moved to Losantiville Country Club in Cincinnati.

I had always enjoyed teaching, and at Losantiville I enjoyed it even more. We established a fine junior program there, and because the adult members were so interested, my staff and I began to teach more than any club in the area.

In 1963 I won the Greater Cincinnati Championship, and about this time people from other clubs began coming to me—and I gave even more lessons. I also realized I wanted to learn more about my profession. I began to read everything I could get my hands on. I listened to and watched all the good teachers in the area; I attended national seminars, where I met Bill Strausbaugh, head professional at Columbia Country Club in Chevy Chase, Md., and Irv Schloss, an outstanding teacher from Florida, who at the time became the two most influential people in my career.

My increasing awareness of what was going on with the golf swing made me realize that I was not play-

(continued on page 12)

## BOB TOSKI

before I won my first event, the Insurance City Open in Hartford, in 1953. It produced such confidence that I asked Lynn Stewart, whom I was dating, to become my wife, and she did that December. And 1954 was my big year. I won George S. May's World Championship and three others and became the leading money-winner.

I quit the tour in 1957 at age 30 because I wanted to spend more time with my family. My first instinct was to become a club professional, and I held jobs at Kings Bay in Miami, Country Club of Miami and Ocean Reef in Key Largo, where I stayed for 12 years. After that I taught at Hound Ears in Blowing Rock, N.C., and the Old Baldy Club in Wyoming.

My association with *Golf Digest* began in 1960, and in 1971 we started the Golf Digest Instruction Schools, which have become phenomenally successful.

During all this time, I feel I have been learning to be a good teacher, and I hope I never stop learning. Teaching was frustrating at first. I realized I had to increase my knowledge. I read books and discussed golf with as many successful teachers as I could. It took me 10 years

## JIM FLICK

ing or teaching the way the successful pros were playing. I had been teaching a very right-sided game—aiming to the right, releasing and rotating the club with the right hand—and I had been able to get away with it. Most of the Cincinnati golf courses were old, without watered fairways and with very few bunkers in front of the greens. You could hit the ball with a low, hard hook and bounce it onto the green.

But the modern courses all had watered fairways and severe bunkering. I saw that if I were going to play and teach my students the modern game, I had to find a way to keep the ball in the air longer.

I asked for help from Strausbaugh and Schloss; I studied pictures of the good players and the positions they were in at various points during the swing. I still refer to and use them on the lesson tee today.

In 1969 I spoke at my first PGA seminar and this launched what has become a very important part of my life. I immensely enjoy my participation in PGA and National Golf Foundation educational activities, and I think by being exposed to many good teachers and players, I've learned as much from them as I've given.

before I felt I was good. I had to learn to teach all types of players—beginners, high and low handicappers and professionals. And you learn yourself from teaching all of them.

I've come to realize that it's impossible to teach a perfect swing, even if people agree on what that is. This has led me to develop the touch system, which emphasizes light grip pressure and learning to swing by beginning with short strokes.

Along the way I met Jim Flick, for whom I have tremendous respect. Through my association with him, my knowledge of the game and the swing has increased greatly. I more fully understand the importance of fundamentals, and Jim has made me especially aware of the roles correct posture and alignment play in the golf swing. It is because of our mutual work for *Golf Digest* and the relationship we have developed that this book has come about. In it we have attempted to communicate the knowledge that we have acquired, working apart and together, so that you, our golfing readers, can play a better game. If we succeed to even a small extent, the effort will have been worthwhile.

One of the teachers I met during this time was Bob Toski. At first I didn't realize how similarly he and I were teaching. We used different words to describe the golf swing, but we hadn't spent enough time on the lesson tee together to see the parallels in our teaching.

It wasn't until 1973, as I watched him work with 36 people in a Golf Digest Instruction School, that I realized we were in the same camp. We had arrived at the same conclusions about the mechanics of the golf swing, but we had got there from different directions—Bob from the standpoint of a player and I from trial-and-error teaching and from the books I had deciphered with my methodical, engineering-type mind.

From then on I tried to watch Bob and be with him at every opportunity. This led to an exchange of our ideas. Bob has gained much from my ideas, as I have gained from his, and at this point we probably teach as nearly the same as any two people can.

Our observations and constant exchanges have evolved into a sound, total teaching methodology you can absorb from this book. We hope you'll profit from it by playing better golf.

# INTRODUCTION

# THE JOY OF GOLF

What is golf, this game that millions around the world play with varying degrees of intensity?

Golf, of course, is many different things. To us, Bob Toski and Jim Flick, it is our livelihood—our passion. It has given us almost everything we have in life. To some, golf is work; to others, it is only play. It has been said that golf should always be fun, yet the fascination of the game lies in the fact that it goes beyond merely having fun.

Golf is uniquely appealing because it offers a challenge found in virtually no other game. Golf defies you to master it. It wants you to be a slave to it, and the game has succeeded in enslaving many of us.

The game always provides a true measure of ability. While it is true that golf can be a game played with and against other players, there is always one opponent—the golf course. It is always challenging, always difficult. A golf course does not always seem fair. Sometimes your ball will bounce the wrong way. Yet, if you are patient, it will often bounce the right way. The course will penalize your bad shots and reward your good ones.

The golf course, in all its natural beauty, lies there waiting to test your skills. It does not harass you. It does not distract you from doing your best. The grass doesn't talk back to you. It is this that often makes golf an antidote to despair. Golf is a friend. It is relief from your problems, from the pressures and tensions of life. It offers you self-satisfaction and recognition from your peers. It gives you companionship. It gives you exercise. At the same time, it offers you solitude and serenity, a walk in the fresh air and sunshine on green grass amid lovely trees, a chance to listen to the birds sing. How many of us take time for that anymore?

Golf is an individualistic sport. You can play at your own pace—for an hour or all day. You can play one hole or 36 holes. You can compete in tournaments, or you can simply go out and play a leisurely round. You can be as intense or as casual as you choose. You can play alone or you can play with friends. You need not react to others, as in tennis or team sports. You can establish your own goals and try to attain them, and if you achieve one goal, you can strive for a higher one. You can be as good as you want, depending on the time and effort you can or want to commit to the game. And, unlike most other sports, you can do this during your whole life. Golf's special attraction is that you can play whether you are young or old.

Golf is also a fantastic character-builder, provided you understand what it can do for you. The game tests you as a human being. There are 18 holes on a golf course, each testing your ability to control the problem in front of you. And how well you solve the problem depends on your ability to control yourself. Golf wants to see how you react, whether you can meet its challenges and how you respond if you can't.

All this is why, whether you are a scratch player or a 36-handicapper, a man or a woman, a junior or a senior player, golf is indeed fun. But because of the game's underlying challenge, it becomes fun of a different sort. Fun can be lying on the beach, basking in the sunshine. Fun in golf is learning to control your body and your mind, striking the ball to the best of your ability, making the lowest score possible within the limits of your potential. *The joy of golf is that success, at whatever level you seek it, comes with learning.*

*To help you acquire that learning, to help you meet the challenges of golf and to enjoy its rewards, is our purpose in writing this book.*

# 1

# HOW TO BECOME A COMPLETE GOLFER

Golf may be a game played by intelligent people stupidly, but it doesn't have to be, and our purpose is to help you learn how to play it properly. We intend to provide you with the knowledge that will help make the game more fun for you.

Achieving a low score is the purpose of the game, but a golfer must have good ball-striking ability to do so. When he first begins to play golf, he uses an instinctive method to move the ball forward and often develops habits that keep him from scoring well. He fails to realize he must prepare himself to acquire the art of playing the game.

This book will help you make that preparation because it encompass-es all phases of golf instruction. It gives you an understanding that reduces the swing to its simplest terms and tells you how to apply that understanding to become a more successful player, whether you are a high, medium or low-handicapper.

That understanding begins with a knowledge of what makes a golf ball fly the way it does—the ball-flight influences. Understanding includes a knowledge of swing *principles* that relate to those laws and make the ball go where you want it, along with your individual *preferences* for putting those principles to work. Understanding encompasses the knowledge of how to do all that consistently on the course.

There are two aspects of becoming a complete golfer: ball-striking and management of the course and yourself. The first relates to swinging at golf balls, the second to playing golf. We will help you learn both the fundamentals of a sound swing and good playing ability. By teaching thousands of golfers of both sexes and all handicap levels, at our Golf Digest Instruction Schools and in individual lessons, we have learned that these fundamentals work for players of any ability. We can't claim to have all the answers, because our own concepts have changed as our knowledge has broadened over the years. But within the limits of that knowledge, the concepts we will help you learn will work for you.

No one can standardize the golf swing, and we are not attempting to. Each player has his own particular physical and emotional characteristics. But one *can* standardize a method of instruction. Every golfer can be given sound fundamentals, a clear understanding of the proven best way to play, which he can adapt to his individual physique and mental outlook.

That is the overriding goal of this book—to let you relate this material to your own needs and thereby get more enjoyment out of the game.

A lot of people with some experience at golf can tell you what you are doing wrong. A good player can tell you what to do right. But only an excellent teacher can tell you *how* to do it. And why, because he understands the cause and effect of golf swing problems.

We will debunk some myths in this book—myths stemming from erroneous ideas of what really goes on in a golf swing and those perpetuated for years by people who haven't made sufficient effort to find out the truth. The instruction schools we have conducted over the last several years have served as laboratories, giving us invaluable insight into what golfers really need in order to play better. And the success we have had in our schools has proved that our method is valid for amateurs at all levels as well as for the professionals we have taught. We see an ever-increasing percentage of repeaters at our schools, which means that more and more players are evaluating our system and finding it productive.

This, then, is what we propose to do for you in this book—we will take you to the lesson tee with us. We will help you evaluate yourself and your own swing and playing problems, and we will give you the tools that, over a period of time, will help you put your golf game together.

This is accomplished by using the learning triangle of knowledge, communication and application, or, if you will, the what, how and when of learning. One side of this equilateral triangle is knowledge: *what* you must know to be a better player. The second side of the triangle is communication: *how* you communicate with yourself and find the correct mental keys that help you build a better swing and play better golf. The third side is application: *when,* or at what stage of your development, you must apply a particular bit of knowledge to best incorporate it into your method of play.

We believe in the *whole-part-whole learning process.* In the case of the golf swing, we will give you the whole concept of what it's about. Then we will give you the parts, teaching in specifics rather than generalities. Then we will help

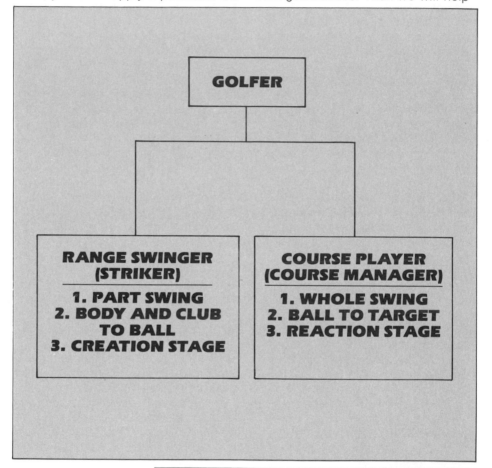

**GOLFER**

| **RANGE SWINGER (STRIKER)** | **COURSE PLAYER (COURSE MANAGER)** |
|---|---|
| **1. PART SWING** <br> **2. BODY AND CLUB TO BALL** <br> **3. CREATION STAGE** | **1. WHOLE SWING** <br> **2. BALL TO TARGET** <br> **3. REACTION STAGE** |

### *How a complete golfer is made*
*You become a complete golfer by first learning to strike the ball on the practice range. Concentrate on the parts of the swing, aligning your body and club to the ball and creating the whole swing from that point. Then you must learn to make that swing work on the golf course, to manage your shots and fit them to the course layout so you can get around in the lowest number of strokes possible. On the course, you think only of the whole swing and the target.*

you put them back into a whole for use on the course. The parts of the swing must work for the whole to be effective, but too many golfers spend their time working only on the parts. As a result, the parts get better but the whole gets worse.

While we teach certain fundamentals of grip, alignment, setup and swing concept, we realize everybody cannot or may not immediately want to do it in the ideal manner. If not, we will urge you to make the deviation that will hurt you the least. For example, it is better to grip the club too lightly than too tightly, because that error causes the least serious swing problems and is easiest to

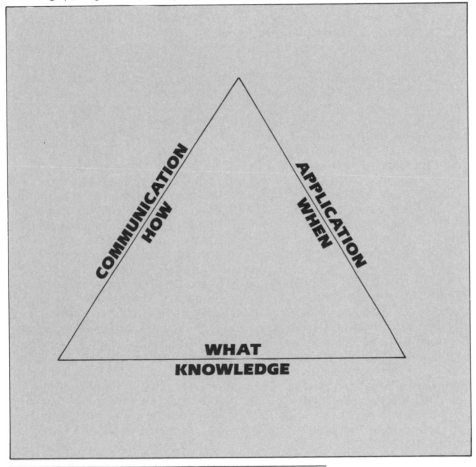

### The triangle of learning

*The triangle of learning involves three equal parts—knowledge, or what you must know to be a better player; communication, or how to find the correct mental keys to build a better swing; and application, or when in your development you must apply a particular piece of knowledge to best incorporate it into your method of play.*

correct. We would rather have you leaning too far out over the ball with your weight too much toward the balls of your feet. From that position you can at least keep your swing on the target line longer than if you were too much back on your heels, which will make you swing off the target line. We will give you many other such alternatives and the reasons why you should choose each so that in time you can become your own best coach and learn by trial and error to perfect your swing.

This awareness is achieved by starting from close to the hole on the putting green, learning to feel the force of the club against the ball, learning the feel of the correct movement your club must make and the correct speed with which it should move. Then you will move gradually to the chip shot, the pitch shot and finally the full swing. Whether you are a beginner or a long-time player, you will find this method invaluable in learning the proper feel of the swing.

We will give you drills to help you ingrain the various fundamental elements of the swing into your muscle memory. And since we cannot physically be with you on the lesson tee to see what you are doing right or wrong, we will show you testing procedures that will help you pinpoint not only what you are doing with your swing in practice but what mental and emotional problems you must overcome on the course. We hope to make you aware of your weaknesses and will help you overcome them while maintaining your strengths.

Finally, before you are given an act to perform or a thought to put into effect, we will give you a mental concept that puts that act or thought into clear perspective. When you know why you are doing something, it becomes much easier to accomplish it.

We are not quick-cure teachers. It is easy to overcome the effect of a bad slice by aiming to the left and letting the ball spin to the right back into the fairway. But that does not cure the slice. Instead, we prefer to give you a method that will build a sound, repeating golf swing. Obviously, that will correct some faults that you already have, but it also will give you the knowledge to keep correcting those faults when they crop up again, as they do with all of us. Because you know what you are doing wrong, you eventaully will be able to do it right.

Almost all beginners play golf in generalities. They have some general idea of what it takes to advance a golf ball—swing the club backward and then forward, for example. But as they become more interested in the game and want to play better, they begin to pay attention to the details that will enable them to swing the club backward and forward more effectively.

In this book we will set forth the

### Curve the ball toward the target
*As this diagram shows, golf becomes a much simpler game when you aim the clubface on the line on which you want the ball to start and swing the club on that line, curving the ball toward the target instead of away from it. If you can hit the ball straight to the target, then aim and swing in that direction (1). But if you want to fade the ball from left to right (2) or draw it from right to left (3), or if those are your natural tendencies, then aim the clubface and swing accordingly. If you aim right, swing right. If you aim left, swing left.*

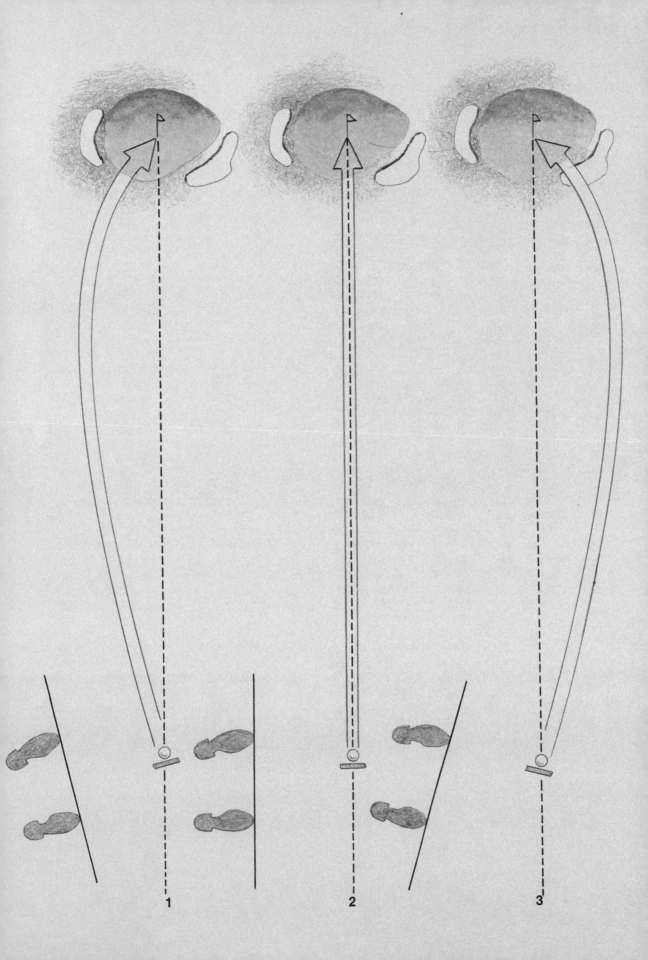

specifics that relate to a sound golf swing and an effective method of play. Admittedly, that requires us to segment the golf swing. It goes back to the whole-part-whole method. We cannot emphasize too strongly that you must play with a whole swing. But first you will learn the proper segments, so that you can react to them subconsciously and efficiently.

The mechanical fundamentals we will give you and the individual swing concepts we present should be molded into a whole that accomplishes one basic, major concept we espouse: *You should aim and swing the club on the line on which you want the ball to start, depending on your individual needs. Then develop the instinctive reaction of your hands to control the face of the club and make the ball curve back to the target.*

Corollary to that basic concept is that direction comes before distance. Every long hitter of the golf ball—from Harry Vardon to Jack Nicklaus—has had to give up some distance for control and direction before he has become a good player.

That concept is developed by learning what we call the *Five P's— preparation, position, posture, path* and *pace.* These give you orderly checkpoints as you build your swing and develop your play thoughts.

We believe the golf swing is natural, and that this naturalness is a result of proper setup related to blade position at the target and body position to the starting path of the ball. This proper setup allows the arms to swing and the body to follow on the backswing, which puts the lower body in position to lead on the forward swing. This gives you a free-flowing motion that lets you relate to the correct swing path.

Golf is a two-sided game. But you will learn that the speed of the right arm and hand is controlled by and is responsive to the speed of the left. The left arm is the swinging lever, because it is the straighter of the two arms and it is the arm in front of the clubhead (the reverse, of course, is true for left-handed golfers). The right hand and arm have a responsibility to provide speed and power, but the speed and aggressiveness of the right arm must be controlled by the speed of the left.

You also will learn the value of a light and constant grip pressure, which helps rid your upper body of unwanted tension, increases your sensitivity and keeps you from over-controlling the golf club and trying to overpower the shot.

This in turn will help you develop a *swing impulse* and overcome the *hit impulse* that is inherent in all of us. The ability to strike a golf ball straight and for good distance is based on proper tempo and timing. We want you to strike the ball squarely while swinging the club with as much speed as you can control. Speed comes from flexibility and the proper application of centrifugal force rather than leverage—terms we will explain later in the book. You do not need great size or strength to generate speed in the golf swing. More than anything else, speed is created by proper technique, by putting your body and the club in proper position to effectively use the strength you have. You don't have to *hit* the ball. The *hit* is simply the result of the ball getting in the way of the clubhead as it passes through the impact area. An on-center hit plus speed equals controlled distance.

It is important to be target-oriented on each shot and goal-oriented in your overall outlook. The object of golf is to advance the ball from one spot to another and get it around the course in the fewest possible strokes. To do that, you cannot be position-oriented or swing-oriented while you are playing the game.

You play the game by feel—after you've incorporated solid fundamentals into a feel for the game. And maintaining that feel is greatly dependent on your mental approach. For example, have you ever considered that almost every physical mistake is caused by a mental or emotional error? Intriguing thought, isn't it? It adds a whole new dimension to your ability to play golf, and learning what you can do about it will make golf a lot more fun for you.

You play golf with the arms, the hands, the legs and the mind, and the first three won't work properly if the mind isn't adequately programmed before every shot. To do that, you must keep your mind in the present tense. You often hear that golf should be played one shot at a time. Again, that's pretty nebulous. It's *how* you play each shot, how your mind handles it, that's important. All lasting improvement comes from the mind first. We believe we can help you orient your mind toward the direction it needs to go.

You must evaluate each shot and your pattern of play, and we will help you learn how to do it. The mental aspect includes proper strategy, of course—how to plan the play of a hole, when to attack it, when to play defensively, what to do relative to your situation in the round and your ability to carry out your plan. Each hole is played by relating the strengths and weaknesses of that hole to your own strengths and weaknesses.

Your playing concepts will be tied together by discussing the *Three A's* and the *Three C's—ability, ambition, attitude;* and *confidence, competitiveness, composure—*and how they control performance on the course.

You may have noticed we keep saying we will "help you learn." That's because we believe that nobody can *teach* somebody to be a better player. We can only teach you how to *learn* to be better.

It's important for you to understand that this book is a source of knowledge, a tool that will help you help yourself. Although you will not be able to go out and play par golf immediately, these new concepts will enable you to improve and give you a lifetime of pleasure as a result.

A top executive at General Motors once came to Bob Toski, introduced himself and stated: "I have come to take some golf lessons from you. Do you think you can teach me to play better golf?"

Toski replied: "Sir, I wouldn't walk into your office at General Motors and ask you to teach me to run your organization in an afternoon. That wouldn't be fair to you and it wouldn't be realistic in view of the size and complexity of your organization. And I might not have the talent to do it. The same is true with the game of golf. So the problem isn't whether I can teach you. I've already proved I can *teach* people. The problem is whether you can *learn* to play better golf."

You should have a desire to learn, and your desire can take different forms. It may be simply a matter of pride in wanting to play as well as you can. You may want to be recognized as a good player at your club. You may want that club championship trophy for your mantel. You may want to become a professional golfer and make money at the game. Whatever your motivation, it should be strong enough to make you emotionally as well as physically involved in your task.

You should be a good planner, establishing a step-by-step program that will best let you build your success patterns and achieve your goals. We see people playing golf as if they are going to die tomorrow—they seem to have to learn it all today. As a result, they don't learn at all.

There is always a time element involved in understanding how to become a good striker of the ball and a good scorer, in understanding the art of being a good player. Some individuals are faster learners, more adaptable than others. Be aware of how fast you can learn, and don't become discouraged if you don't seem to be progressing as quickly as you think you should. It is vital that you have faith that what you are doing is right.

Harry Vardon once said that anybody who thinks he can play golf without practice is paying a very poor compliment to a very difficult game. We will tell you how to practice more effectively, how to evaluate your practice so it will do the most good. You will practice in specifics and play in generalities, and we will tell you how best to do that.

# 2
# ON THE SWING IN GOLF

"Golf is a game played in a state of grace," said Seymour Dunn, one of the game's most insightful writers and teachers, and we've never heard a better description.

It means that the good golf swing promotes a feeling in the player—and an impression on the observer—of grace, ease, fluidity and control.

Ernest Jones, another great teacher, put it beautifully: "The golf swing is a measure of time that few people ever learn to pace." Therein lies the problem for most golfers. The reason you do not learn to pace and time your golf swing is because you do not have a knowledge of what it takes to propel a golf ball forward. You instinctively feel that you have to swing hard to achieve the necessary distance. You succumb to the "hit impulse," which takes away your sense of timing.

Consider that a golf ball weighs 1.62 ounces and is made of rubber. A golf club weighs from 11 to 17 ounces or more and is made of wood or steel. An adult golfer weighs from 100 to 250 pounds or more. Now, how much effort does it take for a person that big with an implement that heavy to advance that little ball? It's just sitting there waiting for you to strike it. It's not going to jump off the tee the moment you take the club back. So why do you swing so fast at it?

Because you equate distance with

speed. You equate speed with effort. You feel you have to swing hard and fast to generate that speed.

When we ask our students what determines the distance a ball travels, nine out of ten say the speed of the clubhead. Well, clubhead speed *is* important, but you can swing a golf club 100 miles an hour with the clubface wide open and the ball will go dead right. You can swing it 100 miles an hour with the face shut and it will go dead left. You can swing it 100 miles an hour and catch the ball on the toe or the heel, or hit the ground behind it, or top it, and you'll get nothing out of the shot. On the other hand, you can swing a club down your target line at 50 miles an hour, with the face square, and catch the ball solidly and watch it go a lot farther and straighter toward your target than all those other shots.

The *speed = distance* formula only works when it is based on the premise of on-center hits, a square clubface at impact and an on-line clubhead path. But a golfer can't live by distance alone. Golf is a game of distance *and* direction, and the great majority of players must learn direction and control before they achieve effective distance.

You learn that by developing your sense of pace and timing. First, realize that the golf swing is nothing but a stroke. There are long strokes, short strokes, slow strokes, fast strokes. We swing the club at many different speeds over the course of a round—the speed of a putt, of a chip, of a drive. But the proper player tends to have much less variation in the speed of his swing than the good player. No matter the length, the speed always seems the same—usually too fast.

The speed of your swing is a reaction to the distance you want to hit the ball. The speed of a tee shot will be greater than that of a putt. *But there should be no conscious effort to make it faster.* The speed is greater simply because the swing is longer. If the swing is properly timed going back and starting back down, the length of the swing and the centrifugal force acting on the clubhead will greatly increase the speed coming through the ball.

Bobby Jones put it best when he said you not only must swing the club *back* in a leisurely manner, you also must *start it down* in a leisurely manner. Most players use far too much physical effort in moving a golf club away from and back through the ball. The hit impulse takes over. Instead of properly timing the swing, they simply overexert themselves when they don't have to.

If this is your problem, you overcome it by learning to use your left leg to support your left arm as it controls the pace of the swing through the ball.

## Pivot—a result of arm swing

Your pivot—the movement of your

body—is a result of your arm swing, and the length of your arm swing is a reaction to the distance you want to strike the ball. If we put a driver in your hands and tell you to hit the ball five feet, you will take the club back a foot or so and just tap the ball. There will be no pivot. If we tell you to drive the ball 250 yards, you will wind the club around your body and pivot, because you need time and leverage to make a swing that will strike the ball that far. Often you hear a player who just putted from 80 feet say he pivoted. He didn't try to pivot—it was the result of his arms swinging. His arm swing had to be so great to roll the ball that far that his body was pulled to the right and back to the left.

To understand the function of a pivot, you must understand how power is created. Most persons equate power with brute strength. In reality, power in golf is created by clubhead speed, and that in turn is created by the swinging of the hands and arms. If you think power and speed come from the center of the body, hold the end of the club there, turn your body and see how fast the clubhead moves. If you think the left shoulder creates speed, hold the end of the club against your left shoulder and see how fast the clubhead moves.

That should convince you that clubhead speed comes from the swinging of the hand and arms, not from any effort of the torso. The movement of the body simply supports that swinging action.

Thus, a properly paced arm-and-hand swing—going back, starting down and coming through—will give your body time to respond to that motion. The legs will follow the swinging of the arms going back and will be put into position to lead the forward swing, accommodating the movement of the upper body and arms and putting them in position to accelerate the club through the ball properly.

If, instead of relating to a gradual increase in arm speed as you start back down, you react to the power urge by spinning your shoulders or otherwise making an effort with your upper body, this correctly timed sequence of hand, arm and body movement will be disrupted and the shot will be ruined. Without a doubt, the overuse of the shoulders or hips, or both, is the No. 1 cause of inconsistency in the golf swing.

To repeat, *relate the length of your arm swing to the distance you want to strike the ball and let that control your pivot and your golf swing.*

However, don't be misled into thinking that proper foot and leg action happens automatically. For many golfers it does not. If this is the case with you, you will have to work—guided by the comments and drills we'll give you later—to develop the good footwork that will result in good lower-body action.

## Control the speed

We've heard it said that if you swing the club back too slowly, you will snatch it down from the top. Maybe. But for every player we've seen take the club back too slowly, we've seen 10,000 who go back too fast.

What is too fast? If you take the club back so slowly that you have no sense of rhythm and flow, no sense of motion, that's too slow. That can happen, but it's a rare problem.

More important is how you determine what is too fast. You may have heard that the speed and tempo of your golf swing should be the same as the speed and tempo of your lifestyle. If you're a quick, fast-moving individual, you will throw your emotional system out of whack if you try to slow your swing down too much—or so the theory goes. Well, that's pretty vague and not really very accurate, because it fails to consider the more important determinant of golf swing speed— *you can swing the club with control only as fast as the strength of your hands and forearms can bear.*

The force of the club swinging around your body has to be controlled if you are to strike the ball squarely with any consistency. For most players, this means swinging the club back slower. If you accelerate the club too quickly going back, the speed of the swing and the weight of the club will cause you to lose control. You probably will overswing and be forced to make a compensation with your hands and body that will throw your swing out of kilter.

In swinging the club back and during the change of direction at the top, you should have a feeling of ease. You should never feel you are swinging the club hard. If you lose that feeling of ease, you have swung the club too fast and are going out ot control. Your muscles are tightening in an effort to regain control and you are heading for trouble.

Swing speed, then, is relative to your physical capabilities. A frail woman of 60 must swing more slowly than a 180-pound young man. How fast or slow you swing is something you must accommodate to your own strength and coordination, with control the determining factor.

## Feel the swinging force

At the same time, you must have *motion* in your swing. There must be a smooth, rhythmic flow to your swing that allows you to generate clubhead speed as effortlessly as possible. A stilted, contrived swing that lacks motion, no matter how much control you have, will cause a tightening of the muscles that will cost you the distance and accuracy you need.

On the practice tee it might help you to sense the feeling of motion by swinging a little bit out of control. But to play effectively, you can't create a motion that completely runs away from you. Maximum motion with maximum control is your objective, and you achieve it by developing a feel for the swing, a communication with the club.

One of the major premises upon which we try to build a swing is that *you must develop a feel for a swinging force with the body complementing that force.* That simply means that before you can ever hope to strike the ball any distance with control you must be able to identify and control the weight and momentum of the clubhead as you swing it backward and forward rhythmically, with all the parts of the body moving in proper sequence and speed.

That feel for the swinging force starts in the hands and arms and in the feet. Your hands and arms control the force of the club swinging around your body, and your feet control your lower body as it supports the movement of your upper body. Most of our students have little feel for the golf swing because their *grip pressure is too tight.* This tightens the arm muscles and denies a good, free arm swing and a full turn. Proper pressure promotes a sense for the timing, the path and the length of the swing.

When your grip pressure is minimal and your muscles are at ease, you have a better sense for striking the tee shot, pitching to the green and rolling the ball on the green. *An ounce of touch is worth a pound of brawn.* The more you minimize your grip pressure, the more touch you have and the better you are able to find the golf ball with the golf club simply by moving the club back and through the ball, striking it squarely.

This helps you eliminate the hit impulse and cultivate the swing impulse, which creates a feeling of pacing and measuring the time and length of the swing. The ball becomes incidental to the golf club and simply gets in the way as the club passes through.

The best way to demonstrate this is for you to place a ball on a tee, then step away and make a practice swing. Pick out a spot on the ground and swing the club through that spot. Just *let* it move forward. As you swing back and through there is no attempt to force the club to come to that point, no sense of lashing or hitting with the hands. You will swing the golf club with some degree of motion in your arms and you will move your legs to some degree. You will be aware of the rhythm and pace of the swing, how the arms are swinging, how your hands are holding the club lightly with a pressure that doesn't perceptibly change once the swing is under way.

Then step up to the ball. Chances are your motion will change. Now you see an object in front of you. Instead of feeling that the ball is simply getting in the way of the club, you try to get the club in the way of the ball. You don't trust the feeling you had in your practice swing of that spot simply being in the way of your club. Now the ball has intimidated you.

You forget that the practice swing was not just a practice swing but a *preparatory* swing. Let your swing be the same at the ball as it was away from the ball.

We have talked of lightness and ease in the golf swing. We do not talk of *complete* relaxation or *complete* freedom from tension. You cannot stay completely relaxed and free of tension during the swing because the extension and stretching and coiling of the muscles creates tension within the body. The swing of your arms and the turn of your upper body create tension. Tension comes from your moving the weight of the club. Your grip pressure will instinctively increase as you begin to swing the club back, but this is a reaction to movement, not a conscious effort. The tension that comes from the movement of the swing is an alive, springy tension that allows your muscles to act, an "at-ease" tension that allows flexibility in your swing, which in turn lets you generate clubhead speed. On the other hand, the nervous tension that most players develop at address tightens the muscles, inhibits their action and greatly reduces clubhead speed.

## Swing with less effort
Golfers, almost all of whom are too power-oriented, usually don't know how to apply the power they have. So they waste most of it. They don't realize that the amount of effort that goes into a swing is not nearly as important as how that effort is applied. There are three factors that create the power that gives us longer shots—strength, speed and flexibility. Some examples can help us determine which are more important.

Why can little guys like Chi Chi Rodriguez, Gardner Dickinson and Bob Toski drive the ball farther on a yards-per-pound basis than Jack Nicklaus or Tom Weiskopf? Bob Toski weighs 125 pounds yet can drive the ball 250 yards or more under normal conditions. That's two yards per pound. On that basis, Jack Nicklaus, who weighs about 185 pounds and is much stronger, should be able to drive the ball with control some 370 yards. Yet he can't, even though he, too, has speed and flexibility in his swing. That means strength is not nearly as important as the other two factors.

You read that Arnold Palmer and Jack Nicklaus learned to play golf by hitting the ball as hard as they could at the start, then later learning to control it. Well, that's one school of thought. It takes an exceptionally gifted athlete to strike a ball that aggressively with any consistency, and few players have the ability to attack a golf ball like a Nicklaus or a Palmer. The person who doesn't have the inherent hand-eye coordination, and the great strength and

### Swing under control
### with grace and ease

Note with what ease Bob Toski makes the full driver
swing, always keeping his arms and body and the
club under control. He is set behind the ball with his
upper body at address and moves even slightly farther behind as his arms swing the club back. On the
forward swing, he allows everything to work in the
proper sequence, his lower body leading and his

arms following. His head and upper body remain behind the ball as his arms swing through the shot, properly supported by the legs. Only by swinging under control can you achieve this correct timing. A swing pace that is too fast will cause your muscles to tighten and your arms and upper body to move too quickly, which will throw your swing out of sequence.

flexibility that these super-athletes have should start out learning direction, control and consistency. By learning to hit the ball solidly and straight, you have not doomed yourself to be a patty-cake player all your life. Your natural instincts are to hit the ball hard, and those instincts will keep surfacing as long as you play golf. You still will be able to hit the ball as far as you could if you had learned the other way—probably farther and certainly more consistently —because you've learned to control your hit impulse, meet the ball solidly and hit it where you want it to go.

What do the great players do when they are unsure of controlling their muscles? Bobby Jones said that on the first two or three holes of a round he just tried to meet the ball and keep it in play. Then, as his mind and muscles became keener and more attuned to the act, he could begin hitting the ball harder. Nicklaus says that on the first tee, when his tension level is usually high, he makes sure he hits a good drive by trying to reduce that tension level and just meeting the ball solidly by swinging slowly with good tempo.

So the strength factor should be combined with proper technique, which puts the club, your arms and your body in position to use that strength most effectively. Proper technique reduces your level of nervous tension, which puts your mus-

cles at ease at address and creates flexibility, speed and a feel for the swing. If you can combine those factors, then you have learned the true essence of the golf swing.

How does one learn to combine these factors, to create this feel for the golf swing? Basically, by learning to time the stroke. Start with the putt, because that is the simplest to learn to time. Learn to time your chipping, your pitch shots, your iron shots and your drives.

Learning to time these strokes correctly is what the game of golf is all about. It's a measure of time of different strokes at different angles and lengths, with every club in your bag. In that respect, the game is a learned process, yet golfers rarely approach it that way. You have the physical capacity to learn that measure of time but fail to realize that your muscles are untrained. They're not golf-oriented, and you have to have the right mental approach and the determination to orient them properly. *You have to learn to do naturally—through muscle habits and training—what comes unnaturally,* if you want to improve your skills.

Acquiring awareness by working with the same concepts and developing a feeling for when a movement is correct or incorrect is essential. Let your mind identify where the club *is* during the swing instead of consciously trying to *direct* it to a position. We learn through our mistakes—awareness gives us accurate feedback. In other words, we must *feel* that the club is out of position before we can correct it.

## Control curvature

One of the biggest hindrances to playing golf effectively is an inability to properly aim the club and align the body. There are several reasons for this. Faulty optics or eye alignment is one of them, and we will deal with this in a later chapter. But we feel that perhaps the main cause of the problem is that most amateur golfers simply are unable to control the curvature of their shots. So, because they seldom know which way or how much the ball is going to curve in flight, or if it is going to curve at all, they really never know where to aim.

The good player is not afraid to curve the ball because he can minimize the amount of curvature. The poorer player gets in trouble because he usually curves it too much. The good player curves the ball into the target. The poorer player usually curves the ball away from the target.

The ideal way to play golf is to *aim and swing the club on the line of aim.* There is no law that tells you in what direction you should start a golf shot or how much you should curve the ball in flight. But we know from experience as successful players and teachers that the closer you start the ball toward your target

and the less you curve the ball, the better and more consistent players you will be.

Let's put it this way. If you had a six-foot putt for the club title or the state championship, would you want it straight or with a break? Obviously, when the ball doesn't have to curve it has a better chance of rolling in the hole. You can aim your clubface at the hole and strike the ball directly at the hole.

Perhaps the straightest player in Europe at one time was Jean Garaialde, who won the French Open many times and has represented France in the World Cup. We once asked him what he thought of when he struck a golf ball. He said, "All I do is try to hit the ball the same way every time with the clubface—I try to make the clubface come back to the ball square."

But, while the theory is unassailable and it is quite possible to hit the ball perfectly straight, trying to do so often creates unwanted tension in golfers. We would rather you take a more relaxed approach and accept the fact that you are going to curve the ball, as long as you minimize the curvature as much as possible and try to curve it the same way every time for a normal shot.

We prefer that you draw the ball, swinging the clubhead into the ball on a path from inside the target line and releasing or uncocking your hands so the clubface is rotating from an open to square to closed position through impact. Thus the ball will start right of your target line and curve left, hopefully into the target. We believe this is the strongest way to play.

If you have not reached that stage of your swing development yet and are a chronic slicer or fader, curving the ball from left to right, at least be aware of that tendency and aim accordingly so the ball will curve into the target rather than away from it until you can get to the practice tee and work on a better method.

No matter which way you curve the ball, the concept of aiming and swinging on the line of play still applies. If you draw the ball you may play from a slightly closed position and aim slightly right of your target. Then swing on that line and curve the ball back to the target. If you slice, aim a bit to the left, swing in that direction and let the ball curve right into the target.

In any event, a minimal curve is your goal, and the way to achieve that is to develop good hand and arm control. The better player has this, complemented by his body movement, because he knows it is the hands and arms that control the clubface and thus the curvature of his shots. You should strive for that.

Your ultimate reward will be not only lower scores but an esthetic joy as well. There is no greater feeling in golf than to see a ball, whether it is traveling perfectly straight or cur-ving, hone in on your target.

If you now understand our concept of the *whole* golf swing, how to control it and how to apply it toward striking the ball to your target, you are prepared to learn the *parts* of that swing, the mechanics that will make you a more consistently effective striker of the ball. But keep in mind, as we dissect the swing and discuss these parts, that the parts eventually must be molded back into a whole if you are going to become a better player.

# 3

# WHY THE BALL GOES WHERE

Learning what makes the ball fly as it does is the first step in learning to swing correctly. And it's really a simple step. There are only four flight characteristics to a golf shot—*distance, trajectory, initial direction and curve.* And there are only five factors that create those characteristics. These are called the *ball-flight laws,* or *influences.* They are:

1. Clubhead path at impact.
2. Clubface position at impact.
3. Squareness of contact.
4. Angle of attack.
5. Clubhead speed.

Understanding these factors will enable you to know why a ball hooks or slices, why it goes high or low, why it travels a long way or not very far at all. This understanding will help you make specialty shots that will get you out of trouble. Peter Kostis of our Golf Digest Instructional staff is fond of saying, when he lands in the bushes, that the ball-flight laws got him in trouble so he will use the ball-flight laws to get out of trouble. If you understand them, you can do the same.

To put the ball-flight laws in perspective, if you arrive at the impact point in your swing with the clubhead traveling on a path that matches your target line, on the proper angle in relation to the ground and with sufficient speed, if your clubface is aiming directly down the target line and if you contact the ball squarely on the "sweet spot" of your club, then the ball will travel straight down the target line with the proper trajectory and will go the distance you intended it to.

The deviations from these five ideas are what get you into trouble, let's examine them.

## Clubhead path and clubface position

These two factors determine both the initial direction of the ball and, to a great extent, how it curves. Because their effects are so interrelated, we will deal with them together.

Forgetting trajectory—the up-and-down curve on which the shot travels—there are only nine basic shot "shapes" or ways the ball can fly. It can start straight to the target and continue straight. It can start straight and curve right or left. It can start left and go straight left, or it can start left and curve right or left from there. Similarly, it can start right and continue on a straight path to the right, or it can start right and curve right or left from there. Obviously, there are unlimited variations.

Let's look first at initial direction, the path on which the ball starts off. This initial flight path will fall somewhere between the path on which your clubhead is traveling and the direction the clubface is aiming at impact, so both factors obviously have an influence.

Such authorities as Frank

Thomas, technical director of the United States Golf Association, and Alastair Cochran and John Stobbs in their book, *The Search for the Perfect Swing,* tell us that the ball will start off approximately 70 percent in the direction the clubface is positioned. In other words, if your clubhead is traveling directly down your target line and your clubface is facing 10 degrees to the right at impact, the ball will start off approximately seven degrees to the right of your target.

This particular bit of knowledge is only important when you want to hook or slice a shot intentionally. For practical application to your swing, you need only be aware of the general relationship between path and face position.

For example, if your clubhead is traveling on a path directly toward your target but your clubface is open, the ball will start off *reasonably* straight toward the target but will then curve to the right or slice. If your clubface is closed, the ball will start off reasonably straight and then curve left or hook.

If your clubhead path is from outside your target line to inside it—traveling to the left of your target—and your clubface is square to that path, your shot will fly straight to the left of your target, that is, in the same direction the clubhead is traveling. If your path is to the left of your target and your clubface is either open or closed to that path at

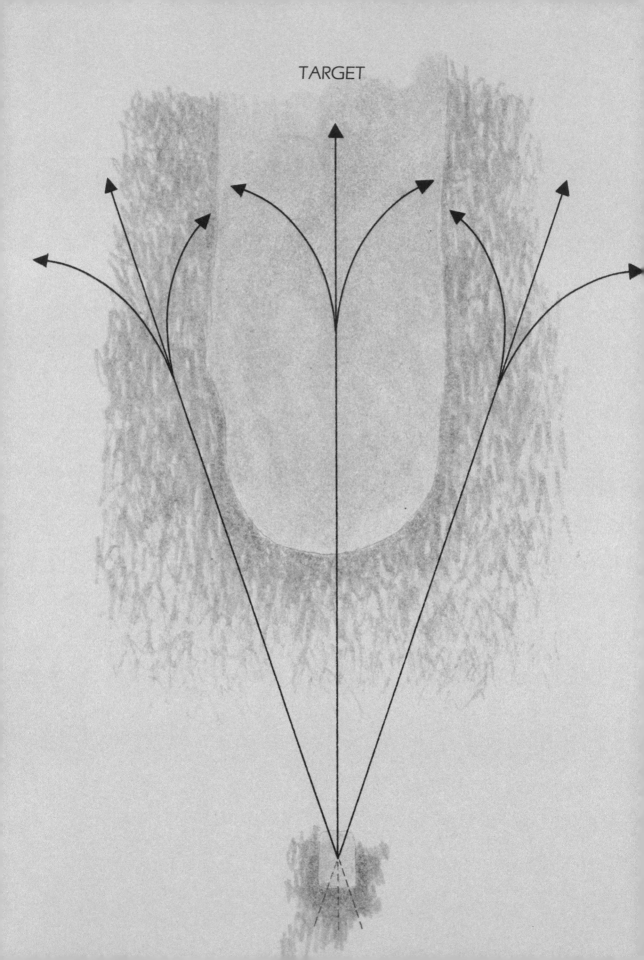

impact, the ball will start left and then curve either right or left. Similarly, if your path is from inside to outside your target line—to the right of your target—the ball will go straight right or start right and then curve either right or left depending on your face position.

Keep in mind that the slower your clubhead is traveling and the more loft it has (usually the two go hand-in-hand), the less curvature you will get on your shots. You may have noticed, or soon will, that while you can curve your driver a great deal in either direction, you have a difficult time hooking or slicing your pitching wedge.

Once you understand these relationships, you can analyze your shots and determine whether your errant shots are caused by incorrect path, incorrect face position at impact or both. Being able to identify the problem will help you solve it more quickly and easily.

## Squareness of contact

This is one of the factors that determines distance, and it can also affect the curve of a shot. Failing to strike the ball squarely on the "sweet spot" will cost you distance. Further, striking the ball toward the heel or toe end of the club will cause it to curve. A toe hit will cause the ball to hook or curve right to left. Contact on the heel will cause the ball to slice or curve left to right. You can feel it when these

off-center hits occur, and knowing what they cause will further help you analyze why the ball goes as it does.

## Angle of approach

As far as you are concerned, this is the angle or steepness of path, relative to the ground, at which your clubhead swings into the ball. As far as the golf ball is concerned, we must add the factor of *dynamic loft.* Each club is designed with a certain degree of face loft relative to the ground line when the club is properly soled. Dynamic loft depends on both the angle at which the face is being swung into the ball and the position of that face relative to the ground at impact. These factors of dynamic loft and angle of attack determine trajectory, the up-and-down curve on which the ball travels.

With a driver, when the ball is sitting off the ground on a tee, it is possible to swing into the ball from above, level with or below it. If your driver has a standard 11-degree loft and you contact the ball with the clubhead traveling level or horizontal with the ground, and with the face square, your club will have a dynamic loft angle of 11 degrees. The ball always is launched at a lesser angle than the loft of the club, so in this case the ball will come off at an angle of approximately eight degrees and will travel a normal trajectory.

*The nine ball-flight possibilities*
*Except for trajectory and distance, there are only nine ways your ball can travel. It can start on a line to the left of your target and from there can continue straight, go farther left or curve right. It can start straight to the target, continue straight or curve left or right. Or it can start on a line to the right of the target, keep going straight or curve right or left. All these flights are determined by the direction of your clubhead path and the position of your clubface—either open, closed or square at impact.*

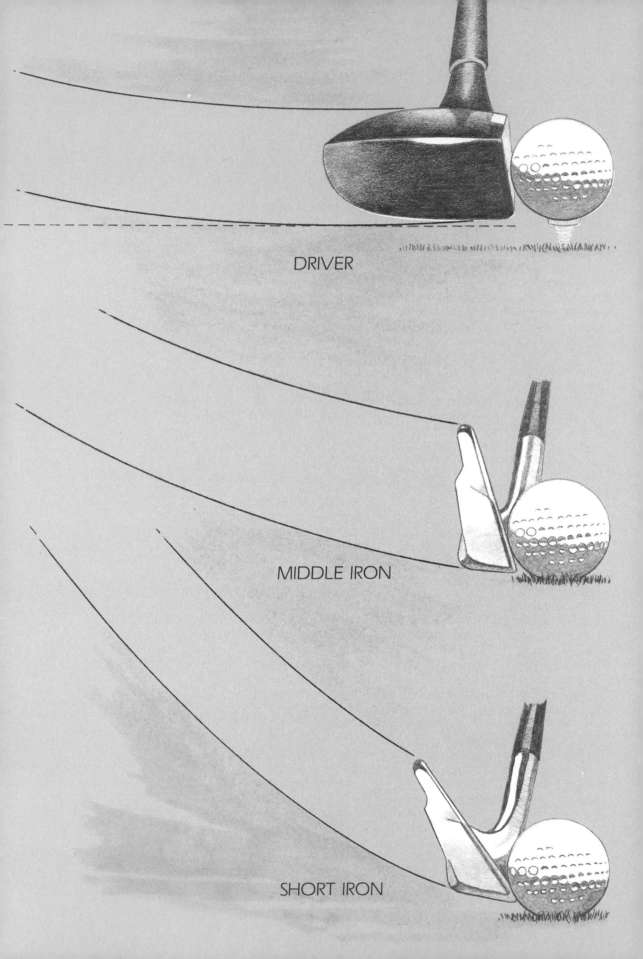

DRIVER

MIDDLE IRON

SHORT IRON

However, if your club is approaching the ball at a steeper angle—say two degrees above horizontal—you now have a dynamic loft angle of 13 degrees, assuming your clubface is still square. The ball may not be launched at a greater angle. It may even be launched slightly lower because your club is traveling on a downward path. But greater loft produces more spin, and the more spin you put on the ball, the higher it will fly. So this shot will travel on a higher trajectory and probably won't go as far.

On the other hand, if you have reached the bottom of your swing arc and the clubhead is traveling at an upward angle of two degrees when it contacts the ball, you have a dynamic loft angle of nine degrees. The ball may actually start a little higher, but because it has less spin it will tend to travel on a flatter or lower trajectory and may, under certain conditions, go a longer distance.

Practical application of that theory explodes the myth that you should tee the ball back in your stance if you want to hit a low tee shot into the wind. Instead, move the ball forward toward your target and catch it on the upswing.

The theory also explains why golfers often hit high, weak slices and low hooks or pulls to the left (did you ever see a high pull-hook?). The slice commonly occurs when the club is being swung from outside to inside the target line—we'll get into those causes when we discuss the swing itself. That outside-in swing also is bringing the clubhead into the ball at a steeper angle. If the clubface remains square or open to the target line, its dynamic loft has been increased. The angle of attack produces a higher shot, and the clubhead path in conjunction with the face position makes the shot slice. If you swing on that same path and angle and also roll the clubface square or closed to that path, you have taken dynamic loft off the face and a low pull or pull-hook will result.

Conversely, a clubhead traveling on a path from *inside* or *down* the target line to the ball will be swinging in a flatter arc. You will be more apt to catch the ball on the level or on the upswing. Depending on the position of your clubface, you will get a lower straight shot or a lower right-to-left hook. If you do happen to leave your clubface open, aiming right, while swinging on that path and angle, you will have added to its dynamic loft and will get a higher push-slice, a shot that starts right and curves farther right.

The principles of this theory remain the same for a fairway wood or an iron shot, but the practicalities change a bit because your ball now is sitting on the turf. Normally, you will not be able to swing up on the ball without topping it, because the ground will have got in the way at

## Angles of approach differ

*The angle of approach at which your clubhead swings into the ball should differ with the various clubs. In general, the longer the club, the shallower your swing arc should be at impact. Your driver should approach the ball on a horizontal path, even traveling slightly upward (which is possible with the driver because the ball is teed above the ground). Your middle irons should come in on a more downward arc and your short irons even more steeply downward. This is accomplished by setting your weight more to the right at address for the longer shots and more balanced for the shorter ones.*

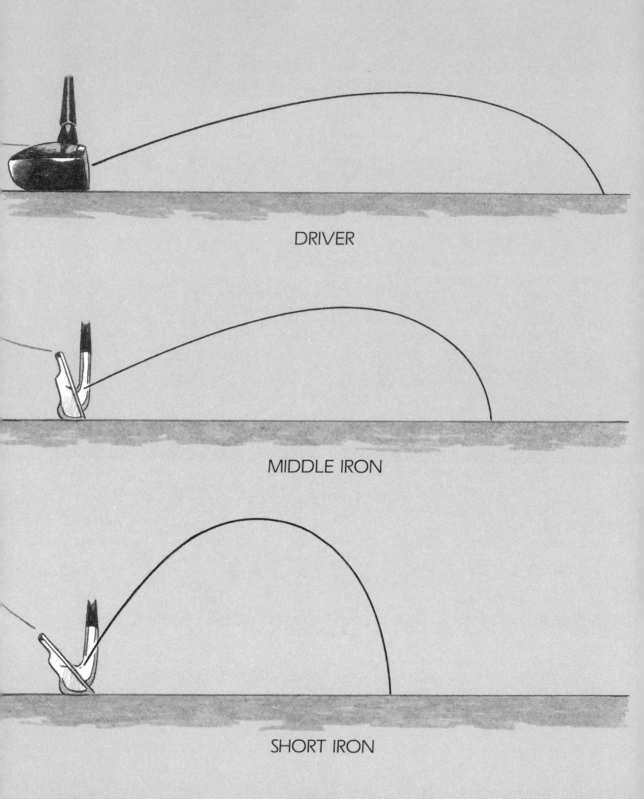

DRIVER

MIDDLE IRON

SHORT IRON

the bottom of your arc. So your angle of attack must be either on the level or from above. (The exception is when your ball is sitting up in rough or fluffy grass or when you can tee the ball on a par-3 hole, and it's often good to apply these principles in such situations.)

On the usual fairway shot, you will get basically the same results with the same types of swings we described for the driver—a steeper outside-in swing will give you a high slice or a low pull or pull hook, depending on the clubface position. A shallower angle of attack from down the target line or from inside it will result in a more normal trajectory.

But to hit the ball lower from the fairway, you *do* address the ball back in your stance. While this results in a steeper angle of attack, it also *de-lofts* your clubface. The ball will be launched at a lower angle—how much lower depending on how far back in your stance you addressed the ball—and will never rise as high as a normal shot.

To hit a fairway shot higher—perhaps you need the distance of a 4-iron but need to clear a tall tree—address the ball *forward* as far as possible in your stance to the point where the clubhead is swinging exactly at or a fraction past the bottom of its arc. You then will get as much dynamic loft as you can out of the club. Be careful not to have the ball too far forward or you will not hit it solidly and perhaps

even top it. You will have to experiment to find the optimum position.

## Clubhead speed

This, in combination with square contact, determines distance. The greater your clubhead speed, the farther you will strike the ball, provided you swing with enough control to make square contact and meet the other requirements of clubhead path and face position.

Learning to swing in this manner will be your objective in the following chapters. Understanding what causes the ball to go where it does will, we hope, make that learning process a little easier.

---

*How trajectory varies*

*Just as the angle of approach varies with the different clubs, so does the trajectory of the resulting shots. The ideal driver-shot trajectory starts low and rises gradually, then falls gradually from its peak. With a middle iron, the shot will start out on a higher angle, come to peak more quickly and drop more steeply. With the short irons, this higher trajectory and steeper descent is accentuated.*

45

# 4
# ALIGN YOUR PREFERENCES

Learning to play golf is best accomplished by establishing an order of priorities. Dr. Gary Wiren, former director of learning and research for the Professional Golfers' Association and one of the game's keenest students, lists these priorities as *laws, principles* and *preferences.*

*The ball-flight influences,* which we have just discussed, rank highest in the order or priorities. They are, so far as is known, invariable under given conditions. They do not refer to the swing but to physical forces of nature that influence the way the golf ball flies. The are absolute. The ball responds every time to the five influences we described. Good players recognize these in-fluences and are keenly aware of ball flight. Poorer players do not understand ball-flight influences and are not nearly as aware of how the ball flies.

A *principle* is a first cause or force, a factor of high order which has a direct relation to and influence on a law or laws, the plane of the downswing, for example. While these principles are not necessarily irrefutable, they are the commonly accepted building blocks of the swing and so constitute a clear, well-instructed plan for helping you learn to play better golf.

A *preference* is a particular approach, method or device which you might choose to satisfy a principle (such as choosing an open stance instead of a closed stance.) Preferences are virtually unlimited, but to be valid they must be aligned and working in concert with each other. If they are not, you will never play with consistency.

For clarity, we divide the principles of the golf swing into two categories—pre-swing and in-swing. The pre-swing principles include grip, aim, setup and routine. The in-swing principles are plane or path, width of arc, length of swing arc, position, lever system, timing, release, dynamic balance and swing center. Let's examine each of these for its primary influence on a ball-flight law or laws.

## Pre-swing principles

The *grip* has its greatest influence on direction, because it is the prime controller of clubface position.

*Aim* includes first clubface aim, followed by body alignment. It has a strong influence on clubface path and thus direction, although it is not the only influence.

*Setup* includes posture, stance, weight distribution, muscular tension and ball position. It can influence all five ball-flight laws and so is important both for distance and direction.

*Pre-shot routine* is perhaps the most important of the pre-swing principles. It directly affects the efficiency of your swing because it relates to your mental preparation for ball flight and your muscular

readiness to react to the target. Every good player has a programmed routine that allows him to grip, aim and set up to the ball correctly and consistently. It bridges the gap between a consciously correct setup and a swing that is properly performed by the subconscious.

## In·swing principles

*Plane* is determined by the more-or-less vertical route your club travels going back and coming forward. Hence, there is a backswing plane and a forward swing plane, and they will not necessarily be the same. Your forward swing plane is the determinant of clubhead path, so it obviously is the most important plane. Just as obviously, the forward swing plane is strongly influenced by the backswing plane.

*Width of forward swing arc* is determined by the extension of your left arm and clubshaft at impact and has a great influence on distance—the farther from your swing center the clubhead is, the faster it will be traveling. If your left arm bends or your left wrist breaks down before impact, you narrow your arc and reduce clubhead speed. The width of your backswing arc is not nearly as important, except as it might affect the width of the forward swing.

*Length of arc* refers to how long your swing is, how far your clubhead travels. It is a primary influence on

# BALL-FLIGHT INFLUENCES

Clubhead path

Angle of attack

Position of clubface

Clubhead speed

Squareness of contact

# PRINCIPLES

Grip

Left wrist position

Aim

Lever system

Setup

Timing

Downswing plane

Release

Width of arc

Dynamic balance

Lenth of arc

Swing center

# PREFERENCES

Early wrist cock

Open stance

Two-knuckle grip

Etc.

distance, simply because the farther your clubhead travels before impact the faster it will be moving.

*Position* refers to the relationship of the back of the left forearm, the back of the left hand and the club-face. Ideally, this relationship should remain relatively constant through-out the swing.

The primary *lever system* in the golf swing is that formed by the left arm and club. If you cock your wrist in a plane with your forearm, you establish a two-lever system that greatly increases your distance because it multiplies your potential force three to four times. If you were to swing without cocking your wrist at all, you would have only a one-lever system that would not give you nearly as much distance.

*Timing,* one of the most important contributors to distance, refers to sequence of movement, and good timing allows the actions in your swing to happen in their proper order. When they do, you create the greatest possible power and club-head speed.

*Release* occurs when you allow your forearms and hands to return to a position at impact that approxi-mates your starting position. This frees the potential energy created in your backswing and returns the clubface to its position at address. Thus, release influences both dis-tance and direction.

*Dynamic balance* is the ability to maintain control while you change the positions of your body to create clubhead momentum. Since this movement from back foot to front foot while swinging your arms can affect swing arc and path as well as clubhead speed, dynamic balance is a contributor to both distance and direction.

Your *swing center* is the point around which the arc of your swing is made. It influences both distance and direction, because moving it also moves the arc of your swing and makes it difficult to consistently strike the ball squarely and on line. Technically, your swing center is located about at the top of your breastbone, although we will give you a different thought you may want to use when we discuss swing preferences in subsequent chapters.

## Preferences

Preferences are the means we use to best put the principles to work. There is a virtually limitless number of preferences. There are many dif-ferent ways to swing a golf club and achieve about the same results. An individual's swing preferences are based on his own swing model or concept. Some players may want to hook the ball, others may want to fade it, so they establish prefer-ences that let the principles work toward that particular objective.

The goal is to make the ball go *reasonably* straight, because that's the most consistent way to play golf. The preferences we will present are

### The order of priorities

*This chart shows the order of priorities in learning to play golf. The ball-flight influences determine what the ball does when struck, the swing prefer-ences determine how the ball is struck and your preferences provide methods for accomplishing the various principles. To play your best, your prefer-ences must work in harmony with the principles and influences.*

directed toward that goal.

All good players, no matter what their swing objectives, have aligned their preferences. If you want your left hand and forearm in a flat position at the top of your swing, they should be in relatively the same position at address. If you prefer to swing on a more upright plane, establish a setup position that will best allow you to do this.

This book will enable you to build your own swing concept, even though it may be different from ours, because you will acquire enough knowledge to make it work. One word of caution. We suggest you *don't* take preferences from Toski and Flick and try to combine them with preferences from other instructors who may be teaching different methods with different goals. If you do that, you won't benefit fully from the Toski/Flick method and you'll confuse yourself.

# 5
# SET UP FOR A FREE SWING: THE PRE-SWING PREFERENCES

Probably 90 percent of the amateurs who come to us for lessons want us to do something about their swings. That sounds logical enough. They are not striking the ball well, so they think that the obvious problem must lie in the way they are swinging at it.

Yet, almost all the touring professionals who call on us for help want us first to check their setup—their posture, clubface aim and body alignment. They realize one of the most-ignored principles in golf: *Your setup dictates the way you swing a golf club, and your swing can only be as consistent as that setup.*

The tour player recognizes that if he isn't hitting the ball well, the swing itself is probably not at fault.

It isn't working properly because his setup isn't allowing it to work. If he gets his posture, ball position, aim and alignment back in working order, his swing will again take on the correct shape related to the target and he can again play consistently.

The tour player knows that proper setup and a good pre-swing routine prepares a golfer for greater success, while improper setup and poor pre-swing preparation creates a greater chance for disaster. *Good golfers prepare for success. Poor golfers prepare for disaster.*

To strike a golf ball, you only need two things—some kind of setup and some kind of swing motion. To strike the ball well and consistently on line, the setup and motion must be compatible with each other and with the target.

The setup accounts for a large percentage of the swing's effectiveness—or ineffectiveness. The rest of the equation is directly related to the freedom of your arms and hands and what is causing that arm freedom to be lost, why you can't get enough motion in your swing, why you can't swing the club on the path you want.

So if, when you are having trouble, you check back to your starting position and the degree of muscle tension you have there, you will almost always find the answer to your problems.

Those problems occur because your swing instinctively will relate itself to your posture, aim and alignment. In other words, no matter how you stand to the ball and no matter where you aim, you will find a swing that will try to get the ball to the target.

That's fine if your setup is correct, if you are aiming the clubface where you want the ball to go. But if you're not, compensations or adjustments in your swing are needed.

For example, if your body and club are aimed to the right of your target and you make a good swing, the ball is going to travel to the right. That's not where you want it to go, so if you consistently aim to the right, you will soon do something

to bring the ball back on target, and you will have changed your good swing into a bad one. You also may have knocked a couple of balls out of bounds.

By that principle, if your setup or aim keeps changing from shot to shot, you must keep changing your swing, and pretty soon your shot pattern will be so inconsistent you'll have no idea where the ball is going.

The compensations needed to overcome improper setup will involve overworking your hands or shoulders, or both, and that costs distance as well as direction and consistency. Interfere with the rhythm of the swing, which costs clubhead speed, and you stand more chance of getting off-center hits.

Is this a common problem? Here's a statistic: 90 percent of the students on their first visit to our Golf Digest Instruction Schools set-up incorrectly, and 80 percent of them aim the clubface and/or the body to the right. These are players of all handicap levels, so you can see how common the problem is.

The good player aims the club in a specific direction and in a specific manner. The poorer player aims in a general direction and fails to position his body so he can make the proper swing motion on the correct path.

The solution, then, is simple, and it's the basis for playing golf well:

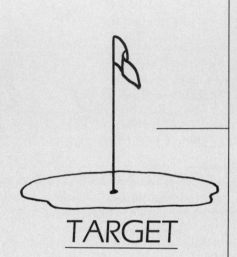

TARGET

# 1. PREPARATION
SHOT DECISION
VISUALIZATION AND FEEL
INTERMEDIATE TARGET

# 2. POSITION
CLUB FACE
BALL
BODY

# 3. POSTURE
ARMS
BALANCE
AXIS

# 4. PATH
BALL
CLUB
ARMS

# 5. PACE
CLUB
ARMS
LEGS

*Aim the club down the line on which you want the ball to start and accommodate all parts of your body so the club can swing down that line.*

The rest of this chapter will be devoted to giving you concepts that will let you learn to do just that. But before you begin, try to erase from your mind one of the most damaging myths in golf instruction and accept instead this paramount concept: *A contrived setup produces a natural swing and a natural setup produces a contrived swing.*

Think about that for a moment. Chances are it is contrary to everything you have read or heard about addressing a golf ball. Countless good players and teachers will tell you that you must feel natural and comfortable at address. Even Jack Nicklaus falls into that trap. In his excellent book, *Golf My Way,* he tells us that setup is "the single most important maneuver in golf," and nobody is more meticulous about it than he. Yet a few pages later he warns against anything being "forced or contrived or exaggerated at address." He tells you to be comfortable and as natural as possible within the simple fundamentals of good setup."

As sound as that advice seems to be, you are led astray for one primary reason: Jack Nicklaus feels comfortable in a good setup position because he learned to play from that position when he was 12 years old and worked very hard on it all during his formative years. Of course he can address the ball naturally; he's been doing it for more than 30-years.

Unfortunately, what feels natural and comfortable to you may be wrong. So when you first get into the correct setup position, it will feel unnatural and uncomfortable. You may have to force some positions and exaggerate them for awhile. Certainly your body position will be contrived or arranged.

We've never put a student in the correct position—either grip, aim and alignment or body arrangement—without evoking a negative response. We're invariably told, "That's uncomfortable." Then we must reinforce the student, just as you must reinforce yourself, with the thought that no matter how uncomfortable you feel at the moment, what you are doing is right and will prove out in the long run. Accept the fact that this contrived feeling can give you a natural, free-flowing, on-line swing.

If you are to be a good player, you will *never* stop working on your setup—Jack Nicklaus never has. And you probably will never be able to address the ball "naturally" (which usually means carelessly) without thinking about it. Nicklaus still thinks about it on every shot. But you *will* eventually feel comfortable over the ball.

At that point, your natural setup

---

## The Five P's
*The chart at left illustrates the Five P's—preparation, position, posture, path and pace—and what is involved in each, all related to getting the ball to go to the target.*

will be a correct one.

## The first two P's

The structure of our teaching and your learning system is clear and simple, encompassed within the Five P's we mentioned in the first chapter—*preparation, position, posture, path and pace.*

These Five P's give you a framework within which to assemble your knowledge without becoming ''over-conceptualized'' and confused. They give you a simple means of organizing your mind so you don't have to worry about every particle of information you have absorbed.

Although an understanding of what makes the golf swing work will make you strike the ball better, that's only part of the answer. People who are not familiar with the athletic act have a tendency to feel that the more knowledge they gain, the better they will play—automatically. That's not so. To perform well, you must be able to channel all your knowledge, all your thoughts, into a simple approach.

The Five P's give you a simple, overall concept that will enable you to condense all your information into clear guidelines for swinging and playing more effectively.

In this chapter we will discuss the two P's that apply to your pre-swing preferences—*position* and *posture*. It might appear that preparation belongs in that category, but that actually is the factor that ties your pre-

swing and in-swing preferences into an effective whole on the course. So preparation will be dealt with in a later chapter.

Position and posture have to do with arranging your body to allow you to build a consistent swing. Each consists of four basic actions, in sequence.

*Position.* (1) Place your hands to the club; (2) place the clubface to the ball, on the path and aiming down the target line; (3) align your body to the clubface and the target line or path; (4) position your body to the ball.

*Posture.* (1) Bend at the hips so your arms are hanging; (2) flex your knees slightly; (3) place your weight toward the balls of your feet; (4) position your upper body behind your lower body, with more weight on the right leg.

Now let's discuss these actions in detail.

## Position

*Grip.* If the grip is not the most important element in a golf swing, it certainly ranks right up there. The purpose of the grip is to insure that the arms can swing the club freely on the correct path and the hands can react to square the clubface at impact. To accomplish this, you must accommodate the grip—the position of your hands on the club—to your body type, the way you swing, the way you play the game.

The *ideal* grip is one that puts the hands in what we like to call *a posi-*

*tion of neutrality.* To visualize the neutral grip, place your hands together, fingers extended, as if you were praying. Now lower them to an approximate address position. Slide the right hand down until the curves of the thumb pads fit snugly together. Notice that the back of the left hand and the palm of the right are facing down a line parallel to the target line. This is approximately the position in which your hands will be when you place them on the club.

Remember, though, that we said *ideal.* To fit your particular body structure and/or swing tendencies, you might have to deviate from that ideal. We'll elaborate on that later on in this section.

Whatever grip position you use, it is important that the hands work together as a unit. When they do that, you have less friction between the parts of the swing and can create more clubhead speed with control. To work as a unit, the hands must be positioned as close together as possible.

There are two basic choices of grips— the interlocking and the overlap, or Vardon, grip—plus a third we call the eight-finger or "unlap" grip that might be desirable for certain players. With the interlocking grip, the little finger of the right hand is interlocked or entwined with the forefinger of the left, and in the overlap or Vardon grip the right little finger is hooked around the left forefinger, laid between the forefinger and middle finger of the left hand.

There is no evidence that either of these grips works better than the other. Jack Nicklaus and Tom Kite, whose fingers are shorter than normal, use the interlocking grip, which is pretty good testimony to its effectiveness. The majority of good players use the overlap grip. The criteria you should use in deciding which is best for you are the size of your hands, the thickness and length of your fingers and the thickness of your palms. We suggest that you experiment with both to see that the club rests in the base of the palm of the left hand and the fingers of the right, and that both hands are as close together and as unified as possible.

The eight-finger or unlap grip, which we sometimes recommend, will be discussed later.

Regardless of which method you use, the same fundamentals apply in finding the correct grip position. Remember as you follow these fundamentals that they are only parameters and that you may have to make the alterations we discuss later to fit your individual needs.

The first thing to understand is that you don't want to change the normal relationship of your shoulder, elbow, wrist and hand when you attach the club to your body. Stand erect but relaxed and let your arms hang at your sides. In 90 percent of the golfers we see, the hands will be turned slightly inward. This is basic-

### How to form the neutral grip
The correct neutral grip is accomplished by placing
your left hand against the club square or perpendicular to the target line (1). The club should run diagonally from under the heel pad as shown. (2). The fingers
of left hand then close around the club, turning up
toward the palm, the pressure in the last three fingers
and the thumb runnng staight down the handle, slightly right of center (3). The right hand is placed square
against the club (4), then is closed around the handle,
the right forefinger "triggered" and the thumb resting

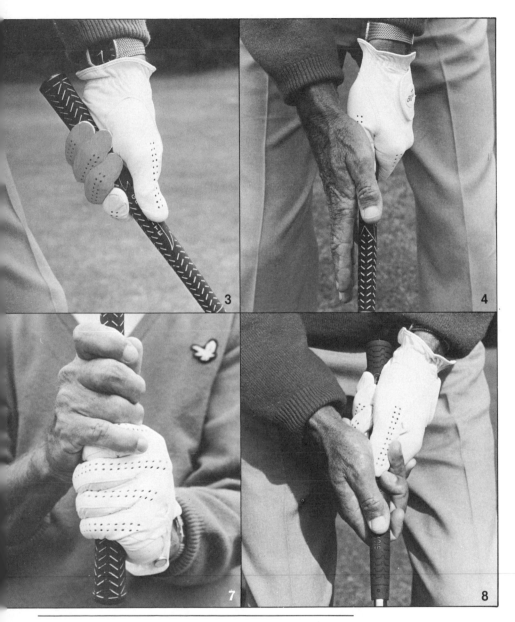

on the left side of the handle (5). Note in the complet-ed grip how the V's formed by the thumbs and forefin-gers of each hand point approximately straight up each arm. The right hand pressure is primarily in the last three fingers (6). Picture 7 shows another view of the completed grip, illustrating how the right little fin-gers hooks around the forefinger of the left hand. Pic-ture 8 shows the "putting" grip used for chipping, with the hands more opposed—the left hand turned more to the left and the right hand turned more to the right—to stabilize the wrists.

59

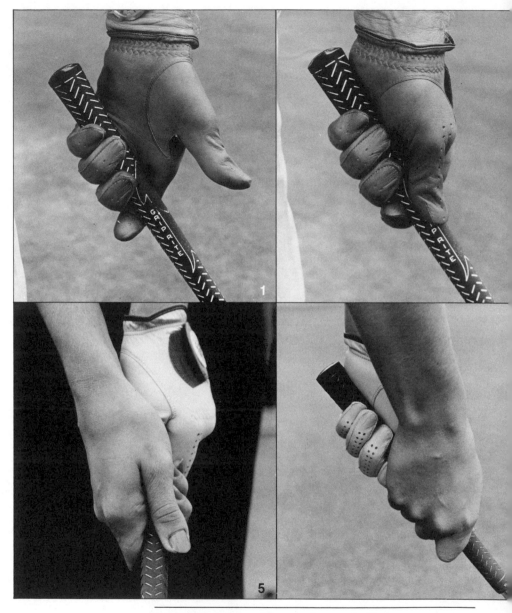

## How to form other grip variations

*To form the so-called stronger grip you might need if you have trouble releasing and rotating the club, place the handle deeper in the palm or more toward the fingers (1 and 2). The hand then is turned more to the right, the back of the hand more on top of the club (3). The right hand also is turned more to the right or under the handle so that both V's point approximately*

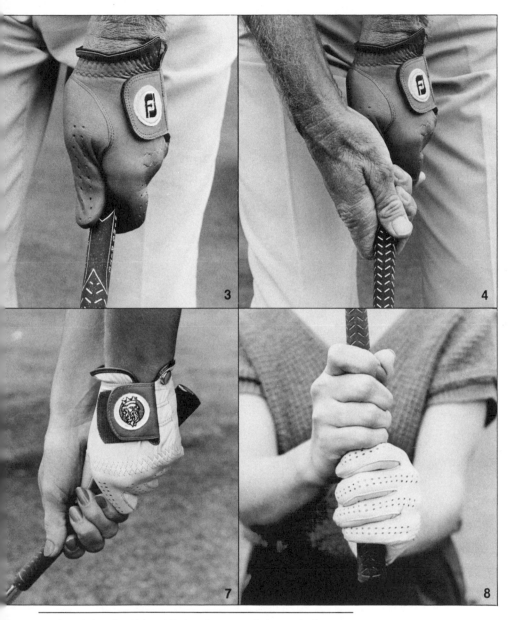

to the right shoulder (4). In pictures 4 through 8 you
see different views of the unlap grip, all eight fingers
and the thumbs placed on the club, that might be appropriate for some women and players who lack
strength and have extraordinary difficulty in turning
over the clubface through impact. The same pressure
points as shown for the neutral grip apply in both
cases.

61

ally the position in which you want them when they are holding a golf club. This allows flexibility, rotation, a good wristcock and freedom of motion. If you do anything to disturb this normal configuration, you will restrict your natural rotation and tend to create too much tension in your golf swing.

With that in mind, take a club and place your left hand against it, fingers extended as shown on page 58. The club should run diagonally from the base joint of your forefinger across the palm, resting *underneath* the heel pad of the hand. Now turn the fingers toward the palm, closing them inward, around and up on the handle of the club. When you do this, the back of the hand will change position only slightly and your thumb will end up resting on the right side of the club, just past center. Don't turn the palm toward the fingers, because this will position your hand too much on top of the club.

By placing the club at the base of the fingers and in the palm and closing your fingers in this manner, you create a much more secure grip, one that will stabilize the left hand and wrist and give you more clubface control when you swing, especially when you want to hit the ball hard. If you hold the club too much in the fingers or let the handle ride up over the heel pad, or both, you build a concave wrist position that could cause excessive hand rotation and loss of clubface control.

To position the right hand, place it against the side of the shaft, the handle resting against the roots of the fingers, snug against the callous pads. Again, the first three fingers close upward and around, toward the palm. The right little finger hooks around the left forefinger, resting in the groove between that and the left index finger, if you are using the Vardon or overlap grip *(See photos, page 59.)* With the interlocking grip, the little finger of the right will hook under the forefinger of the left, resting between the forefinger and index finger. The manner in which the little finger hooks around the forefinger in the Vardon grip is important. If it is too much on top of the forefinger, it sets the right hand too high or toward the left. If the little finger is snuggled too much into the groove, it turns the right hand too far under or to the right. Either way, complications are created.

The left thumb fits snugly into the channel between the heel and thumb pads of the right hand, while the right thumb falls naturally to the left side of the handle, forming a V with the forefinger. Don't pinch the closed end of the V too tightly together, because that creates tension in the wrong place.

At this point, the palm of your right hand should be facing approximately toward the target and should be pretty much aligned with the back of the left hand. The Vs formed by the thumb and forefinger of each hand should be pointing to a spot somewhere between your right shoulder and your chin.

Again, we emphasize that this is the *model* grip we have just described. It may or may not fit your particular needs. Everybody's physical structure is not the same. Everybody's hands are not built the same way. Everybody cannot or may not want to swing the same way. So you may want to make some adjustments to find the grip position that best fits your body and swing shape to give you maximum control over the clubface.

A player of normal height or taller, with reasonable strength and a swing that is relatively upright, probably should use a grip that approximates the model. This is especially true if he has no problem creating enough hand speed to release and square the club through impact and draw the golf ball. However, a shorter player with a swing that is more around his body might want to turn his hands a little more to the right to accommodate that swing shape. Similarly, a weaker player who needs more hand action to create clubhead speed might want to put the club a little deeper in the

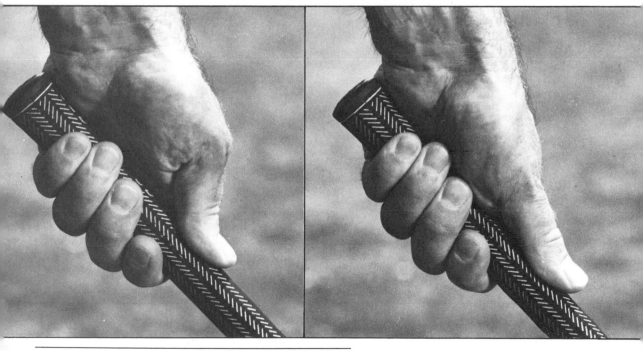

### The long versus short thumb
*The left thumb can rest on the club either in a "short" or arched position (left), or it can be extended into a "long" position by sliding it comfortably down the handle (right). This extension should not be so great that you feel constricted or uncomfortable. The long thumb is preferred by most players because it provides greater wrist stability throughout the swing.*

fingers of his left hand, also putting the left hand more on top and the right hand more to the right or under to facilitate the wrist hinge that will give him that hand action. This could also be necessary for a player who lacks flexibility in his wrists.

An even weaker player, especially one with very small hands, might consider trying the eight-finger or unlap grip. Many women, particularly, fall into this category. We see a lot of them who, because of the strength factor or hand size, cannot play effectively with the interlocking or overlapping grip.

The unlap grip is formed in exactly the same manner as the other two, except that the little finger of the right hand is placed on the club rather than being hooked around or entwined with the forefinger of the left. With all eight fingers thus on the club, the right hand is placed lower on the shaft in a more dominant position. This makes it easier to release and square the clubface through impact and to recock the hands after impact, thus creating the needed hand and clubhead speed.

You may have to experiment to find the grip position that best keeps the clubface square as you swing back and release and square up through impact. Remember that the best determinant of your grip's effectiveness is the way the ball flies—where it starts, how much curvature there is to your shots and how much distance you are getting. If your shots slice from left to right, or start weakly to the right and tail off even farther to the right, chances are your hands are set too much to the left on the club, your left hand tending to be under and your right hand too much on top. If you hook the ball from right to left, or your shots start out left and go farther left, your hands could be turned too much to the right, the left too much on top and the right too far under.

Remember also that if you are going to make a mistake, it is better to have your hands set too far to the right, your left hand over the shaft and your right hand under. The more the right hand sets under, the more it relaxes and softens the right arm, causing it to fold inward and get out of the way during the backswing. It drops the right side underneath the left and allows the club to be taken straight back, then inside and up. If the right hand is too high on the club, it activates the outside muscles of the arm and prevents the wrist from folding on the backswing. Thus, the first move on the backswing is usually to the outside of the target line, from where the clubhead quickly circles back inside and gets ''laid off'' with the face too shut. This causes a reaction that forces the club quickly to the outside of the target line on the forward swing, resulting in a pull, a pull-hook or a pull-slice, depending on what you do with your hands.

Almost every good player starts out with his hands in the left over-right under position, because it is a more natural way to hold the club. Almost every motion we make in propelling an object forward, whether it is throwing a baseball or a football or swinging a baseball bat or a golf club, is done with the right hand coming from under to over. Eventually, as a golfer begins to curve hls shots too much with the hands in this position, he adjusts in the direction of the model grip. This lessens the rotation of the hands during the swing, allows him to stabilize his left hand and wrist against the force of the blow to keep the club from turning over too quickly and lets him hit shots with less curvature.

So, to repeat, the model grip is best if you have the strength and talent to swing on a plane that lets you generate enough arm and hand speed to get the job done. The model grip promotes good aim and alignment, it encourages swinging the shaft on the proper plane and it does help stabilize the hands and wrists against excessive rotation, which results in a simpler swing and more clubface control.

However, if the talent level and the body you bring to the task, and the time you have to devote to that task, preclude your using the model grip, you may have to make one or more of the accommodations we have suggested. You may need more hand rotation to generate as much clubhead speed as possible and to hook the ball to get more distance. This is not a copout, and it will not make you fall short of your goal, which is to play better golf. Rather, it can help you play much better golf than you ever thought possible . . . and play it longer. We watched Gene Sarazan play excellent golf at the age of 82 because he used his hands to produce clubhead speed that he couldn't get from the other parts of his body.

After you have finished this book and understand all of our setup and swing concepts, experiment with your grip until you find the position that works best for *you*. Your shots will tell you if you are on the right track.

*Grip pressure.* The matter of pressure points in your two hands and the amount of pressure you apply is at least as important as the position of the hands. A poor player not only must learn how to hold the club, he must learn how to grip it, which means applying pressure in the correct places and in the correct amounts.

Here is the cardinal rule for applying grip pressure:

*Apply only as much pressure as you need to control the force of the club throughout your swing.*

Therein lies the reason the good player has a long, flowing motion and continuity of rhythm.

Grip pressure should be applied in

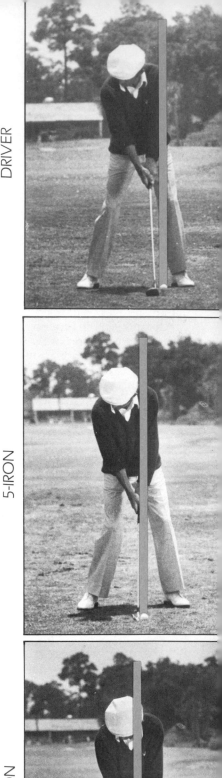

DRIVER

5-IRON

9-IRON

### Address and swing positions change, depending on club

*Notice in these sequences with the driver, 5-iron and 9-iron how the positions of the head and swing center change, both at address and during the swing, in relation to the ball. With the driver, Bob Toski's head is set more behind the ball and stays there throughout the swing, causing him to be in more of a "C" position at impact. Thus he swings the club into the ball on more of a level to upward arc, which, because the ball is on a tee and above the center of the clubface at address, allows him to strike it with that center. With the 5-iron, the ball is positioned farther back in the stance, the head and swing center are set less behind the ball and the swing is more downward, and the body in more of an "I" position. With the 9-iron, the ball even farther back, this is accentuated, the head and swing center almost ahead of the ball and the swing angle more steeply downward. It can easily be seen that the position of the swing center and the angle of descent are directly related to the loft of the club and the length of the shaft.*

the last three fingers of each hand. This includes the little finger of the right hand, even though it is off the shaft and hooked over the forefinger of the left. Pressure in the last three fingers activates the muscles in the inside, or underneath, portion of the arm, which are the muscles you want to use during the forward portion of your swing.

Further, pressure in the last three fingers rather than in the thumb and forefingers of each hand eliminates unwanted tension and creates freedom for the arms to swing. Without our getting technical, those inside muscles are basically attached at the elbow and most of them run no farther up the arm. On the other hand, muscles activated by the thumb and forefinger run all the way to the shoulder. So you can grip relatively firmly with the last three fingers and still leave the upper arms and shoulders free to swing and turn. Pressure in the thumb and forefinger stiffens the muscles all the way up and restricts your swing and shoulder turn.

To prove this to yourself, assume an address position without a club, using your left arm only. Tightly clench the last three fingers of your left hand and swing the left arm back and up as far as you can. Now repeat, this time clenching the thumb and forefinger tightly. Notice that your left arm feels more restricted and cannot be swung back as far.

Applying pressure in the last three fingers only is especially important in the right hand, because the common tendency is to grab and exert pressure with the right thumb and forefinger. When this happens, the right arm—instead of being pulled inward and down by the inside muscles—is forced higher and toward the outside by the outside muscles. This causes the club to be taken back to the outside and creates the problems we discussed earlier. Also, the right hand is lower on the club and closer to the line of play, which gives it more chance to throw the club out of position if pressure is being exerted too close to the clubhead.

Watch any good touring professional as he finishes a swing; the right thumb and forefinger are almost always the first to slip off the club. Notice how the right hand then comes completely off the club, leaving it entirely in the left, an example that tells us clearly which hand is applying the most pressure. The drill on page 93 may help you get the feeling for this.

If you are going to control the golf swing with your left arm and side, more pressure must be in your left hand than your right. (Remember, in all our instruction, left and right should be reversed if you are a left-hander.) Maintaining control in your left hand helps keep the right hand from taking over at that critical moment when you change directions at the top of your swing.

Please don't interpret this to mean there is *no* pressure from the right hand. In the first place, you need *some* pressure in the right thumb and forefinger to provide a cradle that supports the club at the top of the swing. And pressure at the point where the thumb pad of the left hand presses against the butt pad of the right will unify the hands, wrists and arms during the swing. It also tends to make the elbows stay closer together and closer to the body, where you want them while you are swinging. So right hand pressure, particularly in the middle two fingers, *is* important, but it should not be as strong as with the left.

Almost every player below the level of professional or top amateur grips the club too tightly. Assuming this may be your problem, too, we urge you to think about gripping the club as *lightly* as you possibly can—much lighter than you ever imagined—while still being able to swing it with control.

A light grip frees your muscles to produce a relaxed but swift swing. The lighter your pressure on the club, the easier your arms swing, and thus the faster they swing.

A light grip allows you to feel the force of the club being swung around the body, and until you can feel that force you cannot capture the essence of the golf swing. When you lighten your grip, you will rid your arms and upper body of tension and your swing will become longer, freer and more rhythmic. You'll be able to feel the weight of the club as you swing it back and through and you'll play with grace and ease.

How light is light—for you? Let's go back to two earlier premises: swing the club only as fast as your strength will allow and apply only enough pressure to control the club during the swing.

Two related factors come into play here: individual strength and the weight of your golf equipment. A good checkpoint is to hold your driver in mid-air, pointing straight out in front of you, with your left hand. Exert only enough pressure in the last three fingers of your hand to keep the driver parallel to the ground. If you cannot do this in a relatively relaxed manner, if you must tighten you muscles to their fullest and create a great deal of tension in your arm and upper body, then your club is too long or too heavy.

If this is the case, you might want to do some exercises that will increase your strength over the long haul. In the short run, it would probably be better for you to get some lighter and perhaps shorter clubs that you can handle without overexerting yourself.

We would guess, however, that no matter how heavy your clubs might be, you could control them with a lighter grip pressure than you are now applying. The only sure way to find out how light that grip can be is to hit practice shots, starting with as little pressure as possible and gradually increasing it until you can control the club while maintaining a tension-free arm swing.

Al Koch, a Dallas, Texas, electronics expert, has developed a device that records pressure in the last three fingers of the left hand throughout the swing. Koch has found, in general, that the better player, who might have a grip pressure potential of 25-35 pounds per square inch, will hold the club· with only three to five pounds of pressure at address. From that point, the pressure in the left hand will increase at a relatively smooth rate until impact, and even then the player is usually gripping with less than half his potential strength.

Tests on poorer players show more grip pressure at address and at the takeaway, after which the left-hand grip pressure slackens through impact. This means that the right hand has taken over and is controlling the swing.

Light grip pressure, then, is one of our basic precepts. But please don't confuse *light* with *loose*. We believe strongly in grip *firmness,* a grip that remains *solid* without slipping during the swing. There is a great difference between lightness and looseness. You can keep your grip firm and solid while still holding the club lightly.

The key to a solid grip, no matter how light, is maintaining *constant* grip pressure throughout the swing, especially in your left hand. If your grip pressure changes during the swing, you will change your arm swing and disrupt your rhythm and pace. You are also likely to alter your swing path and clubface position. This is especially true if the pressure increases in your right thumb and forefinger, which it usually does.

To be able to maintain *constant* grip pressure, realize that the pressure differs slightly for different clubs and different swings. The pressure for a full driver shot will be greater than for a half-swing with a wedge, just as the pressure using a 2-iron will be a little greater than for a 5-iron. The laws of physics dictate that if you are going to swing a club longer and faster, you must hold onto it more firmly.

We're talking about grip pressure at address. There is no question that the grip pressure increases instinctively as you begin to swing the club back. That is something nobody can avoid. But in the better player it increases minimally.

The less your grip pressure changes when you swing the club back and the more constant it remains throughout the swing, the more constant your arm flow will be and the more sensitivity you will have for the force of the club swinging back and through the shot.

The difference in grip pressure required for each club, from the driver down through the wedge and putter, is not something that can be taught. You become aware of this difference by starting where you learn the feel of the swing itself, with the putt. Experiment for awhile on the putting green and you'll find that when you are putting your best, your grip pressure remains constant; it is very light on the club and your arms and body are free of tension. When you move to the fringe of the green and begin to chip the ball, your grip pressure becomes a bit firmer, but it stays constant and you remain free of tension. And so it will go through the pitch shots, iron shots and full swings with the woods. All the while your grip pressure will be increasing slightly at address, but it will remain within the spectrum of a light grip that keeps you free of tension and allows you the free arm flow you need to achieve the best feel for the swing.

*Aiming the clubface.* Before you aim the clubface at the target, make sure your hands are placed on the club in proper position and *in proper relation to the clubface.* When your hands are in this position, the clubface should be aiming directly down the target line.

Remember our basic objective—trying to hit the ball relatively straight. Except for special shotmaking situations, the only reason golf-

ers curve the ball excessively is because they are not properly aimed at the target. If we want to strike a ball reasonably straight to the target, we had better be aimed there in the first place. Clubface position influences almost everything else in the setup and swing. *(See illustration, page 72.)*

To aim the club properly, we advocate using an "intermediate target." This might be a divot, a leaf, a clump of grass or some other identifiable spot from four to 12 feet in front of your ball that is directly on the line between your ball and the target. The reason for using this intermediate target is that it is easier to aim at a spot close to you than at a target 150 or 200 yards away.

Stand a few yards behind the ball to pick out this intermediate spot. Then move to the ball and place your blade, aiming it at this spot. With an iron club, we find it best to aim by using the vertical lines on the clubface. Most clubs will have these vertical lines at the toe and heel end of the striking surface. They may be scored into the clubface or they may be delineated by the sand-blasted portion of the face.

Imagine these lines as parallel tracks running from the clubface to the target, and simply aim that track line so it runs directly to the target. This will place your clubface—more specifically, the lower portion or leading edge of your clubface—

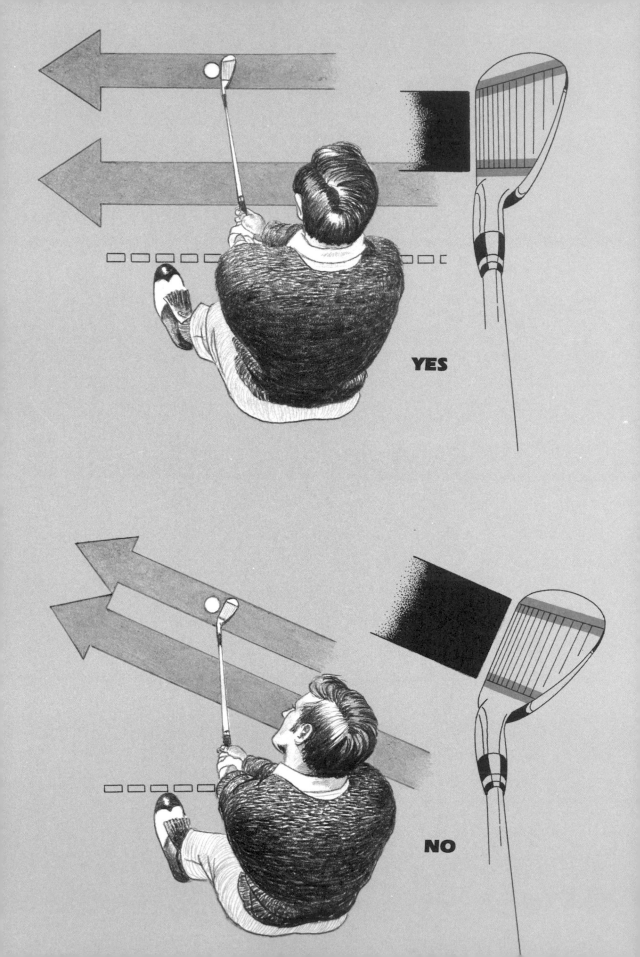

**YES**

**NO**

perpendicular or at right angles to your target line.

There are no vertical lines on woods, of course, so to aim them you must depend on getting the clubface perpendicular to your target line. A great aid in doing this is to place another club on the ground just outside your ball on a line parallel to your target line and set the clubface perpendicular to that club. This is a practice device only, of course, but it's invaluable in getting your clubface aligned properly.

*Aligning your eyes.* How you see determines how you aim and subsequently how you swing a club. That is one of the least understood and most violated principles of good aim and alignment. Faulty optical alignment is one of the biggest contributors to poor play among most golfers.

The most common fault is to cock the chin toward the target at such an angle that the eye line is set to the right of the target. We see few players who have their eye lines set to the left, although that does happen. Whichever direction your eyes are looking, it is going to influence the way you set your clubface, your path and the compensations you must make with your hands and shoulders during the swing.

To aim and swing the club on the line on which you want the ball to start, your eyes must be sighting down that line. This means your eye line must be parallel to the line. Here are some checkpoints:

*1. Be sure your head is straight as you address the ball.* Imagine a vertical line that runs directly in front of you and align your head with it. Don't tilt your head to one side or the other. Practice in front of a mirror to get the feeling of your head being set straight. Next, as you complete your setup, rotate your head slightly to the right, making sure your chin stays behind your forehead. Always look at the target by rotating your head to the left rather than by lifting your head up and around.

*2. Rotate your chin a bit more to the right or counterclockwise* just before you start your backswing, with your head and eyes in the position we've just described. This movement, which can be seen in the swings of almost all the great players, rotates your head along the swing path and helps you get a better feel for that path. Thus, you are able to take the club away and return it to the ball correctly.

*3. Keep your eye line constant during the swing.* Avoid moving it forward or backward and changing its angle to the right or left. There will be a tendency to do just that, especially just before you start your forward swing.

*4. After you have struck the shot, follow the flight of the ball by rotating your head and eyes.* In other words, watch the ball as the same way you viewed the target at address. Don't lift your head as you

## Use vertical lines to aim at target
*The use of the vertical lines on your iron clubface can help you better aim down the line of play to the target. These lines, usually formed by the sandblasted area on your clubface, should be used to visualize a track running directly to the target (top). This will help you set your eyes parallel to the target line. If your optical alignment and clubhead track are set to the right of your target (bottom), it will cause complications in your swing path and mechanics.*

follow through. Watching the shot from "underneath" rather than from "on top" gives you a sense of deliverng the ball on a direct line to your target because you haven't changed your optical perspective. It lets you better identify your image of the ball in flight and will help you establish a feel and a mental picture for correct swings in the future.

To develop your optical routine, again start with the putt. Stroke a putt and hold your eye alignment as you watch the ball roll. When you have practiced this enough that it becomes second nature, progress to short shots and then to full shots.

Your optical routine is incorporated into both your setup preparations and your actual swing. We have presented the entire routine, illustrated below, so you can understand how it ties the setup and swing together.

*Aligning your body.* Aiming your clubface properly gets you only half-

way to your goal of aiming the shot correctly. Now you must aim your body, which means aligning all the parts of your body on a line parallel to the target line.

To accomplish this, we use "the six lines of alignment." *(See photo, page 77)*. These six lines start with the target line and go from there to lines drawn parallel with that target line through the toes, knees, hips, shoulders and eyes. Imagine that you have five boards, and place one against each of those parts of your anatomy. If your body is aligned correctly, each board will run parallel to your target line. This is the position that will be accommodate your arms swinging down the path to the target.

That sounds simple, and it is. The problem in accomplishing this lies in the long-standing myth that your body should be aimed *at* the target. Assuming that the concept of having the body square to, or parallel with,

74

## To sight target, rotate your eyes parallel to line

*During your address procedure, insure proper optical alignment by rotating your head and eyes on a line parallel to the target line as you view the target. Don't lift your head and sight the target directly. Keeping your eyes in proper alignment will get your swing going on the proper path. When you have swung through the shot, follow the flight of the ball by similarly rotating your head and eyes rather than lifting your head up and around.*

the target line is valid, and it is, then aiming the body at the target automatically aims the clubface to the right of the target. That, along with faulty optics, is probably the main reason such a high percentage of our pupils aims to the right.

In actuality, if your body alignment is square to the correctly aimed clubface, and parallel to the target line, it cannot be aimed at the target. Because you are standing to the left of the ball as you view the target, your body must be set *parallel left,* parallel to your target line but aimed left of your target.

This creates the feeling of being aimed far to the left of the target, which is enhanced by an optical illusion created by distance. Many players make the mistake of assuming that because their shoulders are about two feet from the ball at address they should be aimed at a spot two feet left of the target. Because of that optical illusion, they will appear to be set a great deal farther left than that. A general guideline is that at 100 yards your shoulders will appear to be aiming eight yards left of your target, at 170 yards they will seem to be set 12 yards left and at 240 yards 16 yards left. Your individual perception may vary because of your posture, which might put your shoulders closer to or farther from the target line, or simply because of vision peculiarities. Surveyors tell us that the dis-

tance your eyes are set apart has an effect on this illusion.

A good way to determine how far left you should feel you are set is to place two clubs on the ground, either at a marked practice area or at spots on your course where you know the distances to your target are accurate. Put one club on the target line and the other underneath your shoulder line at address, parallel to the target line. Stand just behind the shoulder-line pointer club and sight down it. Note the spot in the target area where the club is pointing. That's the spot at which your shoulders should be aiming, with the rest of your body aligned accordingly. When you set up properly, you should barely see your left shoulder as you rotate your head and eyes toward the target. If you see too much of your left shoulder, it means you are aligned too far to the right.

(For left-handers, the whole procedure should be reversed. Your concept should be that of aiming *parallel right.)*

*Finding your ball position.* The final step in positioning your body to the ball is placing it in the proper spot in relation to your swing arc: the spot where the club will be coming into the ball at the best possible angle.

Start with this guideline: with the irons and fairway woods—anything other than a driver—you want to strike the ball with a slightly des-

## The six lines of alignment

There are six imaginary lines of alignment with which you should be concerned. The first, of course, is the target line. Then imagine lines running across your toes, your knees, hips, shoulders and eyes. All these lines should be parallel to the target line if your body is to be aligned properly, as Jim Flick demonstrates here.

### Swing center, alignment vary with club

*At address, both the ball position and the relationship of your swing center to the ball vary according to the length of club you have in your hand and whether the ball is on a tee or on the ground. Similarly, your body alignment in relation to the target line will vary. In the top row of pictures, Jim Flick's swing center, is about four inches behind the ball with a driver and the ball on a tee (1). With a middle iron (2), the swing center is positioned at the back of the ball, and with a short iron (3), it is directly over the ball. Notice that the ball moves back in the stance as the club gets shorter. In the bottom row of pictures, Bob Toski demonstrates that with a driver (1) his body alignment is more closed to the target line, which promotes a swing that is shallower and more around the body. With a middle iron (2), his alignment is square to the target line, while with a short iron (3), his body set more open or to the left of the target line. His arm hang also varies, more extended with the driver and getting closer to his body as the club gets shorter.*

cending blow; with a driver, you want to catch the ball after the club has reached the bottom of its arc and is slightly on the upswing.

Given that, your ball position becomes an individual matter, dictated basically by your ability to strike the ball with the club coming from the inside. The more difficulty you have returning the club from inside the target line, the farther back you should position the ball.

Our experience has been that amost everybody should play the ball more toward the center of the stance. Try starting by positioning the ball on a tee for a driver shot two to three inches inside the left heel. For the fairway woods, play the ball just ahead of the center of your stance. For the irons, try positioning the ball in the center. Then adjust, depending on what is happening to your shots. If the ball is starting too far to the right and/or you are hooking it too much, move the ball forward in your stance until you get the desired shot shape.

Playing the ball forward in the stance is a luxury usually accorded only the good player with strong leg support, the ability to shift his weight from the ground up and move his lower body laterally so he can still strike the ball from the inside.

If you do not have that good leg support, if you have lost some agility because you are heavy-set or are less supple because of age or in-

firmity and cannot move well with your legs, you probably should play the ball back farther in your stance with all clubs. Experiment to find the best position for your particular swing and physical capabilities.

The angle of descent into the ball will vary with each club, of course, but you take care of that by varying your posture, which we will discuss next. The ball position for each group of clubs— irons, fairway woods and driver—should remain constant, except when you want to hit high, low or other special shots.

## Posture

Posture deals with the position of your body as you address the ball. Since it has a lot to do with how you swing a golf club, it's logical that you adopt a posture that will help you swing the way you *want* to.

We believe the swing should be controlled by the arms rather than by the shoulders. The simplest and most efficient method of striking a golf ball is with a free arm swing that takes the club straight back, then inside the target line, around your body and up, then down from slightly inside the backswing path to along that line and back inside it on the follow-through.

Our posture precepts are based on promoting this freedom of arm swing. Briefly, those precepts are:

1. The weight usually should be set more on the right side than the left.

## Adjust ball position depending on shot

*The positions of the ball in relation to your feet changes with the type of shot you wish to play. For the driver, the ball should be positioned an inch or so inside your left heel (left) so you can catch the ball on a level or slightly ascending arc. With the irons and fairway woods, position the ball two or three inches inside your left heel (right). This allows you to strike the ball a slightly descending blow.*

81

2. The weight should be toward the balls of the feet.

3. The knees should be flexed just slightly, no more than three or four inches.

4. The back should be straight but tilted forward from the hips enough that the arms hang freely suspended from the shoulders.

5. The right side should be set lower then the left, the knees cocked toward the target.

Let's look at these factors in more detail.

*1. Weight right.* Years ago, when we were learning the game as youngsters, we were taught to address the ball with our weight on the left foot. That myth persists today, even though there is no logical reason for it.

In the first place, it is not a natural position. Try this experiment: Stand with your weight balanced between your two feet, bend your upper body forward from the hips, place your hands together in a praying position and let your arms hang as if you were addressing a golf ball. Now slide your right hand a couple of inches lower than the left, as if you were positioning it on a golf club. What happens? Your weight goes to the right side, doesn't it?

Since the legs support the body during the swing, it doesn't make sense to start with the weight on the left leg to support a movement that's going to the right on the back-swing. It would mean shifting position from left to right and back to left again in about a second and a half. It's much simpler to rest the weight on the right leg so it can support the backswing from the start.

Setting the weight right frees up the left side and creates an interesting phenomenon. Good players seem to swing the left side of the body around the right leg on the backswing, putting the left leg in a position to move on the forward swing and the right leg in a position to react to it and move forward into the shot. Poorer players appear to swing the right side around the left leg.

In general, players who set up with their weight on the left side control the swing with their shoulders. This creates a great deal of tension. It also causes a disastrous reversal of position, the upper body tilting toward the target or in front of the ball at the top of the swing. Those who set up with their weight to the right and free up the left side can swing their arms with enough motion to pull them properly behind the ball on the backswing.

The weight should be set more to the right for almost every full shot (there are variations for the short shots that we'll get into later), but the ratio changes depending on the club. That's because the placing of the weight also affects the *angle of approach,* the steepness of the arc on which the club swings into the ball. *In general, the farther you are*

## Weight more to right for longer shot

*With a driver (left), Bob Toski sets his weight more to the right. With a short iron, the weight is balanced about 50/50 without ever putting more weight on the left side than the right. Notice also that with the driver, intending to make a level or upward swing into the ball, the hands are positioned about even with the back of the ball. With a short iron, they are set even with or slightly ahead of the front of the ball.*

*trying to hit the ball, the more
weight you want on your right side*
—this gives you a takeaway that is
lower and slower and a return that
comes in on a shallower arc and
travels parallel to the ground longer
through the impact area.

Your feeling, especially with the
longer clubs, is that your right side
is soft and your weight is moving
toward the right leg. Among other
things, this helps you get your left
heel off the ground more easily and
your body turning more freely.

As the club in your hand gets progressively shorter, your weight
should be progressively more balanced, moving more *toward* your
left side. This is because the shorter
the club, the steeper the descent
into the ball should be. But your
weight distribution for a normal full
shot, even with the short irons,
should never go past 50/50—you
should *never* have more of it on
the left side, for all the reasons
we've mentioned, unless you are
playing a shot that you need to keep
especially low.

The placement of your weight is
pretty much dictated by where you
position your head in relation to the
ball. The farther behind the ball you
set your head for the longer shots,
the more your body tilts to the right
and the more your weight naturally
falls to the right side.

You also should try to develop the
sensation that with a short iron at
impact you are striking the ball from

a slightly downhill lie, while as
the club gets longer you feel as if
you are sriking it from a level to
slightly uphill lie. These sensations,
of course, are pretty much created
by your address position.

One important point—when we
say set the weight right, we mean
set it to the *inside* of the right foot.
This helps keep the weight from
moving too far to the outside of
the right knee and foot during the
backswing. We encourage good motion, body turn and weight shift
going back, but if you overdo it you
can force a breakdown in your right
leg, which is the foundation of your
swing.

*2. Weight toward balls of feet.*
Notice we didn't say on your toes.
The weight should be more toward
the balls than the heels. This promotes a feeling of catlike mobility in
your legs. Think back to the sports
you have played or watched. Can
you think of any that are performed
from the heels? Most every athlete
who needs motion starts from the
balls of his feet. Well, golf too requires good leg movement for the
free motion you need in your swing.

*3. Knees slightly flexed.* The
knees should be flexed only enough
to unlock them. You should feel
some springy tension in the inside of
your legs and the backs of your
thighs. Remember, your right leg is
supporting you as you swing around
it. Too deep a knee flex, a common
fault, creates a weak support for

## The correct posture

*Jim Flick demonstrates proper posture, setting up with his upper body behind the ball, his knee cocked toward the target, his right knee and right shoulder lower than the left and his hands about even with the ball for a driver shot (left). From the down-the-line position (right), his knees are slightly flexed, his back straight and bent from the hips. His upper body is tilted forward so his arms hang freely, his thumb and forefinger just inside his eyeline. His weight is toward the balls of his feet. Note that Flick's head is erect, the back of his neck in line with his spine.*

85

your swing. It tends to set you too much back on your heels and forces your back into too erect a position. Also, the more you flex your knees, the more pressure you place on your spine and the more tension you create in your back.

*4. Back straight but tilted.* Keep your back straight by creating a slight tension in the small of the back. Your buttocks should protrude slightly. But *straight* doesn't mean *erect.* Your straight back should be tilted forward from your hips. You should feel you are "out over the ball," probably much more than you have been used to. Allow your shoulders—not your spine—to slump and hang naturally. This in turn will let your arms hang freely suspended.

Many players have the misconception that their arms and hands must be in a straight line with the clubshaft at address. This causes them to arch their wrists and get their hands high, a position that locks the wrists, tightens the arms and promotes a shoulder-oriented swing that is too flat. Instead, the arms should just hang. The hands, in their starting position, should always be inside the eye line. Check yourself in a mirror, as if you were hitting straight into it or away from it, to make sure of this. The top of your arm-wrist-hand line should appear relaxed and fairly straight, not arched, and *there will be a definite angle between your arms and the clubshaft.*

A word about your head. Stand with your back and head erect, eyes looking straight ahead. As you bend your upper body forward from the hips, keep your head and neck in that same position relative to your spine. Don't let your head slump. This can distort your optical alignment and will tend to get your chin in the way during your swing.

The combination of body tilt and arm suspension promotes a freer, full arm swing and the more upright swing plane which we feel is most effective. It allows you to swing the club on the path we described earlier. If your back is too erect and your weight is back on your heels, you will tend to take the club inside too quickly and swing it on too flat a plane around your body instead of more back and forward along the target line. *(See photos, page 85.)*

This "over-the-ball" posture is particularly effective for large-busted women or heavy-chested men who must swing over the top of the chest. They cannot do it from an erect position.

When you get your body tilted over the ball, your first reaction probably will be that you're going to fall flat on your face. Frankly, we'd rather have you fall that way than on your derriere. At least you have a chance to keep the club on line longer if you are falling forward. But you won't fall if your weight is toward the ball of your feet and doesn't get onto the toes.

You *may* find that when you make a swing from this setup position you'll feel you are going to topple forward, and indeed you might. If you have been setting up with your weight on your heels, you undoubtedly have been taking the club back too quickly to the inside and have had to swing out over the ball with your upper body on the forward swing to get back on the proper path. If you now make this lurching move from your new starting position, you may fall forward and may even hit some shanks with the hosel of the club, because you've forced the club outside the proper path. But stick with it—you'll soon find you no longer have to make this compensating move.

5. *Right side set lower.* Just as having your right hand below the left on the club puts more weight on your right side, so it naturally will set the right side lower than the left. Your right side should feel soft and "broken," which allows it to turn out of the way easily during the backswing. To further insure this, cock your knees to the left or targetward and make sure your upper body is set behind or to the right of your lower body. Look in a mirror and you will see that your body is in somewhat of a "K" position, your right eye approximately over your right knee. As we indicated, this position will vary somewhat with the club you are using, but you should always be in that basic K.

Remember that when you cock your knees targetward, do so on a line *parallel* to your target line.

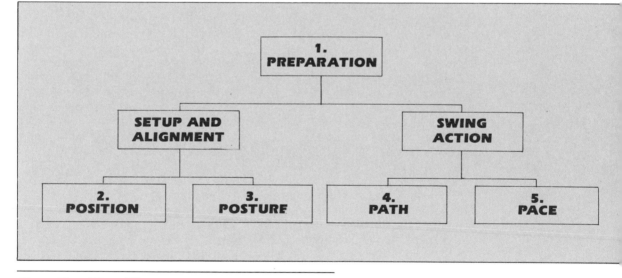

## How the Five P's are applied
The Five P's start with preparation, which involves establishing correct setup and alignment to insure the proper swing action. Position and posture determine your setup and alignment, while path and pace are of paramount importance in the swing.

Avoid the common tendency to twist your left side open or too far to the left of the target when you make this move.

Cocking your knees to the target makes the right leg a firmer support for the backswing. The right knee will move a couple of inches during the backswing—if it stays too solid you will throw too much weight to the left—but the firmer it is the better you are able to control the hip and shoulder turn and the arm swing going back. Setting the knees targetward also frees up the left knee and gives it more time to build momentum as it turns in toward your right thigh on the backswing. This momentum and freer movement allows it to react better and move forward more easily at the start of the forward swing, thus providing a better support for the swinging of your arms and hands. If you start with your left knee tucked too close to your right, the knee will have to move from a static, more constricted position and proper lower-body movement will be inhibited.

For a while, accentuate this position, even to the point where it feels uncomfortable. After a time, the correct knee-cock will begin to feel more natural.

The result of having your right side set lower is the same as having your weight to the right—it makes it easier to revolve your body around the right hip and leg. If your right hip is too high in relation to the left, you will tend to swing around your left leg and make that reverse movement of the upper body.

Incidentally, the K position helps perpetuate the myth that the weight is set on the left side at address. If you look in a mirror or watch the good players who set up in the same fashion, you may get the impression that the weight is left because the left knee and hip are closest to the target. Similarly, you will feel pressure on the outside of the left leg because it is cocked to the target, and you are pushing to the left. Many players mistake that pressure for weight. Don't you fall into that trap. Accept the left-side pressure as correct, but keep your weight on the right side where it belongs.

*Width of stance.* We have not included this among our basic posture precepts, because—although it is important—it is an individual thing, dependent mainly upon a person's flexibility. Our rule of thumb is that *your stance should be as wide as possible to give you a stable foundation, but not so wide that it inhibits a free arm swing and free body turn.*

That's why you'll see many smaller, thinner players—like Ben Hogan, Chi Chi Rodriguez, Bob Toski, Gardner Dickinson—use relatively wide stances which allow them to make a faster, more aggressive arm swing. They are flexible enough that the wide stance doesn't restrict them. A larger, stockier player with less flexibility in his body must play from a narrower stance to retain his free arm swing.

Here are some guidelines: With a driver, start with a stance that is no wider than the outsides of your shoulders, measured from the insides of your heels. Make some swings and gradually widen your stance until you feel you are restricting your hip turn. That's too wide. Now narrow your stance gradually until you feel too much slack in your swing, too loose and sloppy with too much turn. That's too narrow.

Strike some balls while experimenting with various stance widths. You'll find there's an optimum width for the distance you get out of a shot, and there's a point of diminishing return on both ends. You'll get so wide you can't swing your arms fast enough to generate sufficient clubhead speed, or you'll get so narrow you can't swing your arms fast enough because you'll lose your balance. From those parameters, work back to the middle to find the best width for you with each club. As a general rule, your stance will become progressively narrower as you work from the driver down through the woods and irons to the wedge, simply because your swing need not be as full and aggressive with the shorter clubs.

The wider stance will promote a harder, more aggressive swing. So if you are going to err on one end of the spectrum or the other, it's best to have your stance too narrow. Narrowness promotes a free arm swing, but at the same time you must swing slower and more "within yourself" to avoid losing your balance. That's not all bad. Al Geiberger is an example of a great player who swings with beautiful tempo from a relatively narrow stance. You can even play a pretty decent game of golf with your feet together, so keep that in mind when searching for your optimum width.

Let's quickly review the posture precepts and how to incorporate them into your setup:

Without a club or ball, stand with your feet together, your body and head erect, eyes straight ahead. Hold your arms outstretched in front of you at shoulder height, parallel to the ground, your hands in a praying position. Keeping your back straight, bend forward from the hips. Keep your head, eyes and arms in the same position relative to your back and simply tilt forward until your eyes are looking at the spot where the ball would be and your arms are hanging freely.

Now flex your knees slightly. You'll feel your weight go toward the balls of your feet. Move your left foot about shoulder-width toward your target.

Slide your right hand down a couple of inches and, as you do so, push the right knee in toward the left and let both knees cock toward the target line. This will set your weight to the right and place your right side lower than your left. Your right hip is inside your right shoulder, your left knee closer to the target than your left shoulder. Check to see that your right eye is approximately above your right knee, but remember that this is true only if you have a driver in your hand. With progressively shorter clubs, the right eye will be aligned progressively closer to the ball, as we have explained.

Your arms should be hanging in relaxed fashion. Your left arm will be straight and you will feel there is plenty of room under your left armpit, giving you freedom to swing the arm away from your body. Your right arm will be slightly folded and tucked closer to your right side.

Experiment to check your arm position. If the arms are hanging properly you will feel you are in a balanced, catlike position with your weight toward the balls of your feet. There is a slight, springy tension in the insides of your legs, the backs of your thighs and the small of your back. If you move your arms too far away from your body, you will tend to fall forward onto your toes. If you move them too close to your body, you will move back onto your heels.

At all times, your upper body should be free of the tension that tightens your muscles.

Look in a mirror to see that you are in the K position.

Next, try it with a club. Grip the club properly and extend your arms and the club out in front of you. Your arms will be parallel to the ground at shoulder height, but the clubhead will be approximately on a line with the top of your head. Using the same procedure, bend from the hips and lower the club to the ground and move into the same K position. Be sure you end up with the clubhead placed just behind the spot where the ball would be.

Practice assuming this posture until your body becomes familiar with the positions. But don't stop there. Summer and winter, while watching television or doing your morning exercises, practice your setup posture. Check it in a bedroom mirror, or set up a full-length mirror in the garage. Your spouse or non-golfing friends might laugh at you, but you will be a more consistent player for it.

Finally, let's recall our words on aim and alignment and remind you that all aspects of setup are related. Your ability to assume proper posture is dependent on properly aiming the club and aligning your body.

And, as we have said and will continue to stress, it all starts with the position of the clubface.

**Weight right, pressure left**
Bob Toski's address position with a driver shows the majority of his weight set over his right leg. But because his knees are cocked to the target, he feels pressure on the outside of the left leg in the knee and lower thigh area.

## Keep a coin between your thumbs

To make sure your hands stay unified throughout the swing, grip the club properly with your left hand, then place a coin on top of your left thumb, between the two joints. Fit the thumb pad of the right hand over the coin as you make your right-hand grip. Then keep the coin in place as you swing. If the coin drops out, your hands are coming apart and your swing will suffer.

## Constant light grip pressure

Make a full swing while keeping your grip pressure light and unvaried throughout. This promotes proper pace. It's the single most effective way of slowing down your golf swing and gives you a more constant rate of acceleration rather than jerkiness coming forward. Remember, the feeling is *light,* not *loose.* Don't get tight in your arms and loose with your hands.

## Claw

Take your normal grip, then slide your right forefinger over the top of the shaft and curl it under your right thumb. The shaft now will be running between the forefinger and middle finger. This drill is designed to eliminate pressuring with the right thumb and forefinger, preventing casting of the club from the top. It also prevents letting go with the left hand at the top of the swing and makes the hands work together better as a unit. One pitfall is that, because you right hand will feel inadequate, you may try to compensate by overusing the right shoulder. Also, be sure to have some bandages on hand; the tender skin between your fingers may get raw after a few shots.

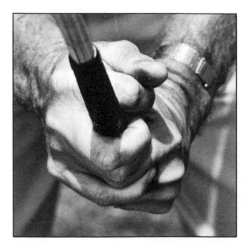

## Right hand off after impact

Make a normal swing and just let the right hand slip off the club *after* impact. Take a couple of practice swings, then hit four or five balls— on the first, take the right hand off at the follow-through position, then let it slip off a little sooner each time until you can take it off just after impact. This drill gives you a sense of your left arm pacing the right arm. It helps promote left arm speed and extension through the ball. It identifies lack of right arm and hand tension during the swing. And, as a by-product, it will improve your take-away. By knowing how much you're going to need your left arm on the forward swing, you'll subconsciously start to use the left hand and arm more on the backswing. Remember, *after* impact. Taking the right hand off *at* impact or before can do you more harm than good. Besides, if you take it off too soon, you might have to shove your left arm back into your shoulder after you finish the swing. Another pitfall is that you'll think you need to apply more effort to your swing, but you really don't. Players who use the interlocking grip should do this drill with an overlapping grip or they'll lose their grip pressure in the last three fingers of the left hand.

## Align with a two-by-four

To get a clearer visual image of a correctly aimed clubface, set a two-by-four on the ground along your target line, place a ball on the board and align the leading edge of your clubface perpendicular to the edges of the board. This will accustom you to seeing the clubface in proper relationship to the ball when it is aimed properly.

## Don't ground club

When you address the ball, don't sole your club on the ground. Use just enough grip pressure to hold the clubhead above the turf. This gives you the feeling of lighter grip pressure, it prevents any pressure *down* on the shaft at address and promotes a slower, smoother takeaway.

## Swing from uphill lie

Find a convenient hill and practice setting up and swinging on an uphill lie. This makes it easier to shift your weight behind the ball and get it supported by your right leg on the backswing. On the forward swing, you'll find you need better acceleration and pace with the left side to get back to the ball. Be sure you don't get on too steep an incline, which can cause you to get your weight on the outside of your right foot on the backswing. Also, in your effort to get back to the ball on the forward swing, don't overwork your right side and come over the top. Taking the right hand off after impact is a good accompaniment to this drill.

## Use clubs for alignment

Place two clubs on the ground parallel to your target line, one a couple
of inches outside the ball and the
other next to your stance line. This
is an aid to creating proper alignment. It's also a good idea to place
a third club (not shown) off your left
heel perpendicular to the others with
the grip end of the club resting
about halfway between. This helps
insure correct ball position. Then set
up and swing . . . but make sure you
don't hit one of your clubs.

## Visualization drill

Stake a ribbon from about three feet
in back of your ball along your
target line and run it several yards
out toward your target. Tee a ball in
the middle of the ribbon. Aim your
club down the ribbon and align your
body to the ribbon. Sight your target
by rotating your head (don't lift and
turn it) and tracking your eyes forward along the ribbon. Next rotate
your head and track your eyes all
the way to the back of the ribbon,
then rotate and track them forward
again until you can just see the golf
ball. Then swing and strike the golf
ball. This drill helps you visualize
your target and the direction in
which you want the ball to go. It
also induces proper body and eye
alignment and encourages the proper swing path back and through.

## Use a mirror for optic line

Take a mirror one and a half inches wide by 12 inches long. Lean it against a two-by-four or a couple of tees just outside the ball and parallel to your target line at an angle so that you can see your eyes reflected when you take the normal address position. This quickly tells you if your eyes are set parallel to the target line and your optical alignment is correct. Then go ahead and swing, making sure not to keep your eyes on the mirror when you do. Until you can find such a mirror, you can tie a piece of dental floss to each bow of your eyeglasses or sunglasses, stretching it in a straight line across the lenses. This line will then let you check to see that your eyes are aligned parallel to the target line at address.

## Swing with heels off ground

Keep your heels half an inch or so off the ground at address and during your backswing. As you start down, let the left heel come back to the ground in normal fashion. This drill is designed to get you more over the ball and keep you in balance throughout the swing. It puts your weight toward the balls of your feet, it helps you maintain your spine angle during the swing and maintain proper knee flex because it won't allow you to stiffen your right leg on the backswing. Make sure you don't change your knee flex to get your heels off the ground. Also, try not to lose your balance by getting your weight too far forward.

## Feet together

Place your feet no more than four or five inches apart, assume your normal address position with the ball off your left heel and make a normal swing, starting with a 9-iron or pitching wedge and progressing to the longer clubs. The main purpose is to promote the concept of arms swinging and body following. People who let the body turn first and the arms follow, who are too shoulder-oriented, will have a difficult time doing this drill. The drill also forces you to reduce tension in your arms and upper body and promotes better balance, a feeling of proper body action and somewhat better foot action. Be sure to bend at the hips and start with your weight more on the right leg. With your feet together, your tendency will be to stand too close to the ball and lose your spine angle. This eventually will alter your swing path, so be careful of this pitfall.

# 6

# IN-SWING PREFERENCES: LEARNING THE PARTS

You may not believe it as you read further into this chapter, but the golf swing is really a very simple movement, done properly. Once you understand the importance of correct position and posture in setting up to strike a shot, it is necessary to learn *where* to swing the club and *how* to swing it with minimum effort and maximum efficiency. That brings us to the next two P's, *path* and *pace,* which we consider the two most important elements in making the swing.

Path and pace are interrelated. For example, swinging on an incorrect path can destroy pace, and poor pace can force the swing off the proper path.

There are five important checkpoints in the swing: (1) takeaway, (2) top of swing, (3) start of forward swing, (4) impact and (5) follow-through. All are influenced by position, posture, path and pace.

In talking about the various positions and swing principles, we'll have to dissect the swing to clearly understand each function. But the last thing we want you to have as a result is a segmented golf swing. Once you thoroughly understand the parts, you must put them back together into a whole swing—one that works fluidly without your having to think of positions or mechanical movements. Golf is a game that is consciously learned but played best with the subconscious mind.

With an eye toward achieving that whole swing, keeping our swing concepts in mind will provide a goal and a plan for putting the parts together in an orderly, unconfused manner.

—Aim and swing the club on the line on which you want the ball to start.

—Arrange your body in the proper position to let the arms swing and the legs and body support. The body follows the arm swing in proper sequence on the backswing, *which puts you in position for the lower body to lead the forward swing at a pace that allows the arms to swing freely from the inside and the hands to release and square the clubface at impact.*

—You must have freedom of motion in your arm swing to generate sufficient clubhead speed.

—Swing the club only at a rate that the strength in your hands and forearms can bear.

—Work to achieve direction in your golf shots before distance.

—Strive for on-center hits, which will help you get both direction and distance.

—The golf stroke is a swing *through* the ball, not a hit *at* the ball.

In Chapter 3 we described why the ball flies as it does. The four flight *characteristics*—distance, trajectory, initial direction and curve—are caused by the five ball-flight *influences*. These are clubhead path at impact, clubface position at impact relative to clubhead path, squareness of contact, angle of attack and clubhead speed.

Directly affecting these influences are the *pre-swing principles* of grip, aim, setup and routine and the *in-swing principles*. You'll recall that in Chapter 4 we listed in-swing principles as path of swing, plane, width of forward swing arc, length of swing arc, position, the lever system, release, dynamic balance, swing center and timing.

The in-swing preferences for applying these principles are our own, of course. Other teachers may differ, but to play using our concept of the golf swing, you should embrace our preferences within the capabilities of your own physical structure and level of talent. This will insure that your preferences are aligned and compatible with each other, working in harmony instead of at cross-purposes, so each portion of the swing fits neatly into the fluid whole that we're seeking.

Let's see how these preferences work for each principle.

## Path

While clubhead path at impact is a direct influence on the way your shot flies, one of the governing principles is the path of the clubhead throughout the swing. The good player is instinctively aware of the path of his swing directed toward the target or toward the line on

### The path is from inside-to-inside

In this sequence, Bob Toski demonstrates the correct path of the swing. The club is swung straight back from the ball, then moves inside, around the body and up to the top of the swing in picture No. 5. At the start of the forward swing, the club is re-routed and approaches the ball on more of an inside path than on the takeaway. At impact the clubhead is traveling straight down the target line, then once again swings inside as the left arm moves left into the follow-through. Note how the path of the arm swing correlates with the path the clubhead travels.

which he wants his ball to start. But for the higher-handicap player, we're afraid path is sadly neglected and greatly misunderstood.

The great majority of amateur players swing too much to the left, from outside the target line to inside it. This instinctively causes them to do something to open the clubface, to "block" it and keep it from releasing it or turning over through impact. This open clubface combined with the outside-in path results in a weak slice from left to right. If a player does manage to get his clubface squared or closed under these conditions, he produces a pull-hook that starts left and goes even farther left, usually off the world.

If you want to hit the ball straight, or reasonably straight, it's obvious that the clubhead must be traveling down the target line at impact. It's just as obvious that the clubhead cannot remain on the target line throughout the swing. You'd have to swing like a Ferris wheel, a physical impossibility.

The ideal path of the clubhead on the forward swing is from *inside the target line to down the line to back inside*. To demonstrate this to yourself, hold a golf club in front of you, parallel to the ground, and swing it backward and forward as if it were a baseball bat. Note the path the clubhead travels—it swings immediately inside the line going back, returns from inside to on the line at the point of impact and swings im-

mediately back inside the line on your follow-through. Because the swing is horizontal, the clubhead is on the target line only for an instant.

Now lower the club to the ground in your normal address position. Because the plane of the swing is now more vertical (another principle we'll discuss later), your clubhead can stay on the target line a bit longer. But because you are still swinging more or less around your body, the clubhead follows generally the same path—inside to inside—on the forward swing.

*However,* and this is an important point to consider, you may need an intermediate step to get to this ideal swing path, depending on your stage of development. If you are used to swinging from outside to inside the target line, you probably will be better off for awhile to think of swinging from *inside to outside*. The inside-out theory has long been held as an ideal, and while it probably isn't that, it may be the perfect solution for those who have been going at the ball from the other way.

The more you think of swinging from inside to out, the closer your right elbow moves to your right side on the forward swing and the longer you retain the angle between your hands and arms coming into impact. You may hit the ball to the right for awhile, but you will begin to sense the feeling of swinging the club into the ball from the inside and retaining that angle until you can release your hands at the most efficient time, squaring the clubface at impact, starting the ball to the right of the target and hooking it back on line.

In trying to swing from inside to out, to the right, you eventually can create some problems, of course. You can overwork your shoulders in an instinctive effort to get the ball starting straight, which most of the time causes you to pull the ball left or hit a pull-slice which starts left and goes right. Or you can end up overworking your hands to get the clubface closed and hook the ball. Usually this brings the right hand too much into play, overpowering the left and ruining the shot.

When this happens—or hopefully before it happens—you should start bringing your swing path back toward inside to inside.

Specifically, the path of that ideal inside-to-inside golf swing is, from start to finish, straight back from the ball for a short distance, then inside, around your body and up on the backswing. As the forward swing begins, the plane of the swing lowers and your arms and the club drop even more inside. The clubhead returns to the ball from inside, goes straight down the flight path and then back inside. In sum—straight back, inside, around and up on the backswing, then from inside to down the line to inside on the forward swing (see photos, pages 100-101).

Setting up with proper posture and aligning correctly parallel left does not insure that you will swing on the proper path, but it does surely enhance your chances. Assuming this proper setup, how do you go about achieving the correct path?

It's important in the beginning to relate to the swinging of your arms and hands rather than the movement of the clubhead. Later on, as your feel for the swing is heightened, you'll begin to sense the clubhead location and the clubface position at all times, as all good players do. But at the start, assume that if the arms and hands swing correctly, the club has to travel on the right path.

For example, if you try to swing the clubhead straight back too far, there is a common tendency to push the hands and arms toward the outside of the target line. This forces the clubhead outside, and at some point when you finally take it back inside you will have destroyed both the plane of your swing and the path of your clubhead. Your hands will be going out while your clubhead is going inside, resulting in the "laid off" position at the top of the swing in which the shaft points behind you or to the left or your target line and the clubface is shut or in a hook position. When this happens, again you will tend to use your hands or your shoulders too quickly in trying to get the club back on the correct path.

To avoid this predicament, imagine a lane formed by two lines, one running back from the ball along

### Keep clubhead in the alley

On the takeaway, the arms and hands should be swung back across your chest and inside the hand line, but the club should remain outside the hands and the ball for a considerable portion of the backswing, as Peter Kostis demonstrates here. This helps keep the club on a more upward path going back and prevents it from being swung too quickly inside into a flat or laid-off position.

### Re-route the club starting down

Bob Toski shows how the club is re-routed from the backswing to the forward swing path. Note the position of the clubshaft at the top of his swing (middle picture). Then compare the shaft in the same positions on the backswing (left) and forward swing (right). See how much lower and more inside is the path on which the club travels coming forward. This re-routing is accomplished by allowing the legs to lead the forward swing and moving the club with the arms instead of spinning outward with the shoulders.

the target line, the other going back from your right thumb and index finger *(see photos, pages 104-105).* Think of swinging your arms back inside the closer line while your hands are cocking the club upward. This will keep the clubhead moving back in that alley—*outside* your hands—for a considerable portion of the backswing, until your hands are about hip-high. It will move inside the target line naturally (you're still swinging around your body, remember), but the longer it stays in the lane outside your hands the easier it is to swing *up* and get in proper position at the top. This feature is especially noticeable in the swings of Johnny Miller, Jack Nicklaus, Seve Ballesteros, Fuzzy Zoeller and Julius Boros, to name a few.

To get a feel for the correct position of your hands at that halfway-back position, imagine as you address the ball that there is somebody standing directly to your right. Extend your right hand and arm toward him as if to shake hands. Now put both hands together as if gripping a club and do the same thing. Now swing an imaginary club back and get in the same position. Then do it with a club in your hands.

Another excellent aid is to visualize, at the top of your swing, your left thumb pointing directly over your right shoulder, aimed straight down a line that is parallel to your target line.

If you incorporate these sensations into your swing, your hands and arms will keep the clubhead and shaft where they belong going back.

This also will put the clubface in the proper position—square with your swing path or slightly open. If the clubface is shut at the top, the natural rotation or release of the hands and arms on the forward swing will be inhibited. If the club-face is square to slightly open, you can make a more aggressive release without fear of hooking or pull-hooking.

So simply swinging your arms and hands back to the inside, around and up while the body turns for support will accomplish the backward portion of your swing path and let you develop a feel for the clubhead. At this point, let's discuss another myth of long standing, the one that says the club swings back and forward on the same path. It doesn't. As the backswing is finishing and the forward swing starting, most good players will re-route their arms and the club more to the inside. In doing so, they also will lower the swing plane. We'll discuss this next, but for now it is enough to think of returning the club to the ball on more of an inside path than the one on which you swing it back.

In good players, this re-routing of the club will happen almost automatically, primarily because excellent timing allows the feet and legs to lead the forward swing and their arms, not the shoulders, to swing the club into the ball. This initial movement of the feet and legs drops the arms and club to the inside, while the shoulders do nothing to interfere with it. The next time you get a chance, watch Zoeller or Lee Trevino or many other top professionals from behind the ball. They provide dramatic examples of how the club is re-routed to the inside *(see photos, pages 104-105).*

Unfortunately, this doesn't happen so automatically with most amateurs. The majority of them make the common move as they start the forward swing that carries the club outside the target line and into the outside of the ball at impact. This move usually is caused by the right shoulder or hip spinning outward. Most will be swinging forward from six inches or more *outside* the target line.

You hear a lot about "staying behind" the ball on the forward swing, which simply means keeping your head and swing center (we'll talk more about that later) behind it while you swing your arms and hands through impact. That's important to a point, particularly with a driver in your hand, although the swing center gets more directly over the ball with the irons and can even move ahead of the ball through impact as your angle of approach gets steeper with the shorter clubs. What is *really* important is that you must

be able to swing through the ball *from the inside* at the same time. While many players actually move *ahead* of the ball on the forward swing, which may or may not be dangerous depending on what club you have in your hands, most players also move *around* and swing across the ball from outside to inside. This is because our right arms are preconditioned to move outward by almost everything we do, whether it be throwing a ball, putting a drinking glass to our lips or lighting a cigarette. When a player makes this outward move in the golf swing, he is in effect re-routing the club in the wrong direction.

The good player feels that on the forward swing the clubhead is moving into impact from inside the target line. He feels the clubhead lagging so far behind and the clubface staying at a right angle to the target so long that it is never going to catch up. It usually does, however, the rotation of his forearms and the release of his hands bringing it into the ball with perfect timing.

The less-skilled player usually doesn't get that sensation. He feels his arms and hands swinging but doesn't feel the clubhead that far behind his hands nor the face at right angles for very long. The clubhead seems to be coming onto the line sooner.

If this is your problem—and it probably is, whether you are a beginner or a more experienced player—you must retrain your muscles. Learn to deliver a blow from inside, underneath and behind the ball and out toward the target. So this re-routing of the club must be done consciously for awhile on the practice tee. Because this feeling must be incorporated into your swing so eventually you don't think about it, the best way to learn the feeling is while making a swinging motion. Here are three simple drills that will help you:

1. Swing without a club, re-routing your arms smoothly to the inside as you finish your backswing and start your downswing, then swinging them forward down the flight path.

2. Again without a club, take your address position in a doorway and place your hands against the wall three or four inches outside the door jamb. Swing your arms back and then forward to a full follow-through without hitting the door jamb.

3. This time with a club, on the practice tee, stick a tee in the ground about a foot straight behind the ball. Swing the clubhead directly over the tee on the backswing, then swing it forward inside the tee and into the ball.

These exercises will teach your muscles the correct sensations. At first it may feel as if you are making a tremendous change in your path, dropping your arms and club a foot or so behind your body. Actually, the re-routing is very slight, ranging from minimal with the short irons to only a few inches with a driver. But

## Left arm and club go left after impact

*Bob Toski's left arm swings away from his body and leads the club into the ball from inside the target line (1). At impact the left arm and clubhead are swinging down the line (2). Then they move naturally to the left in conjunction with the uncocking of the hands and the leftward rotary movement of the left knee (3 and 4). This creates the desired inside-to-inside clubhead path. Note in No. 4 how Toski's hands have recocked and the left arm is folding nicely.*

that's enough to get you coming at the ball from the inside, and when you become accustomed to it, you will have a new, more efficient direction to your swing.

At this point, however, you are only halfway home. Except during the retraining stage we discussed earlier, your arms and the club ideally do not continue swinging from the inside on to the outside. Nor do you even try to make them continue for any great distance down the target line. Your motivating thought should be to swing your arms and the clubhead down the target line, certainly, but as you swing through the ball and into your finish, you should feel *the left arm and the clubhead moving left,* back to the inside of the target line and around your body. When that happens, you will have achieved the inside to down-the-line to inside path that consistent shotmaking requires *(see photos, pages 108-109).*

Try this to learn the feeling: Extend your left arm in front of you parallel to the ground, your hand perpendicular to the ground. Now swing your right arm and slap your left hand briskly with your right. Feel your left arm swing left after impact. That's the feeling you will have if you make the proper motion while swinging a golf club.

It is not a difficult motion to learn. If you have a preconceived image of your line of play and swing the club on that line, your left arm will swing

down that path and then go left or inward after impact, folding at the elbow as it goes, if you don't do anything to stop it. If you don't move your swing center ahead of the ball, if you swing your arms from inside the target line and keep the left arm in control, you have to make a conscious effort to swing the club to the right.

But remember, the *clubhead* must go left with the left arm. This will happen when your hands release correctly through impact. If you think only of the left arm going left, you will tend to get the grip end of the club too far in front of the clubhead, which will inhibit a good release and reduce your distance and accuracy.

Another critical point to remember is that as the clubhead moves left after impact, it also goes *up.* Just as the hands released and uncocked coming into impact, they recock on the follow-through, and it is this that carries the clubhead *up.* If the clubhead is going to go left after impact and still stay on plane, which we discuss in the next section, it *must* go up.

So, just as the path of the club is around and up on the backswing, so is it around and up on the follow-through.

The recocking of your hands accomplishes a full, uninhibited release and also helps the left arm fold correctly as it swings inward and upward. Much is heard about "extension through the shot,"as a means of generating clubhead speed and distance, but often that thought works in just the opposite way. If you work on keeping your left arm extended too long after impact, it usually means you will not release the clubhead early enough, thus *reducing* your speed and distance and affecting your accuracy.

If you have been swinging too much inside to outside, and if you accomplish the leftward movement of the left arm and clubhead correctly, you will have a sensation of almost "cutting" the shot, and for awhile you may expect to look up and see the ball slicing to the right. But if you are coming at the ball from the inside and swinging back inside, you'll find it only going long and straight.

Remember, the left arm and clubhead go left at *their* own speed and of their own volition, aided by the correct release through impact. They are not forced left by the speed and pressure of the right side, as happens with many players.

Almost all first-class players swing on an inside-to-inside path. To satisfy yourself that this is so, go to a professional or top amateur tournament and stand behind the practice tee or one of the par-3 holes on which the players use irons. Watch where the divots go. You'll find almost all of the divot marks pointing to the left of the target, and the divots themselves will land left of the target line. If you have seen this in the past and thought this indicated a pulled shot, think again. It simply means the clubhead is traveling left *after* impact, so naturally the divot must go left.

To sum up, the ideal way to achieve the correct clubhead path is to swing your arms on the proper path—start them straight back and swing them around and up to the completion of the backswing. Then re-route them to the inside at the top and swing forward from the inside to down the line at impact. Then let the left arm and clubhead go left as your hands recock on the follow-through. Your swing center is behind the ball at impact, at least with the driver, and your arms swing out and away from your chest. Your shoulders, therefore, follow your arms on the backswing and also on the forward swing, while your left arm controls the speed of your swing throughout.

## Plane

Path and plane often are lumped together, and they *are* closely intertwined. Plane is simply the angle of your swing arc in relation to the ground. If you were to make a perfectly upright swing, the clubhead would travel on an arc set at a 90-degree angle to the ground. If your swing were perfectly flat, the clubhead would swing around your body and never leave the ground. Obviously, somewhere between these two extremes is where you want your plane to be.

As we indicated in our discussion of path, there are really two swing planes. Because ideally you have re-routed your club to the inside for the forward swing, you also have lowered your swing plane and made it shallower.

Your plane is influenced by your height and body type, by your posture and by whether you use your arms or shoulders to swing the club. That's why we want you to stand more "out over the ball" with your arms hanging. If your upper body is tilted properly, your arms will be free to start the club back on line and swing it around your body and up on a reasonably vertical plane. If your back is too erect, your tendency will be to use your shoulders and take the club too quickly inside and off the flight path on a plane that is too flat.

We'll discuss the advantages of swinging with the arms versus the shoulders in more detail later. For now, it's enough for you to know that a flatter plane induces an outward movement of the shoulders and arms on the forward swing to get the club back on line rather than the inward movement we advocate.

Be particularly aware of the influence your height and body structure will have on your plane. The taller player, especially if he or she is slender, generally will swing on a more upright or vertical plane. The short and/or stocky player will have a more rotary swing, around the body on a flatter plane. The player of average height and build usually has a swing plane that falls somewhere in between. So don't force yourself to swing on a plane that doesn't fit your body type.

Also understand that your plane naturally will be more upright with the shorter clubs and will get flatter as the club in your hands gets longer. *(See photos, right.)* That's because your upper body naturally will be more tilted with the short irons.

## Width of Arc

This is a measurement of the radius of your backswing arc and, more important, the radius of your forward-swing arc. You often hear it referred to as "extension." The better your extension, the wider your arc and the more clubhead speed you can attain.

Arc width is the measurement between your left shoulder and your left hand, not all the way to the clubhead. Satisfactory arc width is achieved by keeping your left arm reasonably straight going back and coming forward to impact, by swinging the club back and forward with your arms. If you pick up the club with your hands, bend your left elbow severely on the backswing, then flail the club back into the ball

### Plane is influenced by posture
*The shorter your club, the more upright your swing plane will be. As Bob Toski shows here, this is because your posture controls your plane. With the shorter club (top), your upper body is more tilted, which causes you to swing the club more vertically. There is less upper-body tilt with the longer club (bottom), so you will swing on a slightly flatter plane. These adjustments should happen without your having to think about them. Note in both sequences how Toski's left thumb points directly over his right shoulder, keeping the shaft on a line parallel to the target line and the clubface square or on line with the swing plane.*

with your hands, you create a V-shaped swing that isn't very wide at all. Or if you tilt your body to the left and swing the club sharply upward, even if you don't bend your left elbow, you create a steeper angle that similarly gives you too narrow an arc for a full shot.

If instead you swing the club back low to the ground in the initial stage of the backswing, letting it turn naturally off the line, then keep your swing center in its correct place going back and coming through, your arc will be as wide as you can make it and your clubhead speed will be greater.

Don't push the club back too far with the left arm and get the clubface hooded or otherwise exaggerate the movement trying to make the arc even wider, because you will destroy your swing center and reduce your chances of striking the ball squarely.

For example, *don't try to force your extension by keeping the left arm rigidly straight, because this creates tension that locks your swing.* Don't be afraid to let the arm bend a little if it keeps you relaxed. As long as you don't overdo it, it will straighten naturally on the forward swing. You get a better sense of rhythm and a much more effective swing if you keep both arms "soft" going back and coming through. There is a symmetry in the swing that you should seek—the right arm folding on the backswing while the left arm is reasonably straight but relaxed, the left arm folding after im-

## Keep a soft symmetry in your swing

*Bob Toski demonstrates the symmetry or mirror im-
age you should create in your swing, the left arm reasonable straight and the right arm folding on the
backswing (1), the right arm straighening and the left
arm folding on the follow-through (4). Note the soft-
ness in his arms and how the left arm bends slightly
at the top of the backswing (2) but straightens naturally at impact (3). Your arm may or may not bend at
the top, depending on your natural flexibility. The
point is, it isn't necessary to try to keep it rigidly
straight.*

pact as the right arm straightens on the follow-through. This will get you the arc width you want.

One final point—perhaps you've heard of "setting the angle" early on the backswing. This means cocking your hands at or near the outset of your swing. This is a personal preference we'll talk about later. Right now we just want you to know that even though setting the angle early may appear to narrow your backswing arc, it really doesn't *as long as you are swinging your arms and supporting with your feet and legs at the same time.*

## Length of arc

The length of your arc is determined by how far back you swing your hands and arms on the backswing. It works in combination with your arc width to help generate clubhead speed. The longer your backswing arc, assuming satisfactory width, the farther the clubhead travels and the more chance it has to build up speed on the forward swing, provided you can maintain control.

As a guideline, it is better that your swing be too long rather than too short (but created by your arms and not by a loose, flippy cocking of the hands). If the length of your swing arc is too short, your tendency will be to overwork your hands on the forward swing to get the speed you feel you need. This gets the clubface out of position and causes wild shots. If you are very strong,

you may get by with a shorter swing, as long as the hands work at the correct time. But most of us need to make our swings as long as possible. It's the easiest, most consistent way to get the clubhead speed we need for distance.

If you have been trying to keep your left heel on the ground throughout the backswing and have been swinging the club with your shoulders, you are cutting down the length of your swing. By swinging your arms back and up and letting them pull the body around, you will get a longer swing and more distance.

Your swing can be so long, of course, that you lose control of it. This is a problem we see in many of our more supple pupils. They let the club dip well past horizontal at the top of the backswing, and the left wrist and elbow break down. This is because they have taken control with the right hand to get the club back that far, and disaster follows.

The guide to how far back you can swing within the bounds of your physique and muscular agility is a simple one: *Swing the club back only as far as you can control it with your left hand and arm.* Once your right hand starts to assist in getting the club back farther, you have control where you don't want it.

## Position of left arm-hand-clubface

This principle is simple to understand once you are aware that *the relationship of the left forearm, back of the left hand and clubface should be relatively the same at address, at the top of the swing and at impact, as well as in the finish position.*

The ideal position at the top of the swing is the "square" position, which lets you return the clubface square at impact. But we don't teach this position as a *cause.* Rather, it is an *effect* of grip position, correct arm swing and correct cocking of the hands. We do not try to make our pupils get in the square position at the top. It will happen if they do the other things correctly.

The so-called "square" position is not necessarily the classic flat look, with the back of the left hand and the left forearm in a straight line. That might be ideal, but not everybody can do it. The position of the left arm, back of the left hand and clubface at the top of your swing is directly related to their position at address. For example, if the back of your left hand is square or aligned with the clubface and is in a relatively flat relationship with the left forearm at address and you then swing your arms back on the correct path with no independent manipulation of the hands, you will be in that same flat or straight-line position at the top. *(See photos, page 118-119.)*

But remember that in the section on the grip we discussed some options, some adjustments you might want to make in your grip depending on your physical structure and needs. Those adjustments will affect your position at the top. If your left-hand grip is strong or turned to the right, for instance, and you make a good arm swing to the top, you'll find that your left wrist is slightly cupped or bent inward, to the same degree it was at address.

If your left-hand grip is turned to the right at address and you try to get into the "ideal" flat position at the top, you will shut the clubface and cause yourself all kinds of problems.

We see two extremes in the position at the top. One is the cupped position—the hands cocked too much inwardly, with too great an angle at the wrists—which is usually caused by the player taking the club back with the right hand and forcing the left out of position. This cupping opens the clubface and forces the clubshaft "across the line," pointing too much toward the target line instead of parallel to that line at the top. The other extreme is the bowed position, the hands cocked outwardly. This can be caused either by starting the hands back outside the target line, the forearms twisting and separating, which instinctively causes you to put the clubhead too far behind you too quickly, or by starting with your shoulders and taking the club too quickly inside. In either event, the clubshaft gets "laid off" and out of plane, pointing too far to the left of your target line, and the weight of the clubhead causes your left wrist to bow. This is particularly prevalent among players whose grips are too "weak" or turned too far to the left and also those who don't have the strength in their left arms and hands to control the club.

Whichever incorrect position you wind up in—cupped or bowed—you cannot return the clubface to a square, on-line position at impact without making some kind of compensation.

To get in the correct position at the top, you must understand that the hands and arms simply rotate around the body and up as they swing back. To help generate the correct sensation, remember the two thoughts we discussed earlier in this chapter in the section on clubhead path—shaking hands with a person directly to your right and getting the left thumb pointed directly over your right shoulder at the top. The latter is particularly important, because from that position the hands and forearms are in position to turn inward and downward on the forward swing and bring the club into impact in the same square position it was in at address.

At the top, both wrists should be *under* the shaft instead of off to either side, and the right arm should be lending support to the left. As we said, many players are not strong enough to control the club with the left arm and hands alone at the top. If this is in the case with you, it can help to feel the right arm aiding as the hands cock and the elbow folds going back.

If you are going to make a mistake, we would prefer that you get more inward cupping, the club pointing across the line at the top. This at least promotes a swing down from the inside and encourages a release of the hand and clubhead, whereas the bowed position that causes the club to be pointing too much behind you invariably leads to an outward move with the shoulders and hands that will bring the club down on an outside path.

But if you simply think of getting

## Left arm-hand-clubface position stays constant

Peter Kostis shows how the relationship of your left forearm, left hand and the clubface should remain constant in a relatively "square" position at takeaway (left), the top of the swing (middle) and at impact (right), as well as at the finish of your swing. This is accomplished by allowing your arms to rotate and your hands to cock and recock as you swing back and through without making any independent manipulation.

that left thumb pointing directly over your right shoulder at the top, on a line parallel to the line on which you want your shot to start, you won't make a mistake and will be in the ideal square position, ready to swing it most effectively into impact.

To repeat, staying "square" means keeping the angle between your left forearm and the back of your left hand basically the same at the top as it was at address, then basically the same again at impact. If you do that, your clubface also will return to the ball square with your line of aim.

Staying square does not, incidentally, mean keeping the clubface square or perpendicular to the target line throughout the swing. If you do that, you will hood or close the clubface and contort yourself to the point that you will never be able to make a free swing. The clubface instead should rotate open, the toe of the club turning clockwise 90 degrees from address to the top of the swing, simply because your left arm is rotating naturally to that extent as you swing. It will rotate back the same amount on your forward swing if you let it.

This means your clubface will be square to—or aligned with— your swing plane at the top. If you look in a mirror you'll find the face is not perpendicular to the ground—it would be that only if you were swinging like a Ferris wheel. Instead, the face should be pointing a bit skyward, depending on how much your swing plane is tilted. From there, you have the best chance of returning it perpendicular to your target line at impact.

Just swing your arms back on the path we have described and get your left thumb pointing correctly over your right shoulder to make all this happen.

## Lever system

The golf swing is accomplished with a two-lever system, the left arm being the first lever and the club being the second. Actually, there are three levers, the body being the other, but for practical application, limit your thinking to the arm and the club.

A lever is generally defined as something that transmits force or motion. In the golf swing, the idea is to create enough motion in the second lever to transmit as much force as possible to the ball. To do that, you must have sufficient motion in the first lever, your left arm, and allow the second lever to work about its hinge to increase that motion or speed even more. *(See photo, right.)*

The flail-like action of the second lever working off the first lever is what produces maximum clubhead speed. If you didn't cock at the wrist during the backswing, you would be operating with just one lever, and it's easy to see that you couldn't achieve nearly as much speed. So what must you do to make that sec-

### How the lever system works
*The basic two levers are shown here in Jim Flick's swing. The first lever is the left arm, the second lever the club. The lever system is activated by the cocking of the hands on the backswing and their uncocking on the forward swing. This produces a flail-like action of the second lever which creates much more clubhead speed than if there were no cock at the wrist and just one lever in the swing.*

ond lever, the golf club, work at peak efficiency?

The answer is to remember you really don't have to do anything. There's more to it than that, of course, but if you keep that premise in mind you'll have more success in the long run.

The levering action of the club is created by the application of physical force that causes a buildup of momentum in the clubhead as it swings. This is true whether you are creating the second lever on your backswing or unleashing it on your forward swing.

Let's start with the creation of the second lever. This is done by cocking the hands on the backswing. When you cock your hands, or set the angle between your left arm and clubshaft, is a matter of personal preference that depends on your physical strength and agility. We happen to believe that the earlier you begin setting the angle the better off you will be, a theory we'll expand on later in this chapter. *However,* we just as firmly believe that the motivating force in your backswing must be a smooth, rhythmic arm swing. This swinging of your left arm creates the momentum that causes a weight buildup in the clubhead as you near the top of your swing. This in turn will cause your hands to finish cocking automatically if you don't interfere.

Notice we said *finish* cocking.

Properly concentrating your grip pressure in the last three fingers of the left hand and maintaining control in those fingers as you start back encourages the hands to begin cocking immediately without much conscious effort. If you have sufficient strength, it will happen. And by the time you reach the top, the job will have been completed.

That's the ideal, combining physical application with momentum. But it will only happen if you satisfy a couple of conditions—first, your grip pressure must be light enough that you can feel the weight of the clubhead going back and instinctively cock it into the position we described earlier; second, your left arm must swing freely going back so the momentum of the clubhead becomes the dominant factor as you near the top.

If your grip is too tight, your hands and wrists will have difficulty reacting to the swinging weight of the clubhead. If your left arm is not swinging freely, the cocking of the hands will be similarly inhibited.

The "ideal" way, of course, might not be ideal for everybody. If you lack the strength to let the cocking happen naturally, you will have to make a conscious effort to set the hands as early as possible in the takeaway. Or if you are a shorter, stockier player with a more rotary swing and an arc that is not as wide, you will need more hand action in your swing to create clubhead speed—and the more hand action you want, the earlier you should begin setting them going back.

Exactly *how* do you cock your hands starting back? It's really very easy. You do not hinge or flap them in one direction or the other. You simply cock the hands so the thumbs stay in basically the same relationships with the sides of the forearms that they were in at address. To get a feel for this, assume your normal grip and address position with any club. Then, without moving your arms, simply pick the club straight up with your hands until the shaft is approximately parallel to the ground and pointing straight in front of you. This is the correct cocking of your hands and the relationship between hands and forearms you want throughout the swing. Remember that the turning of your body and the rotation of your arms will get you into that "handshake" position we described earlier at the halfway point of your backswing and into the correct position at the top.

However soon you begin cocking your hands on the backswing, don't confuse "early" with "quick." If you cock your hands too quickly, you will disrupt the flow of your arms, ruin the correct sequence of motion in your swing and destroy your timing. You can consciously get your hands into the act early if you need to, but do it slowly and smoothly.

Having cocked the hands and created the second lever, let's find a way to apply it most effectively. Our goal is to create motion and force in the second lever and delay the application of that force until the proper moment, at impact with the golf ball.

The best way to accomplish this, we feel, is to *swing the left arm forward* along the proper path. Let's look at the flail. Take a piece of rope about 40 inches long and assume your top-of-swing position with the rope draped across your shoulders. Stand where you can swing the rope against a tree or the corner of your house. Now swing your left arm smoothly forward with no independent action of your hands. Note how the rope swings straight and solidly against the object. Next, take the same position, but this time start the rope moving with your hands as you begin your forward swing. See how the rope buckles and its force is dissipated by the time it gets to impact.

Swinging the left arm forward, without applying the hands, lets centrifugal force do the work. Dr. David Williams, in his book *The Science of the Golf Swing,* tells us that centrifugal force creates a buildup of effective weight in the forward swing from one pound at the start to approximately 107 pounds at impact. This weight buildup forces the hands to uncock and release the full force of the second lever at the right time, as the club is coming into contact with the ball. The hands *do not* force the weight of the club to move.

That's why it's so important to maintain a light, constant grip pressure and keep your arms free of tension during the swing. Once your muscles tighten, the hands cannot respond as effectively or consistently to the buildup of centrifugal force.

We hear good players tell us they hit with their hands at impact. One of Sam Snead's favorite expressions is "give 'er hell at the bottom with the right hand." With all due respect to Snead, one of the game's greatest players and a knowledgeable theorist, we believe that what he and the other good players are feeling is the response of the hands, particularly the right hand, to the buildup of centrifugal force. Ben Hogan has said he wished he had two right hands with which to strike the ball. Well, Hogan had such a powerful arm swing and maintained the angle between arm and club-shaft so long into his forward swing that he *had* to feel the great force of the right hand as it caught up with his arms through impact.

Scientific research has proved that if the centrifugal forces in the forward swing are allowed to build up properly, by the time you reach the impact area the clubhead is moving so rapidly that all your hands can do is hang on. There is no way you can manipulate them independently at that point.

In *The Search For The Perfect Swing,* Alastair Cochran and John Stobbs report on an experiment in reaction time. In a room lighted only by a single artificial light, golfers were told to drive balls into a net. They were told that on some of their swings the light would be switched off, and when this happened they were to stop their swing or, failing this, do something to change it, to slow down or mis-hit the shot.

Not one of the many golfers tested could do anything to alter his swing once he was barely into the forward swing. At that point, he was totally committed to the shot. As Cochran and Stobbs point out, this is not scientifically surprising, because the .2 or .25 of a second which the downswing requires is just about the time it takes for the brain to perceive an external signal and relay it to the muscles for appropriate action.

What this means is that if you are going to consciously use your hands in the forward swing, you must program that action into your mental computer long before you get there. Down that road can lie grave danger if you don't approach it properly.

Byron Nelson puts it so well when he says, "Whenever you consciously try to *hit* the ball on the downswing, to pour on the power in the impact area, you will inevitably do it too early. You will throw the club with your hands or lunge with your shoulders from the top of the swing.

This destroys your timing, dissipates clubhead speed and yanks the clubhead off line.''

Ahh! In those last five words Nelson gives one of the most important reasons for swinging with your arms to create centrifugal force rather than using your hands to physically force the club to work. The application of centrifugal force, combined with correct position and light grip pressure, *will let the hands square the clubface naturally at impact.* And this means you'll hit the ball straight. Since you have to find your golf ball after you hit it, this is important, isn't it?

Now for the qualifiers. Centrifugal force indeed will let the hands square the clubface at impact . . . *if we don't do anything to interfere with it.* Unfortunately, we usually do, either by lunging with the shoulders or casting with the hands at the wrong time or by gripping the club too tightly, creating tension that keeps all the body parts from working smoothly and in the proper sequence. We try to apply power with a heavyhanded approach, with brute strength. We try to force the clubhead rather than feeling the force that builds up in it naturally in a correct, tension-free swing. If you have ever noticed, your best and longest shots feel effortless. They come when you feel you haven't applied any pressure at all. We've just explained the reason for that.

What we're getting around to is that you may have to *train* your hands so they can work naturally, as contradictory as that may sound. You may have to teach them to work correctly and at the right time so they won't jump in at the wrong time and interfere with the natural action of the lever system.

This is especially true for individuals who, for any of the reasons we have mentioned before, need to develop more hand speed. This can apply to the weaker, shorter or stockier player or anyone who perhaps has worked so hard on swinging his arms that he is subconsciously inhibiting his hand action and release. If you fit in any of these categories, by all means work on giving the hands more importance. But do it the right way by developing hand action that blends with a good arm swing and the support of the lower body and comes into play at the correct time.

Jack Nicklaus has said that if the left side leads on the forward swing, it's impossible to hit too early with the hands. That's another way of saying that everything must work in sequence. If the legs are supporting and the arms are swinging, you *can* feel you are giving it hell with your hands. But you have to program that feeling by starting on the practice tee before you take it onto the golf course.

Our colleague Peter Kostis, in his own book, ''The Inside Path to Better Golf,'' prescribes an excellent method for learning to use your hands correctly, in the cocking and recocking manner we referred to in the section on path. Using a short iron, with the ball on a tee, start by using only your hands to strike the ball. Simply cock your hands back with a minimum of arm swing, then recock them after impact. Be sure you cock them correctly, *up* going back and *up* again as you recock them. Gradually add more arm swing, always blending the action of hands and arms so you get the most effective release at impact. As you go to longer clubs and the swing gets longer, your body should begin to move to support the swinging of the arms and hands. Again, this should be blended in at the correct speed and at the right time to keep all the different parts of the body acting in the correct sequence.

If you perform this exercise long and often enough, you will train your hands to work properly in coordination with your arms and legs, and you will develop a feel for proper hand action that you can use naturally and effectively on the course.

That now brings us face-to-face with the question of left side versus right side in the creation and application of centrifugal force.

Centrifugal force is defined as a force which impels something *outward* from a center of rotation; i.e., the clubhead swinging outward around the body.

The opposite of that is *centripetal* force, that which tends to pull *inward* toward a center of rotation. We make you aware of this only because it is this centripetal force or inward pulling that harnesses centrifugal force and allows it to work effectively in the golf swing. Since centrifugal force is outward, it would—in the case of the golf swing—send the clubhead hurtling into the ground if there were not a counter-balancing pulling force keeping it on track around the body.

So while it might not be quite scientifically accurate, for purposes of the golf swing *centrifugal force is created by a pulling action.*

Corollary to this is the fact that you can pull something straighter than you can push it, especially when there is a hinge involved, as there is in the two-lever golf swing. Try it with your child's wagon and see if you don't agree.

It boils down to pull versus push, and you pull with your left or lead side, because it is in front of the shaft and the clubhead from take-away through impact. Because your right side is behind the shaft, any effort from it must be a push.

The only way you can maintain a pulling force through impact is if your power source, the first lever or left arm, remains ahead of the object you're pulling, the second lever or club. If the right hand, arm or side comes into play too soon, you cannot have a predominantly pulling force throughout the forward swing. If you begin to push with the right side, especially the right arm or upper body, using physical force to operate that second lever, you will tend to force open the arm-shaft angle and dissipate the force of the lever too early. You also will tend to force the clubhead off the path and the clubface out of its desired relationship to the target. That's because if the right arm begins to dominate and break down the left, it cannot move *through* the left. It must move out and around.

We are not advocating a one-armed or one-sided golf swing. The right side plays a vital role in supporting the left, adding feel to your swing and, of course, generating extra speed and power through its weight and strength. The right leg is especially important in establishing the initial lateral movement of the lower body, as we'll discuss in the next chapter. Through the early stages of the forward swing the right arm itself is adding to your pulling power as long as it stays ahead of the shaft and clubhead. And in the impact area the right hand and arm do begin to push the club through. This is what provides the extra power.

But that push is a reaction to pull. The right side can work properly only as long as the left side works in harmony with it. Most good players we see have more pull than push in their swings. Some of them may talk about hitting with the right side, but in our opinion they can do this only because the left remains in control. Since in poorer players overactive shoulders and hips cause about a 90 percent pushing action, they should strive to get the feeling of swinging and pulling the arms to allow the clubhead to release properly from the inside.

To accomplish that, there is no question in our minds that your lead side must be the master side.

That, incidentally, is further evidence in support of setting up correctly. If you are aiming to the right of your target, you can't pull with the left side and make the ball go toward the target. At some point you must push with the right to get it on line, and we hope by now we've convinced you that you don't want to do that.

## Release

There once was a pupil at our golf schools who, when he was instructed to release the clubhead through the ball, threw the whole club down the practice range. So we have to be very careful to define what we mean by release.

Actually, we've already defined release in the section you just finished on the lever system. In normal usage, release means to "let go of," and that's exactly what we mean. In the case of the golf swing, you must release or let go of the stored-up energy you created in that second lever when you cocked your hands on the backswing.

Here's a description of the ideal release pattern, at least as we like to see it:

From the cocked position at the top, with the angle set between left forearm and shaft, the arms swing forward. If there is no independent action of the hands, the angle will be retained well into the forward swing. The left forearm will be rotating counterclockwise through the downward part of the forward swing, ideally making a 90-degree rotation and returning to its square address position at impact. As centrifugal force begins to work on the clubhead, the hands will respond to this weight buildup and the effective force of the second lever, the club, will begin to be released. If your timing is proper, the angle of your wrist cock will be fully straightened, the clubshaft will be in line with your left forearm and the clubface will be square with the intended line of flight at impact. Thus the full force of the second lever will have been unleased at the proper moment. *(See photos, below.)*

As you swing through impact, the rotation of the left forearm will cause the right hand to begin crossing over the left and the toe of the club to be passing the heel. While the left arm, left hand and clubface ideally are in a straight line at the very instant of impact, the feeling should be that even then the hands are in the process of recocking—not breaking down or hinging inwardly but simply recocking on the forward side of the ball as they cocked on the back side of the ball during the takeaway. Your arms are continuing

## *How release occurs through impact*

*Effective release occurs through the impact zone when the uncocking of the hands is combined with the rotation of the forearms to create added speed of the clubhead. Note how Bob Toski's hands uncock and then recock as the clubhead swings through the ball.*

129

to rotate at the same time as they swing to the finish.

If those two paragraphs clear up some questions you've had about release, they've been worthwhile. It's really a pretty detailed explanation of something that you shouldn't have to think about at all. Release is just letting the lever system work, with the emphasis on *letting*. If you do the other things properly in your golf swing, it will happen.

This is called *passive* release. There are other ways to turn the club from right to left, to release the angle and make the toe pass the heel, but they all involve more or less conscious manipulations. The less you have to think about, the more natural you can allow your swing to be, and the more consistently you will play.

As we said, you may have to train your hands so they react at the right time in the forward swing, but once you have done that, they should work without your thinking about it.

The effectiveness of a passive release is dependent on a correct grip position that encourages the uncocking and rotation of the hands. For some players, a grip that is too neutral or too far left on the club could inhibit a good release.

Also vital is light grip pressure and the absence of tension in the arms and upper body, because a free arm swing on the correct path and plane is essential. Most players don't get a proper release because

they have too much tension in their arms, especially the right forearm and the thumb and index finger of the right hand. To overcome this, we find it effective to hit balls on the practice range and take the right hand off the club after impact. *(See drill, page 93)* This gives you the feeling of the left side leading and the club extending and accelerating through the shot.

Too much tension in the left arm and failure to swing on the proper path can limit the natural rotation of the left arm during the forward swing. We find that many players with too much tension and stiffness in their swings are helped by consciously working on left forearm rotation, both by using the drill above and when actually hitting balls. Remember, we're talking about rotating the forearm and the hand, not flapping the left hand. Work on developing the feeling of the left arm rotating counter-clockwise while the hands uncock and recock as you swing through the shot.

The pitfall is that an emphasis on forearm rotation can cause you to work outside and over the ball. Actually, if you make a free arm swing and let your arm go left after impact, you will achieve the same effect. You won't have to make a conscious effort to square the clubface, and swinging the left arm left will enable you to stay behind the ball more easily with your upper body.

Your release will happen naturally.

## Dynamic balance

This involves your ability to maintain your balance and body control while you swing backward and forward through the ball. Because balance is so vital to the execution of a good golf shot, we feel this is the place to explode another myth—that of the weight shift in the golf swing.

It is commonly understood—or misunderstood—that your weight shifts from your back foot to your forward foot during the forward part of the swing. Yet we've stressed the importance of keeping the head and swing center behind the ball during the forward swing, especially with the driver. The next time you get a chance to watch a good player, you'll see this is exactly what he does. At impact, with a driver, most of his upper body will be behind the ball. With the shorter irons, his head and swing center will be over the ball or even slightly ahead of it at impact. But in any case, the position of his upper body will be remarkably similar to the way it was at address with that particular club. With a driver, in fact, the swing center may have moved a little to the right, or more behind the ball.

The point is, it's very difficult, if not impossible, to put most of your weight on the left foot while keeping the upper body back. Players trying to shift the weight from right to left tend to get the entire body too much in front of the ball. This causes them to work the upper body around and over the ball, with disastrous consequences.

Instead of a weight transfer, we believe *there is a transfer or change of body position that creates the momentum of the club on the forward swing.* Your left knee is leading a leftward or targetward movement of your lower body. Your right heel is coming off the ground, and you in fact *feel* that your weight is moving to the left. *(See photos, pages 132-133.)*

But let's look at this phenomenon closely. In a relaxed fashion, swing easily into the impact position while keeping your upper body behind the ball. Stop at impact. Even though your left foot is now solidly anchored and your right heel is off the ground, examine how much weight you really have on that right toe. Quite a bit, we'd imagine. Theoretically, if you had shifted your weight from right to left, you would be able to pick your right foot off the ground while balancing on the left at this point. You'll find that's impossible to do, which means that you still have a great deal of weight on your right side.

What you are confusing with weight on your left leg is really pressure as the leg bows toward the target. As we pointed out earlier, it's the same confusion that exists at the address position.

Ideally, golf is a game played

from the *insides* of your feet. Just as your weight is on the inside of your right foot at address and going back, so it returns to the inside of your left foot as you start down and swing into impact. This means your overall weight distribution hasn't changed much at all during the swing.

In fact, we believe that the center of gravity of your body doesn't change at all from address to impact. In other words, your weight distribution stays the same as it was at address, even though your body positions have changed. Your knees have moved forward or to the left, but the mass of your upper body has stayed in approximately the same place.

The fact that the weight mass in your upper body remains stable while your left arm pulls forward and swings left creates the momentum that generates sufficient clubhead speed. From a scientific viewpoint, you are rotating an implement—the golf club—around an axis. As long as the axis—your body—stays constant, you can achieve the greatest rotary speed with that implement. As soon as the axis moves, you lose speed and, in the case of the golf swing, accuracy.

Remember the crack-the-whip game you used to play as a child? If you were the anchor person, what did you do to achieve the greatest speed and send your friend flying at the end of the line? You kept rotating but didn't change your position; you dug solidly and pulled inwardly, didn't you? This is exactly what happens in the golf swing. Keeping your weight distribution

## Upper body moves back for dynamic balance

Dynamic balance, with a driver and the ball on a tee, is created when the head and swing center move slightly rearward behind the ball to counter the effect of the legs moving forward and around. This results in a change of body position that lets the arms swing with the greatest possible momentum, as Bob Toski demonstrates. This means that the weight at impact, while moving toward the left side, is distributed pretty evenly. As the club in your hand gets shorter, this rearward movement of the upper body lessens. With the middle and short irons, with which you want to strike a dynamic, downward blow, your swing center remains in pretty much the same position throughout the swing. This is why, when you swing level or upward with a driver, your finish tends to look more like the so-called "reverse-C" position. With an iron and a more downward swing, you will finish more in the "I" or straight position.

constant while pulling with your left arm creates the greatest possible speed at the end of the line, where your clubhead happens to be.

Also, the longer you stay back on your right during the forward swing, the less apt you are to use your hands, because the clubface can square itself naturally without your having to help it.

But, you ask, doesn't your weight wind up on the left foot at the finish of your swing? Not as much as you might think. As you swing into the follow-through, momentum might carry you a little bit forward and throw a little more weight to the left. But a proper finish will still find you in good balance, which means your weight is still pretty well distributed over both feet. Your upper body

mass is in pretty much the same place at the finish as it was at address and impact.

If you watch the top players, you'll find that whenever they fail to finish in perfect balance they almost always fall back on the right foot. You never see Jack Nicklaus topple forward after a swing, but you often see him recoil backward after his follow-through. That simply means he still has plenty of weight on his right foot at the finish, and if he has made a mistake in his swing it has been toward staying behind the ball too long rather than moving ahead of it.

So crack the whip and send the clubhead flying. All that will happen is that the ball will go high and far and straight.

## Swing Center

This is the center of the arc on which the arms and club are swung. Keeping your swing center constant and maintaining your balance during the swing are interrelated. It's impossible to do one without the other, because so many of the same swing concepts apply to both.

That's why we regard the thought of swinging around the head as very dangerous for most players. Turning around the spine, another misconception, can lead to just as many problems.

The swing center has been defined by Cochran and Stobbs and others as a point halfway between the arms just beneath the top of your sternum or breastbone. Technically, that's probably correct,

but we feel it may not be the best thought for you to use while swinging a golf club.

The thought of keeping your head still and swinging around it, or swinging around the spine or even the technical swing center tends to make you keep too much weight on your left side. Because you're concerned with turning about a point in the center of your body and keeping that point very still, you won't get your upper body behind the ball at the top of the swing. You will tend to work off your left leg and will end up actually making a reverse weight shift, which tips your upper body forward or ahead of the ball.

From that position, your left leg is obviously going to have trouble moving toward the target to lead the for-

### Left side swings around right leg

*Jim Flick shows how the arms swing the left side around the right leg, which supports the backswing. Note how his left shoulder is swung over his right knee and his upper body is well behind the ball.*

ward swing. There is too much weight on it. All you can do from there is fire and fall back to the right.

The right leg supports the golf swing going back and starting forward. Your thought should be to swing the left side of your body around that right leg and back again. This lets you stay in the same position relative to the ball that you assumed at address and provides a constant support for your swing. *(See photos, pages 134-135.)*

This feeling of hanging back over your right leg at the top of the swing allows the left knee freedom to move and lead the way for the rest of the body and the arms on the forward swing. You'll have the feeling the knee is floating weightless in

space, and it really is, because it is not being used as a support. Again, this feeling is most predominant with a driver, progressively less so as the clubs get shorter.

As the forward swing progresses, of course, your feeling should be that of swinging around your *left* leg, the right arm rotating around the left side as you swing through impact and beyond. This keeps you from hanging back on your right side *too* long, which would cause your arms to swing too much up and out instead of around your body.

Why is it important to be back on the right side, behind the ball? Let's put it this way—in any athletic activity in which you're trying to propel an object forward, whether it be throwing a baseball, a football or a

## Learn timing with a mini-swing

*To learn proper timing and the feeling of the correct sequence of motion, make smaller, effortless swings without trying to hit the ball for distance, as Bob Toski is doing here. This feeling of ease with the short swing will result in a pace that allows the parts of your body to work in the right order throughout and will ingrain sensations that you can transfer to the full swing.*

javelin, or hitting a tennis ball, where do you start your motion? From the right side. And the farther you want to throw that object, the more you get your weight on the right side. The same principle holds true in swinging a golf club and propelling a golf ball forward. You would much rather be on your right leg, ready to create momentum in your swing by moving the left leg forward, than on your left leg with no place to go but backward.

For awhile, swinging around the right leg may promote the feeling you are swaying, moving your upper body backward from the ball. As long as your right leg remains reasonably firm and you keep your weight to the inside of your right foot, this won't happen. Your head and your technical swing center will remain pretty well fixed without your having to think about it. Even if you do sway a bit with the driver, we'd rather have you make the mistake on this end of the spectrum for the time being. At least you're creating full motion and putting yourself in position to make a strong forward swing through the ball. Once your muscles learn the feeling of getting and staying behind the ball at the top, you can work to bring your

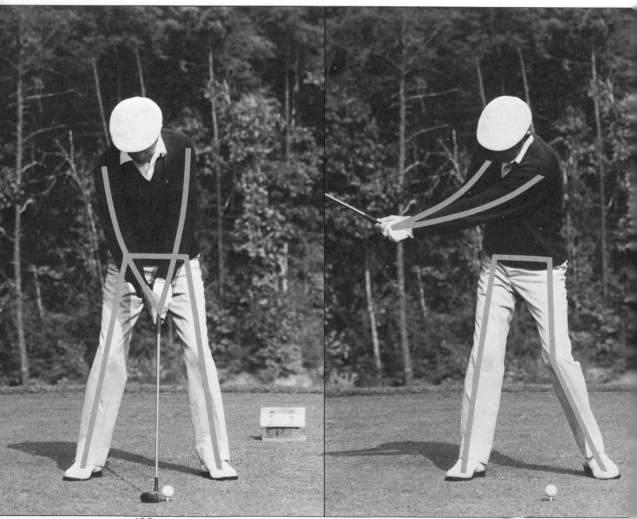

swing under control. From the reverse position, with the weight left, you have no chance at all.

## Timing

Paul Bertholy, the erudite teacher from Pinehurst, N.C., has perhaps the best definition of timing we've heard. He calls it Proper Sequential Movement, which simply means that things happen during the golf swing in the order in which they're supposed to happen.

The proper sequence goes like this: on the backswing, the swinging of the clubhead with the hands and arms pulls the shoulders around, which in turn pulls the hips as the left knee and ankle move to the right and the left heel comes off the ground; on the forward swing, the left heel comes down and the knees move laterally to provide a support for the swinging of the arms, the big support muscles of your legs and hips lead the smaller muscles of your arms, which in turn lead the even smaller muscles of your wrists and hands, your greatest speed producers.

At this point, the smaller muscles are trying to catch up with the bigger ones, and if your sequence of movement happens correctly, they

---

## *Legs respond going back*

*These photos of Bob Toski show how the feet and legs respond to the swinging of the arms and hand on the backswing.*

will accelerate to their maximum speed and unleash the greatest possible force at impact.

In reflecting on this sequence, however, don't get the idea that your arms run off and leave your feet fixed in a static position. The sequence is not a jerky, step-by-step movement but rather a smooth flow of motion. The movement of the feet and legs supports the turning of the hips, which in turn supports the arms, and all this happens early enough in the backswing to give you the arm freedom you need in your swing.

Many, many players, in fact, need to work consciously on the movement of their feet and legs going back to get their bodies to turn properly and get the club inside, then stay turned long enough at the top to make the change of direction correctly and bring the club down on the inside.

As you complete your preswing preparations and get ready to start the club back, your hands should be feeling the club and your feet should be feeling the ground—in both cases lightly and in relaxed motion. Your hands and feet momentarily come to a stop the instant before you take the club away, but the movement now has passed to your knees, which cock slightly forward toward the target the instant before your swing begins.

This sets you up to let your feet and knees move in harmony with your hands and arms, both on the takeaway and at the start of the forward swing. A good thought in both instances is that your left foot and knee are tied to the swinging of your left hand and arm.

This may not happen precisely at the same time. Going back, the hands and arms may start slightly sooner because they have farther to travel than the lower body, a subject we'll examine in the next chapter. The feet and knees may initiate the forward swing before the arms and hands have finished going back, especially in a good player, so they can be in position to provide support for the arms swinging down. In each case, one movement is in response to the other. But the movements do occur smoothly and harmoniously. You can't necessarily depend on the movement of one part to pull other parts along, particularly on the backswing. Depending on your stage of development, as we indicated, you may need to do some conscious work with your feet and knees in practice.

The point is, they happen in the correct sequence—the lower body doesn't get ahead of the arms on the backswing, and the arms and shoulders don't move ahead of the lower body coming forward. The proper blend at the proper time is what makes an effective swing.

After having read so much already in this book about the importance of the arm swing, you might think we are contradicting ourselves by dwelling on the movement of the feet and legs. We are not, and we'll examine the subject of arms versus legs more thoroughly in the next chapter. Keep in mind for the moment that we are discussing here the way things happen at the proper time, not necessarily what makes them happen.

Timing, which is the sequence in which things happen, is often used synonymously with pace and tempo, the speed with which they happen. That's because timing is absolutely dependent on pace. Once one part of your body begins moving too fast, it will not allow the other parts to work in their proper order. And when your timing gets out of whack because of improper pace, all the other swing principles we've just discussed will be affected adversely.

Only by understanding these swing parts can you build an effective whole swing. And to keep that whole swing working efficiently or to repair it when you develop mechanical trouble, you should refer again to the in-swing preferences described in this chapter.

# DRILLS

## Swing left arm down inside the backswing path

This is a conceptual as well as a physical drill which gives you the feeling of the proper path. With no club, set up and swing your left arm back and then down inside your backswing path. Do this several times, then put a club in your hands and try to create the same feeling. You can also develop this feeling by setting up in a doorway without a club, your left hand just touching the door jamb. Then swing your left arm straight back and come forward without touching the jamb. Be sure you complete your backswing before you start your left arm down from the inside.

## Use a board for proper swing path

Place a two-by-four on its edge about two inches to the side of the ball, running parallel to the target line. The drill is designed to help you visualize your target line better and to promote the proper inside-to-inside swing path. Initially, the board may scare you, so you may not make good swings for awhile. Overcome this by starting with little chipping strokes and gradually increase the size of your swing as you gain confidence in your ability to make the inside-to-inside swing path. Also, be careful that the rear end of the board is no closer than 18 inches to the ball. This insures against the club hitting the back of the board.

## Overlap right hand for left-side control

At address, overlap the right hand on the left, fingers over fingers and thumb over thumb, with no part of the right hand touching the shaft.

The primary purposes of this drill are to let you feel the left hand and arm controlling the swing from start to finish and to promote strength in the left hand and arm.

One of the pitfalls is that hitting too many shots with the overlap grip eventually could get you too locked up in the elbows and inhibit the cocking and recocking of your hands. So do this only with shorter swings, not full swings. The other pitfall is that at address you'll have a tendency to get your right shoulder and hip set too high, because your right hand is even with your left. This makes you hang left on the backswing and beat down on the ball with your right side from the top. So make sure you get properly set at address with your right side lower than your left.

## Closed-stance drill

From your normal address position, pull your right foot away from the target line so your stance is closed (pointing right of target) about 20 degrees—pull it back about five inches for a 5-iron shot, for example. Don't change the ball position. Then swing the club straight back along the target line, not along your stance line. This drill is designed to put your path coming from the inside on the forward swing. The pitfall is that you may tend to take the club back along your stance line, which gets it too far inside and around your body and causes you to come out and over the top on the forward swing.

## Swing with left arm alone

Make a normal swing using only your left hand and arm. This drill is the ultimate help in developing left hand and arm control over the right. It's also a strength-building exercise. The drill should be done only after you've worked with the overlap drill for awhile. The pitfall is that if you don't have enough arm strength, you'll tend to make the body turn first to help take the club back. Make sure the left arm swings first and the body follows.

143

## Swing with right arm alone

Make a normal swing using only the right arm and hand. Make sure your arm is free of tension. Feel the clubhead lagging behind and then catching up as you swing through the ball. This drill is designed to give you a feel for what the right arm does in the swing. It promotes the proper hinging action at the wrist and elbow of the right arm. It also gets the pressure into the last three fingers of the right hand and away from the thumb and forefinger. The pitfall is to avoid a tendency to pick the club straight up instead of swinging the right arm back and around the body.

## Rotation with overlap grip

Using the overlap grip and starting with a short club and a short swing, try to hook the ball by rotating your left arm counterclockwise on the forward swing. This develops proper left forearm rotation. The drill is designed to stabilize the left wrist and left elbow and helps eliminate scooping. One pitfall is that you may instinctively feel you need clockwise rotation of the arm on the back-swing. You don't. Just swing the left arm straight back. Also be sure your forward-swing rotation doesn't come from the right hand and right shoulder. This will cause excessive hooking or pull-hooking.

## Extended-arm rotation

Grip a club in your left hand. Hold it in front of you at eye level with the shaft parallel to the ground and at right angles to your left arm, the face pointing skyward. Rotate the left arm counterclockwise so the shaft travels 180 degrees and the face is pointing downward. Rotate back and forth in this manner. This develops strength in the left hand and arm.

The major pitfall is the possibility of injury, so start with a short iron and hold it at the bottom of the grip, gradually working your way to the end of the club. We'd rather have you do more repetitions with a lighter club than to risk doing the exercise with one that is too heavy. Stay with a pitching wedge for at least a month, never doing any more than 10 rotations without stopping to rest. When you feel your strength is sufficiently developed, you can increase the length of the club and the number of rotations.

## Set and swing

Take your proper address position and, without moving the left arm, set the clubshaft parallel to the ground and parallel to the target line with the leading edge of the club pointing straight up and down. Use only the last three fingers of your left hand to do this. Then swing your left arm back and through the ball.

This drill helps correct improper hinging at either of the wrist or elbow joints. It helps a person who is very flippy-wristed with no arm motion, because it creates early wrist action and forces you to swing your arms back. It promotes better hinging of the right elbow, which is pre-set in a broken position. It helps overcome too much bending at the left elbow and makes you feel you are maintaining a constant radius in the left arm. If you pre-set the club with your arms and shoulders instead of the left hand, you'll tend to lose your spine angle. Another pitfall is that, once the club is pre-set in the proper position, there may be a tendency to swing straight up with no width to the arc. This occurs mostly with people who are too hand-oriented. They just pick their hands right up. There also is a tendency, once the wrists are pre-set, to turn the body instead of swinging the arms.

145

## Strike and hold shot

With a short iron, take a half or three-quarter backswing, strike a descending blow and hold your hands below waist-high in the follow-through. Don't let the clubhead pass your hands or arms. This drill teaches you to control the club with the left hand and arm and to strike the ball without letting the clubhead pass the hands before impact. The drill is even more effective if you can do it with the overlap grip.

## Back-to-target drill

First take your regular address position so you can determine the distance your left shoulder is from the ball. Then turn and align your feet at right angles or perpendicular to your target line so your back is facing the target, keeping your left shoulder that same distance from the ball. The ball should be teed opposite your toes. Then cock your hands and swing upward on the backswing. Swing your arms down, letting the right arm cross over the left and recocking your hands through impact as the left elbow folds. The ball should start to the right of the target and hook back on line. You will have swung your arms nicely around your body going back because your body was already turned. The drill teaches the feeling of swinging your arms, hands and clubhead while the body stays turned and shows that you can square the clubface without excessive body rotation.

## Inside-stripe drill

Using a double-striped range ball, align the stripes down the line on which you want the ball to start, then concentrate on hitting the inside stripe as you swing through impact. A single-striped ball or, if you are hitting your own practice balls, the manufacturer's label, will suffice. Just try to strike the side of the stripe or label closed to you. This drill again encourages swinging forward on an inside path.

## Extra ball drill

This drill teaches you to swing on an inside path and can be used in place of the board drill. Tee up a ball, then tee up a second ball about six inches behind the first—away from the target—and two or three inches inside the target line. Then remove the original ball, leaving the tee in the ground. Swing back outside the second ball and strike that ball with your forward swing as the club swings back over the tee for the original ball.

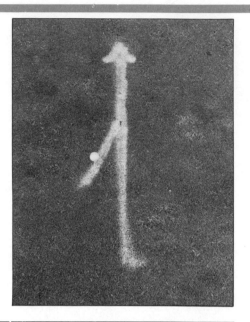

## Inside-loop drill

Using a can of spray paint, some chalk or simply a sharp stick, draw a target line on the ground and superimpose the loop as shown here. With the ball positioned in the middle of your stance, feel that you are keeping the club on the outside portion of the loop going back, then swinging it into the ball on the inside of the loop. This encourages not only a correct backswing path but the correct return to the ball from the inside.

## Hit balls from a chair

Address the ball while sitting on the right front corner of a chair, your right leg tucked back so it is out of the way. Using a fairway wood with the ball on a tee, swing your arms while your hands cock, uncock and recock, letting the clubhead turn over as you swing through impact. Start with small swings and gradually lengthen them. You will have no hip turn and very little shoulder turn, so this drill encourages the development of arm and hand freedom in your swing.

## Hit balls off your knees

With the ball teed high and a driver in your hands, address the ball while kneeling. Swing the club through the air like a baseball bat a couple of times to get the feeling of arm freedom. Then strike balls off the tee. This drill teaches you the feeling of swinging around your body, encourages arm freedom and reduces excessive shoulder movement. You also will be surprised at how far you can strike the ball using only your hands and arms with no supporting leg action.

## Hit balls off each leg

Strike balls while standing first on the left leg and then the right leg only. This is the next step beyond the feet-together drill. You are forced to swing smoothly and with good pace or you'll lose your balance. The drill is good for balance, at the same time quieting down the shoulders and encouraging arm freedom.

149

## Preset impact drill

Using a 6-iron with the ball on the ground, assume the position you feel you should be in at impact—the weight on the outside of your left foot, your left knee bent forward toward the target, your right heel off the ground, your swing center slightly in front of the ball. This gets you used to feeling your impact position. Then, taking about a half backswing, strike the ball easily. This coupled with the step-in drill teaches you to move through impact.

## Toe-up to toe-up drill

With a middle iron, swing your arms and hands back to about 9 o'clock and check to see that the toe of the club is pointing straight up in the air. Then swing through until your hands are about at 3 o'clock and make sure the toe of the club again is pointing straight up in the air. After some practice swings, actually hit balls in this manner. This drill teaches the correct arm rotation and how it turns the clubface going back and coming through. It also encourages you to keep the club on the correct path and plane throughout the swing. The pitfall in this drill is that you can become too arm and hand oriented and lose track of the lower body. Be sure that your feet and legs move in response to the swinging of your arms.

## Tee to re·tee drill

Draw a line along your target line a few feet long. Tee a ball on that line. Stick a tee in the grip end of your 6-iron. Then cock your hands and swing your arms back to waist-high, making sure that at that point the tee in the end of your club is pointing to the target line. Then swing forward, uncocking and recocking your hands through impact, to waist-high on the other side of the ball, trying to hit a shot with a draw or slight right-to-left movement. At the finish, the tee in your club again should be pointing to the target line. This drill helps you keep the club on plane throughout the swing, encourages the feeling of cocking, uncocking and recocking the hands while teaching you to square the clubface at impact in relation to your swing plane and target line.

# 7

# THE WHOLE SWING

In giving you some thoughts which will help mold the parts of your swing into a whole, we'd like to reinforce the importance of our swing concept—that the lead arm and side control the swing, that the arms and legs control the body, that it's essential to have a feel for the swing before you can effectively play the game on the course and that pace is the factor that allows you to put it all together.

## Left side is the leader

This statement is worth repeating: Golf is neither a left-sided nor a right-sided game—it is a two-sided, two-handed game. But the movements of the leading hand, arm and side must master and control the movement of the trailing side, regardless of how fast the trailing force reacts and moves.

In other words, the left side is the leader, the right side the follower, if you are a right-handed player. The reverse is true if you are left-handed. If the left side doesn't lead the swing of a right-handed player, the right arm will say, "Thank you very much, I'm going to take over." That's because the right side is stronger, more coordinated and instinctively anxious to get into the act. That's fine in most unilateral activities like throwing an object, swinging a tennis racquet or writing your name. But golf is a bilateral sport in which both sides play a vital role, and in the discussion on leverage in the preceding chapter we told you of the problems that can result when the right side takes over. You lose the pulling force that is so vital in the golf swing, distort the clubhead path and alter the clubface position at impact, with the loss of both power and accuracy.

That's why in golf you can't hit the ball with your right arm and hand until you know what you're doing with your left. It's instinctive to find the golf ball with your right hand and arm. To play well, learn to find it with your left so you can control the force of the right.

This left-side control begins right at the start of the swing. You will tend to control the forward swing with the side that controlled the backswing. On the backswing, the right arm is simply a support for the left, not vice versa. Your right arm can help you get deeper into the backswing, but only by staying relaxed and letting the left arm pace that backswing. The tighter the right arm gets, the more it actually shortens the backswing, cutting off the backward motion and forcing you too quickly into the forward swing. When you throw a ball underhanded, you just let your right arm swing around your body, bend, set and throw without a lot of effort. You should do the same when swinging at a golf ball.

When the club reaches the top of the backswing, the speed and weight of the swinging clubhead puts greater pressure on the handle end. Therefore, when the club is started on its return to the ball, it is necessary to exert more pressure with the left hand, simply because it's closer to the handle end than the right. That's difficult, if not impossible, to do if the left hand is not in control going back.

How many times do you strike behind the ball and hit a "fat" shot? That's because you have very little control with the left side while the right side dominates. This causes hand action to take place early in the forward swing, the wrists to uncock too early away from the body instead of moving in close to it as you swing through the ball.

You can overcome these shortcomings by programming your left arm to control the club before you step up to the shot. Aim your clubface and align your body properly and swing the golf club on the correct path, down the line of play and left. You will begin to experience the left arm moving left and controlling the force of the right, no matter how hard or fast the right hand and arm try to move. As you continue into your follow-through, the force and weight of the club eventually will cause the left to bend and give way, but by then the ball wil be gone.

## The importance of arm swing
To hit a golf ball consistently, every

part of your body must contribute. But every part does not contribute an equal amount. Yes, the whole body has to move to strike the ball, as some theorists say. But the body must be under control. If the large muscles of the torso, for example, are interfering with, rather than complementing, the small muscles of the arms and hands, you can't control your swing.

Our theory—that for the majority of players the arms should control the body—is borne out by looking at athletes in other sports. Watch a football halfback running with the ball, a figure skater, a dancer, a diver—their arms are flying freely. They're letting their arms dictate what their bodies do, because they know instinctively that arm freedom allows body mobility and balance.

Unfortunately, the more inert nature of golf, the need to create a swing and propel a ball a certain distance, tends to overpower these instincts. When most golfers try to make an attacking motion to get more distance, they tend to over-work either the shoulders or the hands or both. Overworking the shoulders alters the path, and over-working the hands alters the facing of the club. As a result, the ball flies wildly all over the course.

The reason you overwork either the hands or the shoulders is that you don't get enough arm swing go-ing back to achieve the velocity you feel you need. Usually, excessive tension in your arms and shoulders cuts off the swinging of the arms. When this happens, the only agent you have left with which to propel the ball forward is your hands.

Let a free arm swing control the hands and therefore the face of the club. It's the freedom of arm swing we see in the good players that makes them so consistent.

The shoulders, too, should be followers and not leaders. Turning your shoulders on the backswing can get you in fine position, but it can also create unwanted tension in the large muscles and tend to throw your weight to the left side. It also encourages a tendency to take the club too quickly to the inside, off the flight path, on the backswing, which makes you swing outside the flight path on the forward swing. The shoulders turn on a more horizontal plane, the arms swing on a more vertical plane. So which do you want controlling the swing.?

There is also the simple fact that the arms have to go twice as far as the shoulders on the backswing—they must swing approximately 180 de-grees while the shoulders are turn-ing only 90 degrees. Therefore, which should start first?

To prove this to yourself, turn your shoulders 90 degrees and get your back facing the target, but don't swing your arms. Your arms and hands won't get higher than your waist. Then swing your arms back and notice how your shoulders continue to turn as long as your arms keep swinging. The momentum of your arm swing will turn your shoulders completely and at the same time will get your hands into a nice high position at the top of your backswing.

We invariably see in our schools that the shoulder-swinger's worst shot is the three-quarter wedge and other part swings. That's because the shoulders cannot control the arms, the path and the speed well enough to relate to a partial shot. If this happens to be your weakest shot, perhaps this gives you an indication of where the problem lies.

To develop enough motion in your arms so they can lead the hands and shoulders, first arrange and align your body so you can swing on a path related to the target. Motion and path are interdependent. Most players don't trust themselves to make a full-free-swinging motion with the arms because they cannot relate to the correct path. Once you have set yourself to swing on path, you can confidently make the full motion with your arms that will get you behind the ball on the back-swing and will allow you to swing forward from the inside to along the target line. Your arms can do the work, allowing the hands and shoulders to function in their proper roles.

This brings us to the business of setting the angle or intentionally cocking your hands on the back-swing. How soon you do this depends a lot on your size, strength and swing shape. We discussed this in Chapter 6 while explaining the lever system, but let's consider some more factors.

We partially destroyed the myth of the one-piece swing a few paragraphs ago by convincing you, we hope, that the arms must start before the shoulders. Let's finish the job by pointing out that, on the backswing, with a driver, the clubhead must travel approximately 21 feet along its arc (give or take a couple depending on your size), while the hands have to go only about five feet along their arc to the top. That being the case, most players have to do something to get the clubhead started first, that being to cock the hands at the beginning of the takeaway.

If the hands cock too late on the backswing, the clubhead has to catch up and there will be a re-bound, a flail action, at the top that causes you to go out of control. You will be cocking and uncocking at the same time. A Jack Nicklaus has the strength to control a late set and this ensuing rebound action. He turns it to his advantage and gets a downcock (the hands cock even more as the forward swing starts) that, with his ability, he converts into even greater clubhead speed at impact. The great majority of players have neither the strength nor the talent to do that. The grip end of the club gets so far ahead of the clubhead, both going back and coming forward, that their timing gets out of whack. That rebound effect causes an early release of the hands in the forward swing and disaster strikes.

The weaker player, especially, needs to get the weight in the head of the club above his hands as soon as possible so his arms and legs can give the maximum amount of support at the top. If he doesn't, the shaft tends to get laid off behind him and he instinctively makes that spinning move with the shoulders and hands to try to get it back on line. He rarely can accomplish that.

The same is true of the shorter player with a more rotary swing. His arc is not as big, so if he gets the clubhead too far behind his hands going back and at the top, he doesn't have enough time in his swing for it to catch up, even if he did have the strength and ability to make that happen.

So we prefer that the hands start cocking relatively early in the backswing for virtually everybody, because then the mechanism is set and you have things under control. The earlier you set going back, the later your hands will tend to release coming forward. You also will be able to get the club in better position at the top.

Remember our earlier warning that setting the hands early does not mean setting them quickly or jerkily.

As you set them, you must at the same time generate sufficient arm swing to keep from picking up the club too quickly, destroying your swing arc and shortening your backswing. That's why we recommend a "swinging set," which is simply a backswing initiated by the arms in which the hands begin cocking early and continue to do so smoothly and gradually on the way to the top. As we said before, if you maintain control of the club in the last three fingers of your left hand while concentrating on swinging your left arm back, this swinging set can be accomplished smoothly with a minimum of conscious effort.

## The leg myth

Many teachers and players, particularly touring professionals, will tell you that the forward swing has to be started with the legs. For some this may be fact, but for the majority of players here's another myth.

There is no question that the left leg *leads* the forward swing, and conscious use of the legs plays an important part in the swings of tour players and top-caliber amateurs who have learned first to control the club with an absence of tension in their arms, hands and shoulders. But most average golfers would be better off not to use a conscious direction of the legs, other than in the setup position. Not many players, in the short time it takes to make a golf swing, can think about arms going back and legs coming down. You can't change your focus of attention that quickly. Most players who consciously try to use their legs get them too active too early on the backswing and disrupt their sequence of movement.

The legs are important, of course. All good players swing well with the arms and upper part of the body and move beautifully with the lower. But it's a matter of proper emphasis. You don't really strike the ball with your legs. Bob Toski can drive a golf ball almost as far on his knees as when he uses his whole body. So how much do the legs really contribute to power and distance? Sam Snead tells us he hasn't worked five minutes in his life on using his legs. He hasn't done badly concentrating on arm swing, however.

The legs are a platform. They support and balance your body. They allow you to create arm speed and maintain on-center hits. They give you greater control over your angle of attack in playing different shots. *(See photos, page 158-159)*.

To do this, the legs must keep pace with the arms. You must be able to coordinate the lower part of your body with the upper. Because the muscles of your legs are stronger but heavier and slower than those of your arms, they must move earlier on the forward swing to stay in sequence with the arm swing. A good player's legs actually begin to

move forward before his arms complete the backswing.

The point is, your legs can work in this manner if you let them. Most players do not use their legs properly because they get the club out of plane and then have to play catchup with the hands or shoulders, which overpowers the use of the legs. If you aim the club properly, have the correct position and posture, then swing on the right path with the proper pace to allow everything to happen in the proper sequence, your legs have a chance to work correctly.

It won't always be automatic. Some players, because of physical structure or previous swing tendencies, may have to work consciously to develop correct foot and leg action. Practicing with drills such as the baseball drill *(page 176)* or working without a club on the correct leg action that we'll describe in a moment can build that action into your swing. Once that is done, the legs can work instinctively if all the other requisites are satisfied.

Here's an analogy—if you toss a ball overhand just a short distance, your legs will move first, but very little. But if you try to throw that ball a long way, the legs will move a lot, and they'll do so instinctively as long as you don't do anything to interfere with them. The same is true in a golf swing.

For your legs to respond in this manner, your arms must be light

## How the legs work on the forward swing

At the top of Bob Toski's backswing, his weight is well on his right side and his lower body is in position to lead and support the forward swing (1). Toski's left knee initiates the forward swing with a lateral movement (2) as his right knee begins to react. While the gap between the knees widen (3), indicating that the left knee is leading, the right foot and leg are beginning to make an even stronger push. This causes the left leg and hips to begin their rotary action (4), and this turning movement clears the way for the arms to swing through. Note how the left knee moves past the ball just before and at impact (5) but rotates to a point almost back to the position of the ball as Toski's swing continues on to the finish.

158

and free of tension. If your arms are tight, they will cut off your backswing and force your upper body to overwork and outrace the legs. This is why light grip pressure is so important. Your arms also must swing at a pace that gives the legs time to work. In general, the slower you swing your arms going back, the better chance your legs will have to lead the forward swing. You'll have to find the right pace to keep your arms swinging fluidly, but thinking "slow" is always a good guide.

*Remember always that the most important function of your golf swing is to use your hands and arms to find the ball with the clubface and make solid contact.* Don't work so hard at developing stronger leg action that you hinder that function, a fault we have seen in some of our students. If you are having problems in that regard, go back to practicing with soft, relaxed mini-strokes until you can find the ball solidly and consistently. Then, as your swing gets gradually longer, build in support from the feet and legs.

So your first step is to master the swinging of the arms and control of the club that way. Your legs will keep pace, and the movement of the lower body will carry the momentum and the path of the arms, up to a point. If you can become 100 percent proficient with your arms, you can probably get 85 percent efficiency out of your legs. That last 15 percent you need to become a com-

plete player and achieve your full potential can come only by working directly with the legs. But by that time, the tension-free motion of your arms will allow them to respond to your legs, rather than the other way around.

We liken it to a baseball pitcher—at the Little League level he is concerned only with controlling his arm and hand. But by the time he reaches the major leagues, he wants a precise length of stride so his arm can function to the nth degree. So it is with the good player and his leg action in golf.

The freedom of motion needed to execute a golf swing properly is dictated by the target, controlled by the arms and supported by the legs. The degree to which it can and should be supported by the legs is in keeping with the player's level of proficiency.

Since a conscious use of the legs *is* important if you want to climb that final 15 percent to the top of your game, let's talk for a moment about how to use them properly in conjunction with a free arm swing.

We often hear, especially from the better player, that the forward swing is started by kicking in the right knee toward the target. This thought could be dangerous, because it could get your right side too active and tend to move your upper body in front of and out over the ball.

There is no question that the right

knee plays an important role in the forward swing, but it does so as a coordinated effort with the left knee. The forward swing of a good player starts with the left knee leading (actually, the left heel and ankle lead the way, but thinking of the left knee promotes better leg action, as we shall explain.) Watch any top star in action and you'll see that as he starts down, the gap between the left knee and the right knee *widens.* If the right knee were leading, the gap would become smaller.

What happens is that as the left knee starts, the right knee reacts and moves toward the target. That gets your weight off your right leg and supports the motion of your arms swinging forward. As we said earlier, if you hang back on your right side too long, the path on which your arms swing will be affected adversely.

Also, the sooner the right knee flexes forward, the easier it is for the right elbow to fold and move in toward your side, facilitating the club swinging down on the inside path.

Specifically—and this is something you might think about on the practice tee but should ingrain into your swing so you won't have to think about it on the course—the left knee is responsible for the lateral dimension of the forward swing and the right knee is responsible for the rotary dimension. The movement of the left knee toward

the target gets the lower body going laterally, while the pushing of the right knee eventually forces the left knee to rotate or turn. This causes the hips and upper body to turn.

That rotary action of the right knee can be overdone. To prevent this, work in practice on feeling that you are pushing with the inside of the right foot, the outside of the foot coming up but the heel not rising off the ground until the rotation of the body turn forces it to.

If, at the finish of your swing, your right heel has swung past vertical toward the target line, your rotary action has been too pronounced and you need to work on the thought we just gave you.

In any case, the movement of your feet, knees and legs should be blended, the pushing action of the right reacting to the initial movement of the left.

That all may sound pretty complicated, but if you work on those movements in practice, you can marry them into a feel that simply lets you move your feet and legs *laterally* toward the target at the start of the forward swing. We often hear that you should turn your hips and "clear your left side." The problem here is that thinking of this usually causes you to spin your hips too quickly, stiffening your left leg and throwing your upper body out and around. Instead, just move backward and forward with your swing and try to strike the ball squarely from the inside. With practice, your feet, knees and hips then will move correctly. If you don't interfere with that movement, they really can't do anything else.

There actually are two slightly different movements of the legs on the forward swing, depending on whether you are swinging a driver with the ball on a tee or an iron with the ball on the ground. But both movements are predicated on your setup position, so you really don't have to give them any conscious thought in making your swing.

With a driver, the knees make basically the forward-rotary movement we have just described. With an iron, when you are making a more downward swing, there is a bit of a "down-drive," the knees flexing and moving slightly downward as they shift toward the target. Byron Nelson's swing provided a classic example of this, as does the swing of Tom Watson. This down-drive with the knees forces the head to stay down and back, where you want it. The left knee is flexed at impact and the right heel stays relatively close to the ground.

Bear in mind that this kind of action is impossible if you are trying to turn your hips too quickly.

The necessity of shifting your knees laterally is the reason we want you to set your weight to the right at address and stay behind the ball on your backswing—the amount in both cases predicated on what club you have in your hand. If your weight is on the left side at the top of your swing, the lateral motion of your left knee is inhibited. This puts the upper body in position to dominate the forward action of the swing. The hands, arms and shoulders propel the club outside the path, and all the lower body can do is get out of the way. The lower body is accommodating itself to the upper, and it should be the other way around.

Taking the weight off the left leg at the top, then, allows it to move in proper sequence and build the force that keeps the arms swinging on the proper path.

In summary, to build a program for using your legs properly, you first should learn the correct setup, then a good arm swing, then the arm swing on the correct path. After that, you can develop the use of the legs to coordinate the lower body with the upper body. Do this by using the legs as supports, with your weight properly distributed, in the setup position. Then use the right leg as a support for the left arm as it swings on the backswing and pulls the left side around that right leg.

At this point it becomes important to think about completing your backswing, swinging as far back as your body will allow without excessive effort. If you don't do this and instead think about using your legs too soon going forward, your shoulders instinctively will jump into action and overpower the movement of your legs. Think about this in practice so you can develop a feel for it and don't have to worry about it on the course.

On the forward swing, the first move actually is the planting of the left heel. Simultaneously, the left knee moves laterally and the right knee reacts. Both knees move laterally and then in a rotary fashion to the left in conjunction with the left arm. The hips are following the lead of the knees in similarly turning to the left and clearing the way for the arms to swing through.

## The feel of the swing

In any sport, the best players perform as instinctively and as naturally as possible. In other words, they play by *feel*.

Feel is an ephemeral thing that is difficult to describe and virtually impossible to communicate from one person to another. We can't really tell you how our golf swings feel any more than you can tell us how yours feels. But you know, or will soon discover as you progress in the game, that when you have this intangible feeling of correctness and fluidity in your swing, you play your best golf.

While we can't describe what your particular best swing feel should be, we *can* give you some guidelines and a method for finding it. Good swing feel goes beyond the positions in the swing. You must play with a swinging sensation, a feeling of ease and grace, rather than worrying about the mechanics of putting the club into certain positions during the swing. *However,* to achieve this kind of sensation, your positions must be correct, especially your starting position.

For example, when Bob Toski is playing, all he feels in the swing are arms and knees. He doesn't feel his shoulders, body or hands working. That's because he aims his club, aligns his body and sets his posture correctly to begin with, then swings the club on the proper path. You can't feel just your arms and knees if the club gets off the path, if it gets laid behind you or if you get it inside too quickly on the backswing. Then you must feel your hands or shoulders working to re-route the club. You'll have the sensation of swinging out and around, of coming over the top, rather than from inside to down the line. The feel you get making that swing is not going to be the same as you get when coming from a pure position.

Feel is difficult for most players to create and keep from day to day because their complex swings force them into recovery acts, and it's usually a different kind of recovery each day.

If you set up in the same good starting position every time, your feel will be more constant, because you will have to make considerably less recovery than a person who is improperly set up and has to make some correction in each part of the swing. That's why adherence to the correct principles of setup and swing is so important in developing your own sense of feel.

There are three long-standing myths in golf that tend to destroy feel: keep your head still; keep your left arm straight; and keep your eye on the ball. Let's look at each for a moment.

Thinking of *keeping your head still* can have a negative effect on your swing. We're not saying the head should move—at least not very much—but directing your attention to keeping it still can reduce the freedom of motion you need in your swing.

Trying to *keep the left arm straight* can lead to too much tension in the arm and shoulders. We see players who try to keep the left arm rigid and try to force extension so much on the backswing that the arm reflexively relaxes and breaks down on the forward swing. If you are going to err one way or the other, we would rather see the left arm slightly bent on the backswing. This promotes more flexibility and allows you to build up the speed and centrifugal force that will automatically straighten your arm on the forward swing.

The thought of *keeping your eye on the ball* promotes staring at the ball so intently that you lose the vividness of your target picture. You become ball-bound and are unable

to relate your swing to the target, the path the ball must take and the distance it must go to the target. We're not advocating you look anywhere other than at the ball when you swing, but you should merely glance at it while keeping your mind's eye fixed on the target. We'll discuss this more thoroughly in the next chapter.

Seymour Dunn, in writing about the psychology of producing a golf shot, says there must be a keen muscular sense of direction and of striking the golf ball with the center of the clubface. As we said earlier, this muscular sense has to start in the hands and the feet, simply because the hands are the only parts of your body touching the golf club and your feet are the only parts touching the ground. You feel your balance, your posture and alignment and the movements of your lower body with your feet and you relate to the swinging of the golf club with your hands. From there the feel for the golf swing spreads to the rest of your body, especially the muscles you use in making the swing.

Research has been done that shows there is a great difference in muscle use related to the proficiency of the golfer. In general, the poorer the player, the more he uses the outside muscles of his arms. The better the player, the more the inside muscles of both the arms and the legs are used. You can feel this yourself—if you set up properly, there will be a slight tension up and down the insides of your legs. If your grip pressure is properly in the last three fingers of each hand, you will feel that pressure transmitted to the inside muscles of your forearms.

There is an important exception to this, however—on the backswing, properly executed, the outside muscles of the left forearm actually push the club back. If you need proof of this, take a weighted club and make takeaways for a few minutes using just the last three fingers of the left hand. The outside muscles of your left arm will begin burning.

The reason these outside muscles must be used is that that they are tied together all the way to the shoulder, and their use allows you to get the left shoulder and side pulled around. The inside muscles of the forearm are attached to the elbow joint and if you used them it would not necessarily follow that your shoulder would get pulled back. Similarly, if you took the club back with your right arm muscles, the left arm muscles would slacken and you again would lose the stretch or extension that creates a good swing arc. Also, if you rotate the club quickly off the line instead of pushing it straight back, the inside muscles come more into play to the detriment of your backswing.

This pushing back along the line of play with the left arm then puts you in position to make the desired pulling motion with the inside muscles of your left arm and your legs on the forward swing. If, instead, you push on the forward swing with the outside muscles of the right arm, you know what happens next.

You don't have to worry about all this specific muscle activity while making the golf swing, but being aware of it will help you program a feel for the swing into your mental computer.

The best way to accomplish this programming is to start close to the hole and work back. Begin with the short putt, using the mini-swing, to develop a feel related to clubface position and speed and to feel how keeping the club on the right path can make the ball go to the hole without overworking your hands. Move back to longer putts and then to chip shots and pitches to see what effect the angle of attack has on the flight of the ball. As you move back through these short shots, you will begin to develop an awareness of the amount of arm swing you need related to the distance to your target. Remember, you must *feel the force before you can force the feel.* Finally, go to full shots, where you can see more dramatically what the application of speed in the swing does to the ball. Through it all, you begin to absorb the correct sensations in relation to the mental image of what you're trying to do with each shot. This helps you better evaluate the mental and physical feedback from your swing related to how the ball flies. You will be developing your own swing feel and learning to relate it to results.

A final word of caution: Even though you understand the golf swing and think you have developed a consistent swing feel, your timing will get off at times. You may be physically or mentally tired or distracted by external or internal influences which disrupt your concentration. All these factors affect your ability to play the game. And when your timing goes awry, your anxiety level increases, adding further to your woes.

When this happens, all you can do is come back the next time in a more relaxed state of mind and begin working again from the hole back to regain your timing. It returns much more quickly working with the short shots than trying to beat a driver. Even the best professionals occasionally find it useful to hit a bagful of short iron shots to smooth out their timing and tempo. We once watched Gene Littler hit nothing but 7-irons for two hours trying to put his timing back in order and regain his swing feel. There's a man considered to have one of the finest swing tempos in the game, so that has to be a pretty good prescription for the rest of us.

## Pace

*The most important factor in the golf swing is motion, the motion in which the clubhead travels on the correct path like a jackknife on the end of a string, You can't play golf well without it.*

*The golf swing is predicated on correct club position, body position and alignment, which in turn help create the correct path for the swing. Swinging on this path is accomplished by proper timing and controlled by the correct pace. So while all of the first three P's are vital in building a sound swing, you can't put them together and make them work without a proper pace to that swing.*

*The right pace is easier to achieve if you are in the proper position, both before and during your swing. To put it another way, good pace is almost impossible to achieve if you aren't in proper position. But building proper pace into your swing requires more than good positions. Many players work hard on the positional aspect of their swings, and while their positions may be good, their pace isn't constant enough to let the parts fall into their workable relationship. The pace and momentum of your swing are the things that let the positions give you the most reward, the most shot consistency.*

You can't work too much on developing pace. On the golf course, particularly, you need to relate to the pace of your swing rather than to the positions. We've never talked to a good golfer who didn't relate primarily to the pace of his swing while playing.

Developing the pace you're looking for starts in your mind, which is the most difficult to control. In Chapter 2 we presented some thoughts on how the correct swing pace should feel. What we say next may repeat some of those thoughts, but the importance of the subject justifies repetition. These thoughts may help you put your golf swing together better than anything else in this book.

The first thought that you must incorporate into your subconscious is that *golf is a game of effortless power rather than powerless effort.* If you are going to get any consistency in your stroke, you apply power with grace and with a sense of rhythm and relative ease. Effective power is a result of your ability to create maximum clubhead speed while still moving the club squarely down the line of flight and making an on-center hit.

Learn to control the golf ball before you can hit it farther. Most golfers do not play to their potential because of direction problems, not distance problems. To control the ball, first learn to control the force of the club moving around the body. Most especially, learn to *swing at a pace that lets you feel you can change directions at the top without losing control.*

That's why you can only swing a club at the rate of speed that the strength of your hands and forearms can bear. If you swing the club back too fast for your particular strength level, the pressure to stop the club at the top builds up tension in your arms, which destroys your sense of feel and rhythm and wreaks havoc with your change of direction. Among other things, it almost always ruins your chances of getting the club back down on an inside path.

This is especially common among women and junior players, whose legs and hips often are stronger than their upper bodies. They move too fast with their lower bodies to be able to control the club with their hands and arms, so they can't get the clubface squared and usually slice the ball badly. That's why we often have the youngsters in our junior schools hit balls on their knees. It virtually eliminates their lower body action, slows down their upper body action and teaches them to control the club with their hands and arms.

So the less strength you have, the slower you must swing the club back to maintain control and keep unwanted tightness out of your body.

Pace is always controlled by your left arm and side if you are right-handed. If you swing the club back too fast, your left arm may break down and bend too much. Your left wrist may bow in the opposite direction and "lay the club off" behind the plane. You will swing too far back. You will feel you cannot make a good move forward with the left side and swing down from the inside with your left arm. Instead, you feel as if the right arm is going to swing down outwardly and outrace the left. And you won't retain the cocked position of your hands very long into the forward swing.

The faster you take the club back, the more you dissipate control at the top so that when you change directions you reduce the amount of energy available to get the club down. Your grip pressure changes drastically because the club is going so fast up there that to start forward you've really got to grip it tightly to keep it from getting away. Almost always it's the right hand that does the grabbing, which then alters the path and the face of the club. You've now ruined your accuracy and your ability to make solid contact as well as reducing the speed with which you can swing the club forward.

There is such a thing as taking the club back so slowly that you don't create enough momentum and movement to get properly positioned behind the ball. But that's rare. Most players create too much momentum on the backswing, perhaps because they instinctively feel this will help them swing faster coming forward. But the momentum you create going back doesn't help when you change directions and start forward. It doesn't transfer. The speed with which

you take the club back doesn't necessarily relate to the speed with which you bring it forward.

*The purpose of the backswing is to do nothing more than put your body and the club in position to move forward.* We would like to see the club going back at a speed that lets you effectively transfer your energies to the forward swing, rather than using those energies to control the club when you are changing directions. Which means the smoother you can take the club back, the better off you are.

But it also must be swung back with a sense of rhythm that will let you flow into the forward swing. Taking the club back is only the first step. Putting the club at the top and then starting over on the forward swing isn't going to get it for anybody. Pace must be related to a thought encompassing the whole swing rather than just "slow back." Our students often start the clubhead back slowly, but at the change of direction their swings speed up dramatically. That's because they haven't programmed themselves to incorporate a full-swing pace. As Bobby Jones put it so well, you must swing the club down leisurely as well as swing it back leisurely. The change of direction should be the slowest portion of the swing. Your swing should be like that of a pendulum. You should feel that the backswing is simply running out of steam as it gets to the stop, the club then starting back down almost of its own accord as the lower body begins its forward movement. And remember, you instinctively will be moving the club faster by the time you get to the ball. The buildup of centrifugal force alone will insure that you generate plenty of clubhead speed for the distance required, provided you don't let too much tension interfere.

A player needs to swing at a pace that allows the centrifugal force to work. Most often pace is lost and centrifugal force destroyed because the hands get going too fast. Your arms and legs can speed up, but not dramatically. But once your hands get out of correlation with the other parts of the body and are controlling rather than responding to the arm swing, you've got problems. This usually happens for one of two reasons, or maybe both. First, you may have a negative image of your swing, probably because of faulty aim and alignment or improper ballflight visualization, which makes you tight and tense and reduces your arm swing. We'll talk more about this in the following chapter on preparation for the shot. Second, your anxiety to hit the ball too hard and far causes your hands to overwork.

Overcoming this "hit impulse" is a major key to establishing a correct swing pace. The expression "to play within yourself" is perhaps overused, but that's exactly what you must do. Sam Snead says he only swings at about 80 percent of his potential speed. It's the pace he feels he can handle. If he swings full-out, he might hit an occasional good shot, but he can't get away with it consistently. And Sam is one of the longest hitters ever, which tells you 100 percent effort isn't necessary to produce distance in your shots.

How do you control yourself to swing at only 80 percent of your maximum speed? By programming yourself to do it before you step up to the shot and by working with your grip and arm pressure. If you concentrate on a light grip pressure and lightness in your arms during the swing, you can hit the ball just as far or farther with what seems like less effort. And you'll have much more control over where the shot goes. It's a beautiful way to establish the pace of your swing.

It's also vital that you relate the same swing pace to every club you have in your hand. Davis Love, a member of our Golf Digest Instruction Schools staff, describes it aptly when he says you would like the pace of your driver swing to be the same as that of your 7-iron. It will be longer, but the pace of the swing will be constant.

So many people have trouble with the driver because they're thinking of distance. The minute they pull it out of the bag their tension level increases, and this reduces their

## 1. BACKSWING

## 2. CHANGE OF DIRECTION

## 3. FORWARD SWING TO IMPACT

## 4. FINISH

### Tom Watson is slow at the top

This sequence of Tom Watson's full swing, shot at 50 frames per second, provides a striking demonstration of good pace. Watson requires 30 frames to get from takeaway to the top of his backswing. He spends 10 frames with minimal movement at the top while changing directions. From there to impact requires only 11 frames, and from impact to finish is 18 additional frames. The conclusion is clear—although Watson's swing appears to be fast, he makes a relatively slow backswing and is well under control, almost leisurely, as he changes direction and begins to build up speed in the forward swing. This slower pace at the top allows him to establish the proper sequence of movement and his superb timing.

tendency to think of pace. With the driver or 2-iron, they feel distance comes through tension and quickness rather than a sustained pace or speed.

Learn to feel that *every club is just a golf club*—not a 2-iron, not a driver, just a club—and you'll make a golf swing at the same constant pace every time.

A major problem in achieving correct pace in a full swing is that it's difficult to differentiate length of motion from speed of motion. A lot of players need more motion, greater length of arm swing, more freedom in the arms and shoulders. But most, when they are told to lengthen their arm swing, will speed it up drastically and lose control. They cannot measure and trust the greater length of motion at a slower speed. They cannot measure the pace of the swing.

That relationship of arm motion to pace applies in reverse, too. If you shorten your backswing because you have been swinging back too far and losing control, you have a great deal of difficulty because your sense of time in the swing has been disrupted, especially with the driver. You're willing to shorten your backswing to keep your motion under control but you are not willing to do it if you feel you are going to sacrifice 20 yards. As a result, you instinctively increase your speed, almost always at the cost of control.

We once took a man in Paris who had no sense of pace in his swing and asked him to hit 8-iron shots into a valley about 75 yards away, using his full swing. He hit 40 shots and all went well beyond the valley. His sense of pace improved. He had more velocity at impact. He said he thought he was swinging easier, but he was striking the ball better.

That's a proven technique that will help you play golf better. Try it yourself. Attempt to hit an 8-iron 50 yards with a full swing—not a full swing back and a half swing forward, but a full swing both ways. You'll always hit the shot twice as far as you're trying to. Because you have the club under control, it's more productive at the moment of impact. Therein lies the value of pace.

Let's discuss for a moment this business of "torque" and "coil" that we often hear applied to the backswing. Trying to build up torque, which theoretically will cause your muscles to unload automatically into the forward swing, actually, in our opinion, gets your body so tight that you can't start back down at all with any semblance of ease and rhythm.

We contend that even the very good players who talk about coiling and torquing really are only feeling the natural stretching of the muscles at the top of the swing. If you think that, at some stage of your development, you don't have to make a conscious forward-swing thought, that if you "load" your muscles on the backswing the forward swing will be automatic, just try swinging back as far as you can and do nothing else. You'll either stay right there at the top or your club will fall to the ground, depending on how much tension you are exerting. In any event, you won't make a forward swing that will find your golf ball.

That's why thinking of the legs as supports rather than braces is important. A brace, which some players and teachers like to label the right leg on the backswing, is a fixed object against which you have to develop. All that thought does is tighten the body. A support, on the other hand, is flexible enough to allow freedom of motion. The support of your legs allows the arms and body to swing and turn back and through without creating tension and inhibiting motion.

So instead of relating distance and direction to tension and effort, relate it to motion and pace. Don't try to learn this by starting with a full swing, because your natural instincts will promote tension and effort and you'll have trouble getting rid of those bad habits. That's why it's so important to start your learning process with the short shot. If you can relate motion and pace to the distance and direction needed for that shot, you build an instinctive reaction for the rest of your game.

Learn to pace your swing by learning not to over-control your putter. Let it swing back. Finish your backswing and accelerate forward smoothly without pressuring the stroke at any point. Once you ingrain that feeling with a putter, progress to a chip shot, then to a short pitch. Gradually accelerate the club throughout the swing, controlling and timing that acceleration as you move into longer swings.

Slow down, even pause, at the top and allow the change of direction from backswing to forward swing without forcing it. That slowdown gives the lower body time to react and initiate the forward swing instinctively. It lets the long muscles accomplish the change of direction.

Don't try to come to a dead stop at the top. As we indicated, when you do that you have to start all over again. A full stop hinders gradual acceleration, because you instinctively feel you must start the club forward too quickly to build up clubhead speed.

To learn proper swing pace you *must* overcome that hit impulse. You must come to feel that the hit is simply a result of the ball getting in the way of the club. One excellent way to avoid hitting *at* the ball is to imagine that instead of a hard rubber object there is a soap bubble down there. Now, instead of applying a lot of force to hit the object a long way, all you have to do is make contact to burst the bubble. You won't try to strike hard and quickly but will just let your arms swing down and feel as though the weight of the club is just falling into the ball. The result will be a smooth, properly timed swing.

Placing the ball on a tee when you practice also helps. You won't try to lift or force the ball into the air, because it's already there. You'll be more likely to swing your arms at a comfortable pace and not force your hands to hit early. When the ball is in a bad lie, you're more likely to subsciously use your hands to try to force it into the air, causing you to throw the club outward and come down into the ball from outside the target line.

That's why you're more comfortable and generally make a better swing when you have a good lie in the fairway. Once you learn to pace your swing properly, you'll be able to handle the bad lies as well as the good.

When you begin to develop this proper swing pace, you'll get some different sensations than those from the too-fast swing we described earlier. Your left arm will stay extended but soft during the backswing, and you'll feel your left wrist in a straighter, more stable position at the top. You will feel a much easier, earlier weight shift in the lower body going forward, the forward swing starting from there instead of your upper body. This will give you the feeling that you can swing your arms down more from the inside with a pulling sensation instead of a throwing action. At that point, you're on your way to becoming a smooth, consistent swinger rather than a slasher at the golf ball.

This, then, is the golf swing— complicated in its positions and functions but simple in its execution if those positions are correct and are molded together by pace.

Learning to make a consistent, efficient golf swing is not easy. We would be deceiving you if we said it were. If you study what we have written so far, you will understand the swing, and understanding is the first and vital step toward learning. Understanding the swing will help you play better, but to play really well you'll have to train your muscles to apply that understanding instinctively and as consistently as possible on the golf course.

Developing a swing, of course, is only half the goal. Ultimately, you want to take that swing onto the golf course and make it work to produce as low a score as possible. In the chapters that follow, we will tell you how to prepare yourself to make the swing perform on shot after shot, in the vital short game area particularly, and how to prime yourself mentally on the course so you can make your best possible score.

### Right foot—left toe

This drill should be done with a wood, with the ball on a tee. Using a stance about a foot wide, set your weight on your right foot. Pick up your left foot and rest it on its toe. Then swing, letting the right hand come off after impact. The drill gives you the feeling of the right leg being used as a steady axis to support the swing. It magnifies the feeling of the arms swinging, body following and the left arm and club going left after impact. Most important, it encourages the ascending swing you need with a driver and helps you stay behind the ball with your upper body. That makes it a good drill for players who pull the ball. If you don't do it with the right hand off after impact, you'll tend to cast or throw from the top of your swing, coming outside to inside the target line and pulling the shot. Another pitfall to watch for is playing the ball too far forward. This will make you lunge to get to the ball. Remember, you're not using your legs as much as you normally would, so be sure your stance is only a foot wide, placing the ball more toward your right foot.

### Right foot behind left drill

With the ball on a tee, take your normal address position, then place your shoulders and right foot behind your left and swing normally. This drill takes the shoulders and hips out of the swing for players who are overactive with them, who start the forward swing with the shoulders and hips twisting to the left faster than the feet and legs move laterally. It helps coordinate the sequence of movement and is good for balance and pace.

175

## Use a whippy shaft

Get the whippiest golf shaft you can find and strike shots with it. In our golf schools, we use a fishing pole shaft. There also are rubber-shafted training clubs on the market. This drill improves your timing, pace and rhythm. If you don't use your arms well enough and overwork your hands, you'll get a tremendous amount of curvature in your shots. If you get a variation in your shot trajectory, it's because your right side is pacing the left side.

## Baseball drill

Set up in your normal address position, then move your left foot back so it's together with the right. Then swing back, step into the ball and swing forward, just as if you were striding into a pitched baseball. This drill is designed to promote better left leg action, better transfer of the necessary weight to the left leg and better overall leg motion. Be sure to get your left leg planted in the correct spot as you stride forward. If you don't, the upper body will have a tendency to move past the ball. The drill is best performed with an iron and the ball on a tee—teed higher at first, then lower as you gain proficiency.

## Tee ball high

Use a 2½-inch tee and stick it in the ground just far enough so it will stand up with the ball on it. Using a *driver*, this drill will force you to stay behind the ball and create an ascending blow. If you use a descending blow, you may have to get the top of your club refinished. Avoid the tendency to play the ball too far forward. Also, be careful not to hang back on your right side too long. This eventually will get you throwing the club from outside the target line.

## Swish drill

We use a shaft stuck into a golf ball for this one, but you can simply grip a club at the hosel end and make swings with the left arm with the club upside down. Try to create the loudest possible "swish" in the forward swing. Accelerate your left arm to the target and let your body follow. At the completion of the swing, your hips and shoulders should be facing the target. This drill primarily produces lightness and increased acceleration from the left arm. It helps develop the feeling of retaining the arm-shaft angle longer instead of casting the club with your hands. The only pitfall is that some players will try to throw the club with the left arm and resist with the body. Do the swish drill with the left arm and listen to the sound. Then do it with both arms and notice how much less noise there is. This documents the importance of left-side control.

## Swing a weighted club

Using a weighted training club, a weighted headcover or a heavy "donut" that fits on the shaft near the clubhead (available in golf shops and sporting goods stores), just swing with grace and ease, moving this heavy club backward and forward on the correct path. Actually strike shots with it. This stretches your arm swing and promotes more motion in your swing. And it builds up strength in your forearms and hands, developing your muscles in the way they are used in the swing.

Be sure the club is not too heavy, because this may make you want to move your body first. A too-heavy club also can cause injury, especially to your left thumb and wrist. Something in the 20- to 25-ounce range is adequate.

177

## Left foot off ground at top

This is the intermediate step between the baseball drill and the regular swing. From your normal stance, make your backswing and lift your left foot off the ground, then put it back in the same place as you swing forward. This has the same advantages and the same pitfalls as the baseball drill to a lesser degree. It helps you get behind the ball, but it can also cause you to sway somewhat to the right and back forward with the upper body.

## Full motion—half speed

This drill is normally done with a 5-iron, although any club may be used. With your regular full-motion swing, hit shots progressively 25, 50 and 75 percent of your normal distance. This develops proper arm control of the club and correct left-side pace. The pitfalls are that initially you may tend to get tight and almost mechanical with your swing and you might tend to make a decelerating motion to the ball. You also may tend to overwork your hands, so relate strongly to your arms swinging.

## Flip drill

This requires two participants. Take your normal setup. Have a friend place the shaft of a club against the target side of your shaft just under the grip, metal to metal. Then, with a quick, smooth push backward and downward, he should flip your club back. This is an excellent drill for promoting lightness in the arms, a relaxation of tension in the upper body and increased motion. It gives you the feeling of a proper backswing, with the arms swinging and the body following. The pitfall is that it could tend to make your takeaway a little quick and/or jerky.

## Split grip

Assume your normal address position, then move your right hand down on the shaft so there's about a three-inch gap between it and the left. This helps the right hand and arm fold and become passive to the left and helps create a forward swing path that comes from the inside. It also gives you a descending blow. Pitfalls to avoid are an excessive use of the hands and lack of arm motion and a tendency to want to hit with the right hand rather than creating a pulling action with the left arm.

## Walk-through or machine-gun drill

Tee four or five balls in a row about six inches apart and hit them without stopping. This drill is designed to help rigid players who need to get some motion in their swings. It promotes arm freedom and proper grip pressure. The pitfalls are that you get sloppy with your posture, you may tend to get right-sided in your takeaway or you may get too much upper-body movement as you walk through the drill.

# 8

# THE
# FIFTH
# P:
# PREPARATION

No matter how good your golf swing is on the practice tee, it is more important that you make it work on the course. In general, every golfer has three different swings: the practice swing when there is no ball in front of him; the practice-tee swing under no pressure when, if he misses a shot, the golfer can rake another ball out of the pile and try it again; and his swing on the course, where each shot counts.

Your obvious goal is to make your swing on the course resemble your practice swing as closely as possible. To do this, forget about the mechanics and concentrate instead on where you want the ball to go, not how to make it get there.

The where or *target visualization* is one important factor in pre-shot preparation, the fifth P. Then you must find a way to get your swing started, triggering it so that it will happen as automatically as possible without your having to worry about it. This requires a consistent pre-shot routine, done in a certain time interval, that allows you to approach the ball, set yourself at the ball, waggle the club and *go* in the same manner each time.

Once you establish such a pre-shot routine and learn to trust it, you'll find a couple of marvelous things happening. Number one, it eliminates that awful moment when you must start the club away from the ball. For players who start the club back from a static position, that moment of takeaway becomes an awesome, dreaded thing that disrupts the continuity and flow of your swing. When you're on an established routine, that awful moment becomes no different than any other moment throughout your routine. You'll find your swing starting reflexively without the worry that causes tension and anxiety.

Secondly, a good routine gives your body a sense of timing, a feeling for the rhythm and sequence of motion, a feeling of alertness, quickness and fluidity that puts you in a more relaxed state to start the swing. Once you get into the flow of such a routine, your body won't know whether it's the last shot of a tournament or the first shot of a practice session. It will react the same way in either case.

Lee Trevino is an excellent example of this. Whether he's on the practice tee or making a pressure shot for the PGA Championship, his pre-shot routine is exactly the same. He never varies his mannerisms or his time interval.

Billy Casper is another with an ingrained, unvarying routine. Casper's routine happens to start when he takes the club out of the bag. From that point, his pattern never changes as he steps up and makes the shot. If something distracts Casper, he actually will put the club back in the bag and start all over again. He has

his body trained to accommodate itself to a precise series of movements, and any variation in those movements would disrupt his concentration and cause a rebellion in his muscles, undoubtedly resulting in a poor swing and a bad shot.

Before we get to the business of helping you develop your own routine, let's quickly review your basic address procedure. As we told you in Chapter 5, this involves, In order, placing your hands on the club; placing the clubface to the ball, on the path and aiming down the target line; aligning your body to the clubface and the target line; and positioning your body to the ball in the proper posture.

Mechanically, this is done by approaching the ball from behind and to the side, stepping forward with your right foot as you place the club behind the ball and aim it down the target line. Next, place your left foot in position, then adjust your right foot so the line of your stance is at right angles to the clubface and parallel with the target line. Next, set your knees, hips, shoulders and eye line parallel to the line, while at the same time setting up in the posture we outlined earlier.

Those are the mechanics. In how you accomplish those mechanics lies the secret to a pre-shot preparation that will set your swing off instinctively, fluidly and consistently.

Creation requires preparation. When you are creating a golf shot, that preparation involves getting your mind organized to make that shot, then following a procedure that lets your body perform the act as instinctively as possible. As you move into the shot, your mind must be uncluttered by details and instead be focused on a feeling for the whole swing related to the target.

Target orientation or visualization is the cornerstone of this procedure. Fix your attention on the target at the very beginning of your preparation and keep that target picture in your mind as you go through the routine that leads to the actual swing. Visualization ties together the whole shotmaking procedure, and we will devote the entire last part of this chapter to helping you develop your visualization abilities. First, let's examine the physical portion of the routine that takes you into the shot.

Start your preparation from several paces behind the ball, looking through the ball down the path to the target. It is from here that you identify the flight path and consequently your swing path. By now you should have a plan for your swing, a key or, at the most, two keys that will direct you in making the correct swing. You might be thinking "arms swing, body follows" or whatever key words work best for you. But you must have that plan. Make a preparatory swing down the target line, using your keys, to identify the feeling of the swing you are about to make at the ball.

Next, it is vital to pick out an intermediate target—a leaf, a divot or some other easily discernible spot on the target line a few feet in front of the ball. When you step up to make the shot, aim your club at this spot, a much easier and more accurate process than trying to aim it at a distant target. Most players don't have the talent to put the club on line without using an intermediate target, and we see drastic improvement in the aiming and alignment abilities of our students once they start using one. Jack Nicklaus never lines up a shot without using an intermediate target, so why should you?

Now relate the ball and your intermediate target to the target itself and establish in your mind a picture of the shot you want to make. Ideally, that picture should never leave you until the shot has been completed, and we'll discuss that more thoroughly later. At this point, it should be as if you are in an isolation booth, shut off from everything else. The shot picture is clear and you should be identifying in your mind how little effort and tension is necessary to create the swing and clubhead speed you want.

Having made your preparatory swing down the target line, picked out your intermediate target and visualized your shot, you are ready to begin your approach to the ball. Grip your club as you stand behind the ball. Hold the club in front of you at about a 45-degree angle, which helps you establish the proper grip pressure and also enables you to use the club as a plumb line from your ball to the target.

Approach the ball at a right angle to the target line and slightly behind the ball. As you walk to the ball, don't take your eye off the intermediate spot, or you may never find it again. Watch it until your eyes are positioned the same as they will be at address.

Position the right foot squarely to the line and put all your weight on the right leg. This helps establish the proper knee flex for the shot. Your left leg is resting basically on the toes at this point. Next bend forward from the hips so you can place the clubhead squarely behind the ball and aim to your intermediate target. Your arms should be hanging freely. In effect, you have put your upper body in position first, properly aligned to the clubface and to the target.

Now adjust your lower body to accommodate the upper, moving your left leg into place and repositioning the right leg so your ball position and stance alignment are correct and your weight is properly balanced toward the balls of your feet. Do this without moving your upper body or losing your spine angle. *(See photos, pages 184-185)*.

*Keep routine the same*. Your-routine should never vary. Your walk to the ball, your aiming and setup procedures, your waggle and your takeaway all should be done in rhythmic sequence within a specific time span. This puts you into your comfort zone, and promotes a feeling of ease and freedom and a sensation of readiness that tells your body precisely the right moment to start the swing.

This sequence of pre-shot motions and the time it takes need not be the same for everyone. Do it at your own pace. We generally find that the slower and more deliberately you do it, the smoother and more controlled your takeaway will be. But don't get *too* slow, either. A 10-to 15-second interval from first step to takeaway is about right. This forces you to do the routine by feel rather than by mechanical thoughts. But whatever time you take, do it all the same way every time.

It is important as you go through this routine always to be in some sort of motion. You really never stop moving from the time you begin your walk to the ball until your swing is completed. You should be constantly refining your stance and your setup position as you make your waggle or waggles, establishing a keen muscular feel in your hands and feet that spreads to the rest of your muscles and prepares your body for the shot. Once you stop and get into a fixed position, you disrupt the flow and continuity that triggers your swing instinctively. As

1

2

5

6

## The pre-shot routine

*Jim Flick goes through an ideal pre-shot routine that takes him without pause from his point of mental preparation to the act of striking the ball. Your routine should be patterned after this: (1) make your mental preparation (the isolation booth) while focusing on the intermediate target from several paces behind the ball; (2) move to the ball, eyes on intermediate target while identifying proper grip pressure; (3) step in with right foot and establish correct knee flex; (4) set the clubface behind the ball; (5) check your clubface aim with the intermediate target and identify your arm hang while positioning the upper body; (6) place your left foot and adjust your right foot to complete the positioning of your lower body relative to your upper body; (7) identify your target; (8) identify your swing path to the target while waggling; (9) make your final waggle, identifying the correct arm and grip pressure; (10) cock your head to the right and begin your arm swing.*

3

4

7

8

9

10

you become more advanced and polished with your setup routine, you will find less need to refine and adjust your positions, and your motion will lead you more easily into the takeway.

*Waggle.* It is here that the waggle and forward press are so important. The waggle keeps you in motion and helps you create that keen sense of feel that you need. If you waggle correctly, you prepare the muscles you want to use in swinging the club and striking the ball. *(See photos, right.)*

There's an old Scots expression, "As ye waggle, so shall ye swing," and that thought isn't all bad. The proper waggle actually does preview the swing. It excites the correct muscles to be used in the swing.

That's why we prefer a long, flowing waggle when you're preparing to make a full swing, especially with the driver. That builds up an arm momentum that helps you flow easily into your takeaway. The waggle should be made at the pace with which you're going to make the actual swing. Sam Snead is an excellent example of a player who lets his waggle dictate the length and tempo of his swing. With a driver, the waggle is long and slow. If he's going to play a little punch shot, the waggle will be much shorter and quicker, and the waggle will vary similarly for each different shot he's attempting to play.

The waggle is made in a free and easy manner, using the last three fingers of the left hand. This identifies the underneath muscles of the left arm that are going to be used in the golf swing. It is done primarily by cocking the wrists, without a lot of arm movement. The club is waggled straight back from the ball, the clubface going from square to slightly open to the line, and from the top of the waggle there is the feeling of it coming back to the ball on an inside path, thus giving you the sensation of a miniature swing.

All the while your hands are developing a feel for the club and your feet are in slight motion, feeling the ground and creating an anticipation of their action during the swing.

Too many players waggle the club up and down or waggle the clubhead up in front of the ball. We never see a good player waggle the club forward, because that sort of waggle must be done with the right hand, which then tends to take over in the backswing. While you are waggling, be sure to keep your spine angle constant. Don't make the common mistake of raising your upper body during the waggle.

How many waggles should you make? Snead waggles the club once. Tommy Armour seemed to waggle it a hundred times. We would suggest that the longer you stand over the ball, the less distinct your target picture becomes and the more your muscles tend to tighten. For that reason, the fewer waggles you make the better—two or three should be enough.

As you complete your final waggle and return the club to the ball, there should be an instinctive forward press that sets your backswing in motion. There are many ways to forward press, but we prefer that it be done with a slight push of the right knee toward the left. This movement in turn moves the left knee a bit toward the target and pushes the left hip slightly upward, at the same time relaxing and slight-

ly lowering the right side. This helps the right side turn more easily and promotes a freer arm swing. It also performs the vital function of activating the muscles of the feet and legs for their part in the swing. It adds to the feeling of "aliveness" you need if the legs are to support the swing properly.

The forward press not only leads to a smooth start of the backswing, it also gives you the real key to the start of the forward swing. The sensation there is the same as the for-

### The waggle prepares your muscles
*A correct waggle, as Jim Flick demonstrates, prepares your hand and arm muscles as well as the muscles of your feet, legs and knees, creating in them a keenness and readiness to work in the swing. The waggle is done with the left hand. With the driver, especially, it is a long, flowing movement back along the swing path and returning to the ball. In this sense, it previews your swing.*

ward press, except that it is a stronger move and is initiated with the left knee rather than the right.

If you have never used a consistent, repetitive pre-shot routine—and most players haven't—develop it the same place you learn everything else in your swing, on the practice tee. Work on feeling that you are setting up and taking the club away on a count, even though you might not consciously be counting. At first you will find this difficult to do. You will feel you are hitting the shot before you are ready. This is a stage you must go through, but once you get through it you will begin to find your body wanting to go instinctively at the right moment. You'll become like the good free-throw shooter in basketball, who bounces the ball three times and shoots automatically, never giving himself time to think about the actions or consequences of the shot.

If, for some reason, you stay over the ball past that prescribed moment without starting your swing, your body will sense that something is out of kilter, and it won't want to go. When that happens, don't just stand there and try to recapture the feeling while your tension level rises. Do as Casper and the other tour players do—step back and start your routine all over.

Once your routine works for you on the practice tee, learn to make it work on the course. This is a tougher task. On the practice tee,

the shot doesn't mean anything, and you've always got another ball to hit if something goes awry. That reduces tension and instinctively gives you more trust in what you're doing. But on the course, many intimidating factors loom—every shot counts toward making a score, which raises your tension level; each shot you play is different, which affects your routine; you subconsciously have less trust in your swing, which means you'll have less trust in your routine; you're faced with different types of lies, and while it might be relatively easy to make your routine work with a good lie, your mind and body will have difficulty accommodating to a ball sitting in a divot or buried in tall grass.

To make this psychological adjustment between practice and actual play easier, go out in the evening when the course is not crowded and play a few holes with two or three balls. Don't be concerned with your score. Simply get used to walking up to the ball and whacking it, using the routine you've developed, from all kinds of lies and under all sorts of conditions. See how often you can repeat your routine and your swing no matter what the circumstances.

How long this transition period takes depends to a great extent on how much confidence you have in your routine and your swing from the very beginning. And don't try to short-cut the process. If you fail to develop and trust your routine during practice and, instead, try to learn it during a round that counts, you'll hit a lot of bad shots and feel that your routine isn't worth anything.

If you do develop your routine to the point where you can trust it and use it on the course, keep practicing it, diligently, so it stays with you. An especially good time to practice it is during your warm-up sessions prior to playing. Incorporate your pre-swing routine into every shot you strike during a warm-up session.

This will keep you secure in the knowledge that you can walk up to every shot on the course and get your swing going without having to say, "Now!"

## Target visualization

The element that makes your swing path and pace work most productively on the course is *visualization* or *target projection.*

The influence of target projection on path is obvious. A mental picture of the target and the ball-flight to that target gives your swing direction. Golf, like most other sports, is a target game. The object is to propel a ball from one point to another specific point. But unlike other sports, in golf you are not looking at your target during the moment of action that gets the ball there. The quarterback sees his receiver, the pitcher sights the plate, the basketball player watches the hoop. Even

the tennis player, while he may be following the ball, is usually facing the spot where he wants to hit the ball and is seeing it with his peripheral vision. In golf, you are looking only at the ball. This tends to make the ball your primary target. You become "ball bound" and instinctively will swing *at* the ball rather than *through* it. Your objective becomes simply striking the ball rather than getting it where you want it to go.

For that reason, you must get and keep a picture of the target and the path to that target in your mind's eye. Even though you may be properly aligned, without such a picture you will still be swinging only in a general direction. Target projection gets your mind away from the ball. It refines and focuses your swing path and instinctively helps you swing the club and send the ball flying in the specific direction you want.

An even more important result of visualization is that it quiets you down mentally so your swing pace stays correct and constant. To create proper pace, you not only need a feel related to your physical swing, but a positive mental picture of the ball going where you want it to go. Your mind then lets your body react positively.

You can prove this to yourself with a simple experiment. Station a friend a few feet away and toss a golf ball softly to his or her hands. Concentrate only on your friend's hands. Think of nothing else. Notice how the ball travels on a nice, high arc and drops unerringly into the target. Now toss another ball to the same target, only this time watch the ball as your arm swings back and forward and try to be aware of which finger last touches the ball as it leaves your hand. You'll likely not come anywhere near your target. The ball probably will fall well short, because you stifled your throwing motion by concentrating on the mechanics and on the ball instead of visualizing where you wanted the ball to go. Exactly the same thing happens in a golf swing.

Without the proper ball-flight picture in your mind, mechanical thoughts may creep in and force you to change the good pace of your swing. Maybe every swing won't be affected, but sooner or later they're going to get to you, probably when you need swing pace the most, in the tightest spot.

Developing the ability to consistently project to the target is not easy. Actually, it is the final stage in a series of swing developments. Your first stage, as a beginner, is to play by a mechanical thought, to make a conscious effort to do something with your swing. The second stage is when you begin to play with a feel related to that mechanical thought.

Next, you develop a mental picture of another player swinging. The first such mental image probably will be of the best player in your group. Later, your swing model improves and becomes probably the best player in your club or area. Eventually, as your experience in golf widens, you will see some top professionals on television or in person and will begin to pattern your swing after them.

You can never play your best golf if you stop there, because your swing model is still somebody else. *To play really well, you must know your own swing and "internalize" that swing, developing a mental picture and a feel for it.* Developing that picture and feel for your own swing is the purpose of the instruction we have presented so far in this book.

The final stage is taking that swing image and physical feel and marrying it to your target by visualizing the flight of the ball. The top players do that well, which is why they play well. Sam Snead says the only time he ever sees his swing on the golf course might be while he is walking down the fairway between shots. Once he reaches the ball and begins to prepare for the shot, he wants to see only the flight of the ball going to the target.

Bruce Crampton, winner of more than one million dollars on the PGA tour, once claimed he not only visualized ball flight but also saw the ball landing on the green, bouncing and rolling to the cup!

Jack Nicklaus calls it "going to

the movies,'' and says he never makes a shot in practice or in play, without first visualizing the ball resting where it wants to go, the flight of the ball on its way to that target and, finally, a picture of the swing he wants to make.

Here's a tip to help you visualize more vividly. The mind sees in pictures, and words trigger those pictures. So keep your mind focused on your ball flight to the target, talk to yourself—under your breath, while you are preparing for the shot. Describe in words how you want the ball to fly and where you want it to end up. This will firmly implant that ball-flight and target picture in your mind.

Be realistic, though. You can't visualize something you can't execute. If your swing is not good enough to make a particular shot, your mind won't let you visualize the shot. It will rebel, simply because there has been no input, no previous experience in making such a shot that lets the mind picture it and allows the body to go ahead and do it.

Once the mechanics of your swing are good enough that you can physically perform what you are visualizing, *your effectiveness will depend on trusting that swing.* Let your mind's eye picture what you want the ball to do, then let your swing be a reaction to that target picture. Let the body do what you know it can do. Accept that you can

make the shot, then execute it.

When you first start working with visualization, you will find it difficult to keep the entire ball-flight and target picture in your mind as you set up to the ball. Perhaps the top player can visualize the entire scene until the moment he starts his club in motion on the backswing, but you will build to that point gradually.

In doing this, it's again important to start close to the hole with short putts. The relatively short span of the shot will allow you to visualize the path of the putt and see it rolling into the hole and to keep that picture while you're stroking the putt. Because the target is so close, your orientation to it remains more vivid.

Then move back to longer putts, to chips and pitches and finally to the full shots. As you do this, always start from behind the ball and relate to the target, the path to the target and the flight of the ball to the target. As you advance to the ball and move into your setup routine, you can glance at the target to reaffirm that path and ball-flight picture and use it to aim your clubface and align your body. As you make your final waggle and go into the forward press that initiates your takeaway, you may lose the target picture. But you can still relate, through your peripheral vision, to the starting path and initial trajectory of the shot. If you let your swing react to this starting path, it will put the clubhead on the right track. The umbrella drill we describe on page 287 is an important aid in building a reaction to the initial flight and direction of the ball.

You do, after all, get to the target through the path. As you progress and your mind becomes more keenly attuned to the act, you'll find your mental picture stretching farther and farther down the path until finally it is encompassing the target itself and the entire flight to that target until the moment you begin your swing.

Once the club goes into motion on the backswing, you want to be thinking only of rhythm and pace, simply letting your swing react to the target picture you've established.

Don't be concerned if it takes you a long time to develop this complete target picture as you stand over the ball. Training the mind is not easy, and even many good players never quite reach that point. But reacting to the starting path will immediately make you a better player, and the farther you take that mental picture to the target, the better you'll become. Hopefully, some day you'll consistently be able to look up and see the ball flying just as you've visualized it.

That, then, is your prepration— the fifth P that makes your swing work on the course. Stand behind the ball, visualizing your target and the path to that target. Move into your actual pre-shot routine, keeping that target picture in mind for as long as possible, aligning your club

and body along the path and staying in motion so your swing can flow without interruption as a reaction to that path.

If you trust yourself to do this, your swing will become more and more efficient and you will play better golf than you ever thought possible.

## Make a dry run

Without a ball, go through your pre-swing routine and actually make a swing to the target. This will relieve the anxiety that often occurs with the ball in front of you, keeps you oriented toward the target instead of becoming ball-bound and ingrains the routine and swing into your muscle memory. Enough dry practice will help you go through the procedure more smoothly when the ball is actually there.

## Arm swing-knee fling

Without a club, swing your arms freely back and through several times. Eliminate the tension in your arms and shoulders. Feel your swinging arms turning your shoulders, not vice versa. On the forward swing, make sure your left knee leads the way and feel your legs fling your arms. Feel yourself roll onto the outside of your left foot and onto the toes of your right as you finish your swing, as shown below. This drill gives you the feeling of motion and freedom of movement you must have.

193

## Stop at the top

Make a full swing, stopping at the top for a count of two. This will promote a slowed change of direction from backswing to forward swing. It also helps you feel your arms swinging down on the inside. It takes the arms-swing/body-follows concept a step further. The pitfall is a loss of rhythm and fluidity of motion and an increase of tension in the shoulders.

# 9
# THE SCORING SHOTS

Consider your last round of golf. How many greens did you hit in the regulation number of strokes? We'll bet not very many, and we're not being derogatory. Even the best touring professionals miss several greens a round. Some women, juniors and senior players hit very few a round, simply because they don't have the strength. Yet the tour professionals shoot par or better, and we know a lot of short-hitting players who score better than their ball-striking potential. In both cases, good scores are rescued with the short game, the scoring shots around and on the green. The scoring shots let us finish the hole, taking advantage of good shots on long holes and recovering from poor shots anytime.

David Pelz, inventor of the Teacher putter and one of golf's more analytical students, tells us that 68 percent of the shots we take during a round are less than full swings —43 percent are putts, 25 percent chips, pitches and sand shots.

Yet, we constantly see players beating out full shots on the practice tee and seldom, if ever, spending as much time working on their scoring shots around the green. You need to practice your long game, as we have stressed, but you are misdirecting a lot of energy if you don't spend as much or more time becoming proficient in the shots that can really produce a lower score at the end of your round.

The scoring shots—chips, pitches, greenside sand shots and putts —do not require size or strength. They require skill that comes through only knowledge and practice.

Before we explore the differences in the short game strokes, there is one basic you should apply to all of them: the feeling that, *at impact, the left hand and arm are pulling the right hand under.* That applies to chipping and pitching and, especially, to sand play. It even applies to putting, although perhaps to a lesser degree.

This feeling tells you that the left hand and arm are controlling the stroke. You can't achieve this sensation if the right hand gets overactive. If you ingrain this feeling into your stroke, you can become consistent in all phases of the short game.

## Short strokes from grass
Your most important objective in the short shot is controlling the distance the ball goes. When the ball is resting on grass, this control requires consistent ball-club contact. Overactive hands during the stroke make this consistency difficult if not impossible to achieve. Overuse of the hands also changes the trajectory of your shot and affects the roll of the ball. If your trajectory with a particular club is inconsistent, you can't maintain the mental image of ball-

flight that lets you get the ball close time after time.

So while your goal in all shots is to let the hands react to the swinging of the arms, this becomes particularly important in the short strokes from grass, where precise distance and accuracy are so vital to the success of the shot.

Once you have established this thought, the next step in becoming skilled at making the shots from grass around the green is to organize your short-game concept. That simply means knowing which stroke to use at what time and from which situation.

There is a basic rule to follow: *Give your shot minimum air time and maximum ground time.* Loft it as little as possible, get it on the putting surface as quickly as you can and let it run as far as you can to the hole within the limits of the green surface available to you. The more loft you put on a shot, the more variables of spin and turf consistency you add. The more like a putt you can make your shot, the better off you are. *(See illustration, page 199).*

In that light, Peter Kostis has devised what he calls the putt-chip-pitch system, as shown on pages 172-173. Basically, this means you putt the ball with a putter when you can, use your putting stroke with a more lofted club if you can't use a putter, use the chipping stroke as your next option and use the pitching stroke when you have it. These strokes vary basically in the amount of wrist action used and in the angle of attack to the ball.

*The putting stroke*. The most accurate motion is the putt, because you basically use a one-lever system in striking the ball. Keep your left hand and forearm firm, with no break at the wrist, going back and coming through the ball. Use a pendulum-type stroke, with the club striking the ball on the level at the bottom of the arc, or with just a slightly descending arc. The left arm and the clubshaft remain in line throughout the stroke. Anytime you don't create an angle between the shaft and the arm, while you won't get as much distance, you will be able to control the accuracy and distance better.

In this stroke, combine firm wrists with a little more aggressive use of the arms. You will feel slightly more tension than if you hold the club lightly and use wrist action.

Set up with your weight even, the ball in the center of your stance or slightly forward of center and your eyes over the target line, parallel to that line and set slightly behind the ball.

As we said, if the area between the ball and the green is relatively smooth, your first choice may be to use the putter. If the grass is too high or for some other reason you want to land the ball on the putting surface, you may still want to use this accurate putting stroke with a lofted club. You may use any club from a 2-iron to a wedge and can effect any kind of ball flight you want with this stroke. There are two limitations on this shot. The first is the lie—it is dangerous to use your putting stroke from a bad lie, because you need a more sharply descending angle of approach. The second limitation is the distance you must carry the ball and let it run, and this you learn by experience.

Use your putting grip with the more lofted clubs if you feel comfortable with it. But even with your regular grip, use the putting stroke for accuracy whenever possible.

In using the putting stroke, be careful that the club does not set too far up on its toe, because this will result in unpredictable spin on the ball. To get the club soled properly, you may have to set your hands lower or more toward your body than you would for your normal putting stroke. It may feel uncomfortable until you practice it awhile, but the increased consistency will make it worthwhile.

*The chipping stroke*. Once the distance your ball must travel becomes so great that a single-lever arm swing becomes cumbersome, you have to go to a two-lever system. You have to allow your wrists to break to gain clubhead speed for the greater distance you need.

Now, anytime you create an angle

## *Minimum air time, maximum ground time*

*Your rule of thumb for the short game is "minimum air time, maximum ground time." The more loft you put on your approach shot (top), the more you are subject to leaving it short or long. When the terrain allows, use the flag as your target and chip with a lower-lofted club (bottom), getting the ball on the ground as quickly as possible and letting it run to the hole.*

199

PUTT

CHIP

PITCH

### The putt-chip-pitch system

*Bob Toski demonstrates the basic system for short shots from off the green, each to be used according to the terrain, the distance and the amount of available green between you and your target. In order of preference, they are: the putting stroke (top)—your weight balanced, ball in the middle of your stance, eyes over the target line and slightly behind the ball, a level or slightly descending swing with a one-lever stroke; the chipping stroke (middle)—weight forward, ball back, eyes forward of the ball, a more descending swing with a slight hinging action; and the pitching stroke (bottom) —weight back, ball forward, eyes behind the ball, a less descending or more U-shaped stroke with more hinging action and a light grip pressure.*

between the arm and the clubshaft and the ball is not teed up, the only way you can get the ball properly airborne is with a descending blow. You must strike the ball squarely with this downward blow to propel it into the air and get it to run to the hole.

Most players don't trust the loft of the club to get the ball in the air. Instinctively, they try to force the club to get the ball up by scooping it with overactive hands. They take the club too much inside on the backswing, with the result that their swing is very flat going back and very upright coming through the ball. The short-

shot stroke should be just the opposite—upright going back and low going through. Don't try to force the shot; just let the arms swing the weight of the club into the ball. You'll find that the amount of force you need to swing the club into the ball on a short shot is really very slight. Acceleration comes from the weight of the clubhead. *(See photos, below.)*

Using slightly more grip pressure in the last three fingers of the left hand than what you use in the putting stroke, you'll find that your hands will cock the club upward. From there, keeping the left hand

## Upright back, low through for chip

*In this down the-line view of the chipping stroke,
Bob Toski shows how the club is swung back and
up on an upright or steep path (2), then remains low
to the ground through impact and the finish of the
stroke (3 and 4). There is no scooping but rather a
firm tapping-down action that results in crisp contact and better control of distance and direction.*

firmly in control, just tap down on the ball. You'll learn through experience the amount of arm swing you need to strike the ball a given distance.

The short stroke is simply a miniature swing, with one difference. Don't make any attempt to follow through, especially in the chipping stroke. In this stroke, the backswing is always longer than the follow through.

Henry Cotton, the famed British player and teacher, tells a relevant story. His young assistant was trying to teach the short shot to a student and he kept telling the pupil to "follow through, follow through." The student was concentrating so hard on following through that he kept mis-hitting the ball. Henry finally said, "Why don't you teach the gentleman to find the golf ball by simply swinging the club to the ball and tapping down on it. Teach him to get *to* the ball first and *through* the ball second. I'd rather have him stick the club into the ground after he hits the ball than try to lift the ball into the air with a follow-through."

The more you make this kind of a descending stroke, the more your left hand will control the force of your right. The loft of the club you have chosen will get the ball into the air on the proper trajectory.

So the chipping stroke is still a short stroke made at a descending angle. Using your regular grip, set your weight forward, to the left, and the ball back, at the center of your stance or slightly farther back. This puts your hands a little more ahead of the ball, your left hand about at the point of your left knee. Your eyes are in front of the ball. This in itself creates a steeper swing path and the descending blow you want, so you really don't have to worry about it.

Your weight stays on the left side during the swing, and the angle between arm and shaft will create itself. The weight of the club being swung by the arms will force the hands to hinge. If you allow the hands to react to the arms coming down, you'll get the tapping-down motion you want for this stroke. Don't try to over-control your hand action, because this makes the hands and wrists stiffen. A light grip pressure allows the hands and wrists to flow properly through the swing, as if you were throwing a ball.

Again, the lofted club you choose depends on how far you must carry the ball and how much room on the green you have to let it roll. Practice and experience on the course will soon let you make a wise club selection for each situation. But your stroke should remain the same, if at all possible.

*The pitching stroke.* Your final option around the green is the pitching or lob stroke. It is the least accurate stroke with the least chance for success, and there are relatively few times you have to use it. At the same time, it is most important to learn. It offers the greatest variety of shots because it can produce the most variation in ball flight and the most flexibility in applying spin to the ball. You can change your club or your length of motion or your speed of acceleration, and with these changes, you can play an unlimited number of different shots.

The basic purpose of the pitching stroke is to give you a higher flight with a softer landing and less roll. To do that, you need more arm swing and usually a softer arm swing than in the putting or chipping strokes. You'll want a light grip pressure, so the clubhead can more easily catch up and square itself on the forward swing. The weight of the clubhead can accelerate itself better when your grip is light. If your grip gets tight, your hands tend to get overactive and ruin the stroke.

To allow the clubhead time to work, we recommend that any time you make a pitching stroke your arms swing back at least to the nine o'clock position, your left arm parallel to the ground. *(See illustration, page 206).* This gives your legs a chance to work and slow down your stroke. It allows you to control the distance you want the ball to go with the speed of your left arm and left knee and, again, lessens the chance of your hands becoming overactive.

For this stroke, you still want to create a descending blow, but now you move the ball forward in your stance—to the center or just slightly ahead of center—and distribute your weight more equally, positioning your swing center about even with the ball. Remember, your basic preference in any shot is to have your weight start on the right side and move to the left. But you don't need that in making the putting stroke and there isn't enough time for it to occur in the chipping stroke. The pitch is the first shot available in which the weight shifts to the right and back to the left. The longer, slower and softer arm swing, with less hand action than in the chipping stroke, gives you time to get your weight to the left side to make the necessary descending blow with the left arm. As you swing through, you should feel that the club is coming down from inside the target line and is being supported by the movement of your feet and knees. That movement will move your swing center ever so slightly ahead of the ball through impact, ensuring that you make the descending blow you want.

This shot played with the softer arm swing will give you a high trajectory and not a lot of spin—the lob shot. You can impart more backspin by accelerating your arms a bit more, as long as you retain the angle by not using your hands too soon. The more constant your arm

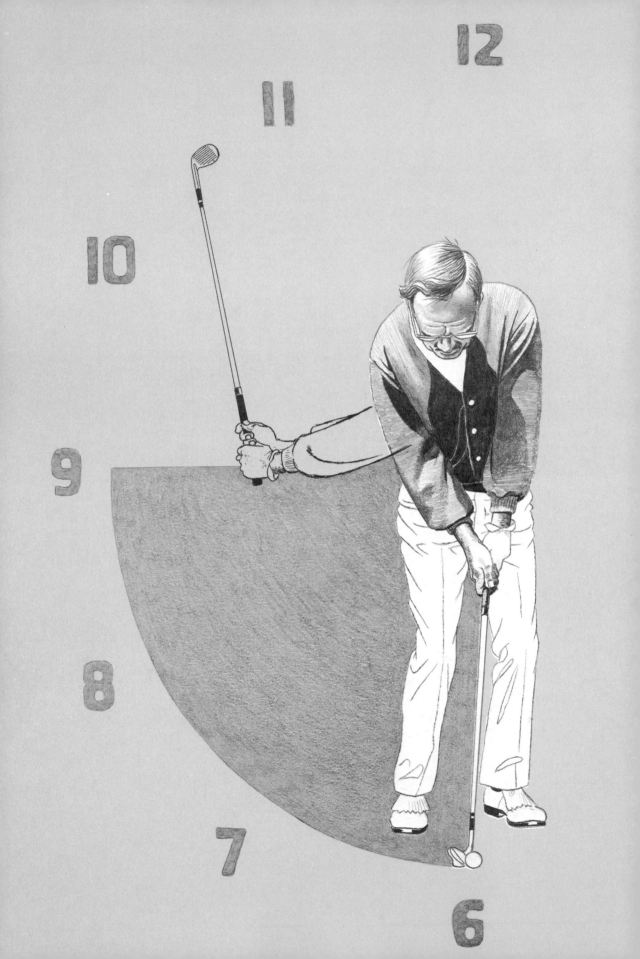

speed, the more you'll get the lob effect; the faster you accelerate into the ball, the more spin you'll get and the lower the ball will fly, only because you'll probably de-loft the club a little as you swing faster and retain the angle longer. Which shot, or which variation, you choose to play depends on the distance, the height you need and the amount of green available to work with. Experience will tell you which to use. *(See photos, pages 180-181.)*

Because the pitching clubs are the heaviest in your bag, we encourage you to grip down a bit on the handle, the amount depending on the length of the shot—for pitches of just a few yards, you can go down almost to the shaft itself, then go up gradually as the length of the shot increases.

It's important to understand that your setup and ball position for the short-game strokes insures that you don't have to consciously create hand action. So let's recap:

—The putting stroke is made with your weight evenly distributed, the ball in the middle of your stance or slightly forward of middle, your swing center in line with the ball, your eyes over the target line and a level or slightly descending swing.

—The chipping stroke is played with the weight forward or left, eyes and swing center forward of the ball, the ball back in your stance and a more descending swing.

—The pitching stroke is played with your weight evenly distributed, the ball in the center of your stance or just slightly forward of it, your eyes and swing center in line with the ball and again a descending stroke with light grip pressure.

Each stroke is a little longer than the previous one. The closer to the hole you are, the lighter your grip pressure must be to feel and control the force of the club against the ball.

If you know these various strokes and learn through practice and experience the variables involved, your chances of playing the desired shot at the right time are better. Your selection can depend more on the type of shot facing you than on the distance. For example, if you are 30 yards from the flag with plenty of green to work with, you should chip the ball instead of pitching it. You might even take, say, a 4-iron and use your putting stroke. If you're close in and don't have much green to work with, you could use your chipping or putting stroke with a sand wedge. With this arsenal of strokes, you don't get stereotyped into thinking that every time you're 20 yards off the green you have to use a wedge.

## Greenside sand play

We long ago gave up telling our students that sand play is easy. It is *not* easy for most players, because of the technique required for effective bunker play. As a result, when-

---

### *Arm swing goes to 9 o'clock for pitch shots*

*Plenty of arm swing is the key to executing the pitch shot well, so in all but exceptional situations you should swing your arms back at least to the 9 o'clock position on an imaginary clock. The distance required then can be controlled by your left arm and left knee speed rather than forcing your hands to become overactive.*

## Use plenty of arm swing for high lob shot

*When you need to make a high-flying, soft-landing pitch, like this shot over a bunker that Bob Toski is facing, the secret is to use plenty of arm swing so your hands don't become overactive. From a slightly open stance, Toski takes the club back on an upright plane (2). The clubface is slightly open and remains that way throughout as Toski swings it softly down from inside the target line (4). The left hand pulls the right hand under and there is no stopping at impact (5). The left arm and the clubhead go left in the follow through (6). Note at this point that the clubface hasn't turned over, remaining slightly open, which means that there has been no undue pressure from the right hand.*

ever the ball lands in the sand they become confused and frightened. The sand becomes an enemy.

If you fit that description, take heart. Knowledge can ease your fear and simplify your concept of how to play an effective sand shot. You still must practice to become a good bunker player, but if you know what to practice it's easier.

The sand shot differs from most other shots in golf in that there normally is no ball-club contact. While this is the factor that upsets most players, it actually *increases* your margin of error. So your first step in learning effective sand technique is understanding the use of the flange on your sand wedge, which is the tool you use to displace the sand under the ball and take advantage of this margin of error.

The *flange* is the rounded sole or bottom of the club. Its purpose is to let the club ride through the sand, undercutting the ball and lifting it out on a cushion of sand. The flange —or "bounce" as it is sometimes called—is used to control the depth at which the club passes through the sand. For the normal sand shot, the flange must strike the sand first. That's why the sand shot usually must be played with the clubface set open or laid back. This puts the trailing edge of the flange lower than the leading edge and allows it to contact the sand first. This trailing edge then acts as a rudder in letting the club make a relatively shallow

cut as it rides through the sand. *(See illustration, next page.) If the* leading edge of the flange enters first, the club will dig too deeply, the force of the swing will be dissipated and you are likely to leave the ball in the bunker.

It will help, as you address the ball, to imagine you are looking *through* the clubface and seeing the flange. Then, simply undercut the ball with this portion of the club, knocking the sand out from under the ball.

The use of this built-in bounce is dictated by your lie in the sand. If the ball is sitting nicely on top of the sand, a positive use of the bounce is indicated—the club is laid open or back to insure that the trailing edge of the flange strikes well before the leading edge. If you have just a fair lie with the ball slightly nestled down in the sand, use less bounce—don't open the clubface quite as much so the entire flange enters the sand at the same time and a deeper cut results. If your ball is buried, eliminate the bounce altogether in most cases; square the clubface so the leading edge enters the sand first and the club digs deeply to pop the ball out. We'll discuss this shot in more detail later.

Effective use of the bounce requires that you strike the sand several inches behind the ball. Three to four inches is a good guideline, but it's important to remember that you have that great margin of error in making this shot. If you use the flange properly, the club will make a shallow cut of 12 inches or so as it "bounces" into, through and out of the sand. If the ball is sitting in any portion of sand removed by this cut, it will fly out on the cushion of sand and land softly on the green.

Remember, the sand is your friend. The sand, rather than you or your club, lifts the ball out of the bunker. Thus, you can strike three to six inches behind the ball, providing you let the flange work properly to make the shallow cut.

That dispels another prevailing myth, that you must strike only an inch or two behind the ball in making a sand shot. Aiming that close to the ball, in fact, encourages catch-ing the ball with the blade first and probably skulling it over the green. Instead, take advantage of the large safety factor you have.

Thus, you should not aim at a particular spot in the sand behind the ball. Simply look at the general area of the sand you are going to displace, and your swing will react accordingly. At the same time, since you are going to strike the sand *behind* the ball, don't make the common mistake of addressing the shot with the club directly behind the ball. Set the club several inches behind it to insure your margin of error. And remember that the rules do not allow you to ground your club in the sand.

*The distance the ball travels on a*

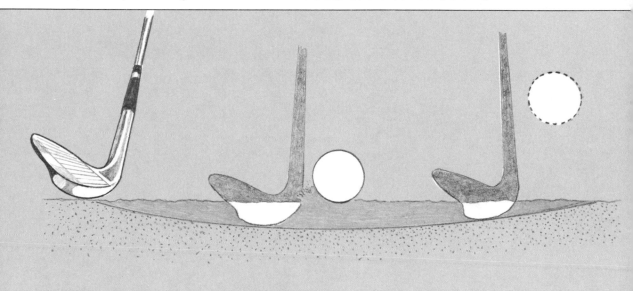

## How the club works in the sand
*This diagram illustrates how the flange or "bounce" on your sand wedge works in the bunker shot. With a descending blow and the clubface open or laid back, the flange strikes the sand first. This prevents the club from digging in too deeply and stopping the stroke. The flange then acts as a rudder, allowing the club to ride through the sand on a shallow arc under the ball. The ball is lifted out on a cushion of sand as the club continues through and out of the sand into the follow through.*

V-SHAPED
SWING

U-SHAPED
SWING

212

## Use V-shaped swing for higher shots

Because the ball comes out of the sand at approximately the same angle the club enters the sand, shots that you must get up quickly and stop more quickly require a steeper or more V-shaped swing arc. Here Bob Toski demonstrates this, setting his weight more to the left, swinging the club back and up more sharply with his arms and cocking his wrists more quickly, then returning it through the sand on a steeper arc. This pops the ball up on a higher initial trajectory.

## Use U-shaped swing for longer shots

When you want the ball to carry farther from the sand, a lower initial trajectory is required. This is accomplished by setting your weight more balanced or even to the right and making a shallower, U-shaped swing back and through the sand with not so much early wrist cock. The ball will come out lower and travel farther in the air.

*normal sand shot is controlled by the speed of your arms and hands, which of course controls your club- head speed, and the amount of sand displaced.*

While the less-skilled bunker player usually is better off swinging more with the arms and less with the hands, feeling that he is simply dragging the clubhead through the sand, the better player often likes to incorporate more hand speed throughout the shot. This creates more spin on the ball, which is desirable if you can control it.

Sand displacement is determined by the angle of attack with your clubhead, not necessarily by how far you strike the sand behind the ball. The angle at which your clubhead enters the sand creates the initial trajectory of your shot as well as the depth of cut through the sand. The steeper the angle, the higher your trajectory will be, the deeper the cut and the shorter the distance the ball will carry. The deeper cut will slow your clubhead speed and the steep- er angle will dissipate power down- ward. The shallower the angle, the shallower the cut you will make, the lower your initial trajectory will be and the farther the ball will travel in the air.

Don't confuse the overall height of your shots with their starting tra- jectories. The longer bunker shot may achieve more height than the shorter one, simply because the ball goes farther. But it probably left the

sand at a shallower angle.

The concept that angle of attack creates initial trajectory is graphical- ly illustrated by a simple demonstra- tion we use in our schools, one you can use yourself. Set a cement block in the sand or in your back- yard and bounce several golf balls off it. If you drop a ball from straight above the block, the ball will bounce straight up. If you throw the ball at the block on a 45-degree angle, the ball will bounce off at a 45-degree angle. If you throw the ball at a shallower 30-degree angle from behind the block, it will bounce for- ward off the block at a 30-degree angle. The same principle applies exactly in the sand—*the ball will ex- it from the sand at the same angle the club enters it.*

This angle of your swing arc is best controlled by your setup. For most bunker shots around the green, you'll want a steeper angle, which displaces more sand and pro- duces a higher trajectory. To achieve this, set your weight on your left side and put your hands ahead of the ball at address. Make sure your clubface remains slightly open and is not closed or hooded, except for buried lies. Then just swing your arms back and through the shot in a manner which we'll ex- plain in a moment. The angle will have been predetermined by your setup. You will make a steeper, V-shaped swing and get a deeper cut through the sand without having

### Angle right foot into sand

In this down-the-line view of the setup for a long bunker shot, note how Bob Toski's right foot is angled into the sand in the direction of the shot to give him a brace against which to swing. The balls of his feet are dug in deeper than the heels to set his weight properly. His upper body is tilted forward and his arms are hanging freely. Note how his clubface remains open even for the longer shot.

to think about it.

For longer bunker shots, you will need a lower trajectory, so you want a shallower, more U-shaped swing arc that produces a shallower cut through the sand. To get this, set your weight increasingly more on the right side and play the ball more forward in your stance. Still keep your hands ahead of the ball at address, although not so much. Practice in the bunker soon will give you the right combination of weight distribution and hand and ball position to achieve the distance you need. (See photos, page 212-213.)

If you are reasonably confident about your work in the bunker, there is another way to play the longer sand shot. With your weight set right, place the club square at ad-dress and *lay it back* rather than open. Using your normal grip, position the left thumb in line with the back of the ball. This will make you feel your left wrist is in a slightly concave position and that your hands are behind the ball. The advantage of this method is that the square blade helps you aim your shot better, and having your hands slightly behind the ball will produce a shallower cut through the sand. You'll get the distance you need more easily. This position will also encourage you to keep your left arm moving strongly through the shot. But there also is a tendency to skull the shot and let the right hand over-power the left. We don't recommend this procedure unless you are a skill-ful player with strong left arm con-

## *Left arm goes left in sand shot*

*It is especially important in the sand shot that the left arm go left after the club passes directly beneath the ball. As Bob Toski shows here, this keeps the blade from closing (3) and keeps the right hand activity to a minimum so you can get a consistent cut through the sand with the flange of your club.*

trol on the forward swing.

Remember that distance is controlled by sand displacement, trajectory and arm speed. For the shorter shot, make an easier, slower swing with your weight set left. When the long shot gets too long, simply swing with greater arm speed. When even that doesn't do the job, you must begin thinking about taking less sand with an even shallower cut and, eventually, striking a normal pitch shot out of the bunker by contacting the ball first. Again, practice will soon let you learn the right combination to fit the circumstance.

It's often said that you must aim your sand shots to the left of your target because the open blade will cause the ball to come out spinning to the right. The only quirk in that theory is that, in the sand, the clubface does not determine direction. The clubface never touches the ball. Instead, it's the direction in which the sand is displaced that largely determines the direction the ball will fly. This makes clubface path the most significant determinant of direction, which means that in the sand you must be just as careful to align yourself properly and swing the club on the proper path to the target as you are on any other shot.

For the sand shot, as for any pitch shot that requires a longer swing, set your lower body slightly open, with the left foot withdrawn a few inches from your normal stance line. This allows you to swing more freely through the shot with your arms. Play the ball a couple of inches back of your left heel, then just swing your arms straight back and up and through the ball toward the target. The cushion of sand you cut out will send the ball flying where you want it to go.

For the normal, short bunker shot, not only set your weight left at address, but keep it there while you make the shot. There's a simple procedure that will help you hang left during the swing. For any bunker shot, work your feet into the sand to get them firmly planted so you won't slip. For the short, high-trajectory shot, plant both feet angled to the left, your weight on the inside of the right foot and the outside of the left. Set your left foot on the same angle you want to swing. This will help you keep your weight left and swing on that angle without having to do so consciously. For the longer sand shots, still bury your feet in the sand and angle your right foot slightly to the inside, but plant your left foot squarely. *(See photo, page 215.)*

More golfers would hit successful sand shots if they didn't become so anxious, swing too quickly, cut their swings too short or use their hands prematurely to make up for their lack of arm motion. If you find this happening, concentrate on swinging with your arms, not your hands, and making a full, free motion. Get used to making a longer swing than you feel necessary for the force of the

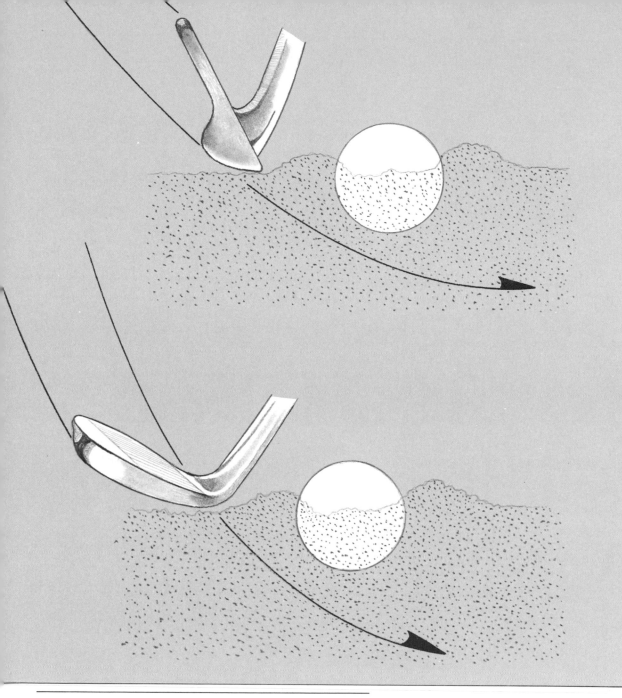

## How to handle buried lies in sand

This illustration shows two effective methods for coping with a buried lie in the bunker. The usual method is to square the clubface and hood it (top). With a steeply descending swing, strike down just behind the crater in which the ball sits. You can apply force with the right hand and simply stick the club in the sand. This will pop the ball out with little or no backspin and it will run a long way when it lands. From the same lie, for a softer shot that won't run as far, open the blade wide (bottom). Controlling the entire swing with the left hand and arm, swing the club up and down very steeply into the sand just behind the crater, with no extended follow-through. You should feel as if you're almost striking the sand with the hosel of the club.

shot. This will encourage a smooth arm swing and will keep your hands out of the act.

*Keep left arm moving, in control.* The most important factor in successful sand play is keeping your left arm moving and in control. The left arm initiates the backswing, initiates the forward swing and remains in command throughout while the left side keeps moving to maintain a platform for the arm swing. *(See photos, page 216-217.)*

The poor bunker player pressures the club too much with his right hand, which causes his left side to collapse. He thus strikes the sand with the leading edge of the club instead of the flange, takes a deep divot rather than a shallow cut and seldom follows through. Or else the right hand flips the clubhead past the left and he skulls the shot. He also swings harder, apparently obeying the instincts that tell him he must whale the ball out of this unfriendly sand.

To the contrary, the easy sand shot (all right, we'll admit it—it *is* easy if you know how) requires only an easy swing. The better the sand player, the easier it seems he's swinging through the ball. See for yourself the next time you get to a tour event or watch one on television. Watch a good bunker player, like Tom Kite, and build an image of his smooth, rhythmic swing in your mind.

To prove to yourself how important it is to keep the left arm swinging, let go with your right hand as you strike the ball. You'll still take a nice, shallow divot and undercut the ball pretty well. Now let go with the left hand at impact, and we'll bet you bury the club in the sand.

So swing club straight back and up. On the forward swing, you should have the feeling that the left arm is pulling the clubface directly under the ball and moving slightly left or inside the target line, swinging leftward and *up* as you finish.

Your left wrist should not collapse while swinging through the shot, and you should have the feeling that your left hand is pulling your right hand under at impact. Check the clubface at the finish of your swing. If you have swung in this manner, the face will be pointing pretty much to the sky. If your right hand has taken over, the clubface will be facing more to the ground.

Don't force the leftward movement of the left arm. It happens naturally if you don't let the left wrist collapse and turn over. Don't roll the clubface shut—the face stays square as the left wrist remains firm and the left arm swings left, pulling the right hand under.

Let's quickly review the sand shot basics:

—Use the flange to ride through the sand with a shallow cut by opening your clubface or laying it back.

—Use of the flange or the leading edge is dictated by your lie in

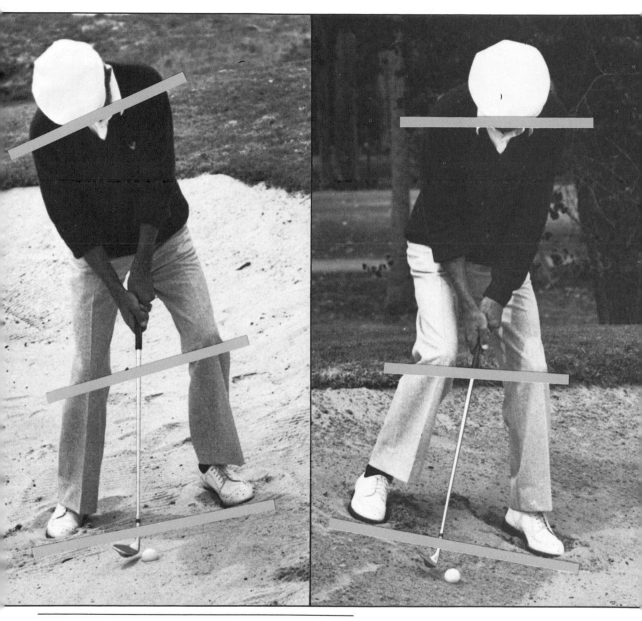

## Set body with slope in sand

*Bob Toski shows how to handle uphill and downhill
lies in the bunker. In either case, set your body to
conform with the slope. For the uphill lie, put your
weight on your right side and get your knees and
shoulders sloping upward. For downhill lies, your
weight will be forward, your right knee will be above
your left and your shoulders should conform to the
slope as much as possible, taking into consideration
the fact that your right shoulder normally sits lower
than your left.*

221

the sand.

—Strike the sand several inches behind the ball, remembering that you have a great margin for error if you make a shallow cut.

—Aim at the general area of sand displacement, rather than a specific spot behind the ball.

—The length of the shot is influenced by sand displacement, trajectory and arm speed.

—Sand displacement and trajectory are created by the angle at which your club enters the sand—the steeper the angle, the deeper the cut, the higher your trajectory and the shorter distance the ball will carry; the shallower the angle, the shallower the cut, the lower your trajectory and the farther the ball will fly.

—Swing angle is controlled by setup. For a V-shaped swing, a steep angle and high trajectory, set your weight left; for a U-shaped swing, a shallower angle and a lower trajectory, set your weight right.

—Direction is determined by the displacement of the sand, not your clubface position, so clubhead path becomes all-important.

—Use plenty of arm motion, not your hands.

—The left arm and side are in command throughout. Swing straight back and up, and on the forward swing keep the left wrist firm, the left arm swinging through the shot and moving left; at the finish, the clubface should be pointing skyward.

—The sand swing is an easy swing; force is not required.

*Some special thoughts for better sand play.*

1. *From a buried lie.* There are two ways to play this shot. The standard method, as we indicated earlier, is to square the blade and then just stick the club in the sand behind the ball. If you have the usual "fried egg" in which the ball sits in a crater of sand, aim slightly behind the back edge of the crater. With your weight set well to the left, take the club straight back and up with the arms, keep a firm grip with your left hand and strike a steeply descending blow with your right. The ball will pop out fast and low with little spin and will run much farther than the normal sand shot, so remember to use much less arm speed than you think is necessary *(See illustration, page 219.)*

There is another way to handle the buried lie that will produce a softer shot with less roll, but it requires practice and confidence in your ability. Again with your weight set well left, open the blade drastically so you are addressing the ball with the very back of the flange, almost at the heel or hosel of the club to negate the bounce. Then strike a very descending blow with the left hand firmly in control but with little tension in your arms.

Because you want no closing of the clubface, there should be little use of the right hand. Don't follow through and never let the clubface pass the hands. The action of the flange digging deeply into the sand will produce a larger, more upward explosion of sand than if the leading edge were used. The ball will still have little or no spin, but it will come out higher and softer. This shot is especially effective from a deep bunker and when you have little green to work with.

2. *From an uphill lie.* If your ball rests on an upward slope in the bunker, just swing into the bank. Play the ball back more toward the center of your stance and be sure to set your shoulders in line with the slope angle. Take a normal backswing and simply swing the clubhead on an inside path into the sand behind the ball. Your left hand will stop when it hits the sand, so don't worry about trying to carry it through. Practice will tell you how far behind the ball to strike and how much force you need to carry the ball to your target.

3. *From a downhill lie.* Swinging down lightly and steeply is the key thought here. Your right knee should be more flexed, and again your shoulder line should approximate the downward slope. Your hands should be set well forward of the ball. Concentrate on keeping the left arm moving down and across the ball at a steeper angle than normal.

Otherwise, you'll hit the ball in the belly and send it sailing. The swing should be light and easy—and don't get anxious with your hands. *(See photos, page 221.)*

4. *To stop the ball quickly.* From a normal lie, if you must get the ball up in a hurry over a high bunker lip and stop it quickly in a limited space, this is one time we suggest that you take the club away outside the target line. This gives you a steeper angle of attack and a deeper divot as you undercut the ball, softening the blow and causing the ball to pop up and drop softly.

5. *Feel the sand depth and texture with your feet.* To determine the depth and firmness of the sand, feel with your feet as you are anchoring them solidly in the bunker. This can tell you a lot about how to strike the shot. The firmer the sand, the quicker the ball will come out, so the softer and easier your swing must be. The softer the sand, the more the force of the club will be deadened as it rides through and the slower the ball will come out, so your swing must be longer and faster.

6. *Play the sand shot from hard pan.* While not technically a sand shot, the shot from mud or hardpan is played the same way. Just imagine that your ball is sitting on extra-firm sand and apply the same principles with an easy swing. You may want to use a pitching wedge, because it has a less-rounded

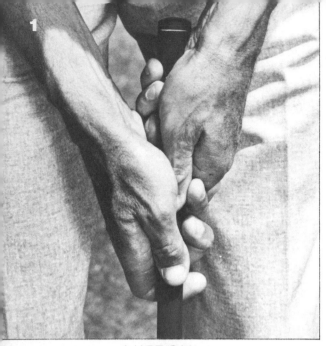

VARDON

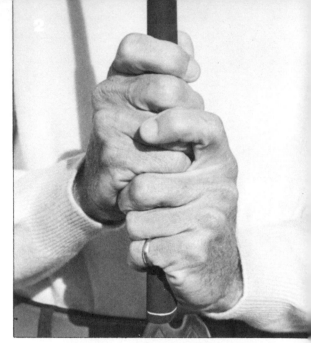

REVERSE OVERLAP

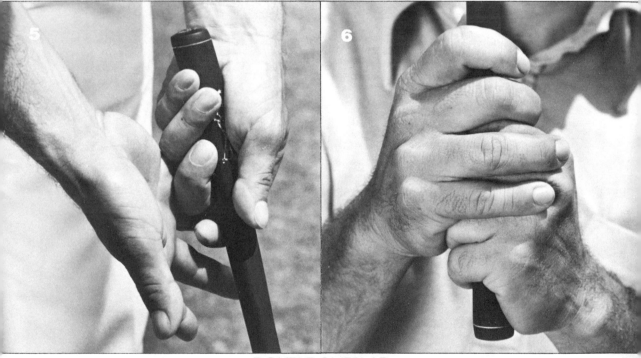

DOUBLE OVERLAP

### The putting grips

Shown here are the various putting grips: (1) the Vardon or overlap grip, with the little finger of the right hand overlapping the forefinger of the left, the same grip as is used for regular shots except that the hands are set in a bit more opposing fashion; (2) the regular reverse overlap grip, the left forefinger overlapping the right fingers in a curved fashion; (3) the same reverse overlap with the left forefinger

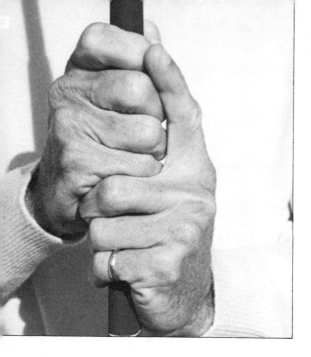

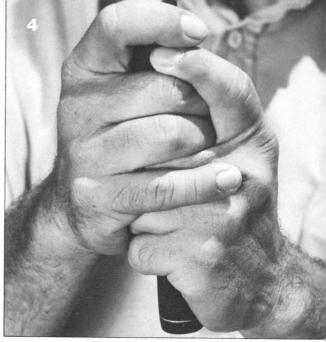

THREE FINGERS

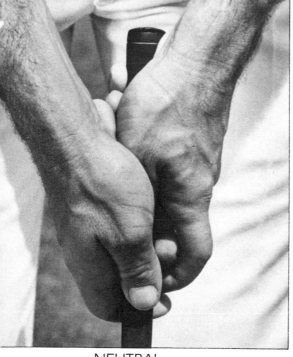

NEUTRAL

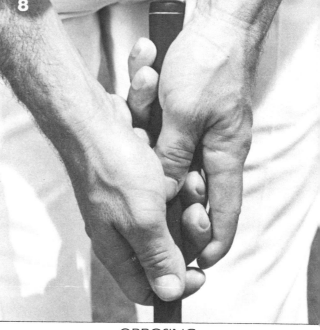

OPPOSING

*straight down the shaft line; (4) three fingers of each hand on the club, the forefinger of the left overlapping the right fingers and the little finger of the right hand overlapping the left; (5) and (6) the double reverse overlap, the last two fingers of the right hand overlapping the left. Photo 7 shows the hands in the neutral position, while photo 8 shows them in an opposing position, each turned more under the shaft.*

flange. But still open the clubface and use that flange, never the leading edge. Drop the flange into the ground a few inches behind the ball. The club will skid through the ball and produce a satisfactory shot.

## Putting

Just as feel is important in the swing, so is it especially vital in successful putting. The mechanics of grip, setup and stroke vary among great putters, but all have a superb sense of feel on the greens.

To sharpen your feel on the greens, you must develop the same traits we discussed in the full swing: a clear understanding of pace in your stroke, great patience and a reaction to the target. Incorporating these traits will help you make more putts and will help you keep your emotional equilibrium when you miss them. *Knowledge builds confidence, and confidence breeds composure.*

You certainly must ingrain good mechanics into a fundamentally sound putting stroke. We will first discuss what we believe are the fundamentals of grip, setup and stroke in putting, and we urge you to practice them. That's the only way to get better on the course. But, as you practice and play, you will incorporate the sense of feel for motion that lets you use these mechanics to best advantage.

*The grip.* There are many putting grips that work. We will describe each of them and tell you how they work in relation to particular putting philosophies.

Basically, the putter is held in the palm and against the heel pad of the left hand, lying primarily along the lifeline in your palm, and the fingers of the right hand. The club is held lightly, with most of the pressure in last three fingers of the left hand and very little in the right. Within that fundamental structure, you can use the following grip configurations:

—The normal Vardon grip, with the little finger of the right hand overlapping the forefinger of the left.

—The regular reverse overlap grip, with all four fingers of the right hand on the club and the left forefinger overlapping the right fingers in a curved or hooked fashion.

—The same reverse overlap but with the left forefinger overlapping the right fingers straight down the shaft line.

—All four fingers of the left hand on the club with the last two fingers of the right hand overlapping the left.

—Three fingers of each hand on the club, with the forefinger of the left overlapping the right fingers and the little finger of the right hand overlapping the left. (*See photos, pages 224-225.*)

The purpose behind each grip is to make it compatible with your philosophy of the putting stroke. The player who believes that the right hand supplies the power and feel while the left hand gives direction to the stroke—such as Jack Nicklaus —would want to put all four fingers of the right hand on the club and overlap the left forefinger. If you feel that the left hand should control the entire stroke and the right hand is just supporting and stabilizing, then you would want all four fingers of the left hand on the club.

Because the latter is our philosphy, that's the primary grip we teach. Our experience leads us to believe that most golfers overwork their hands, especially the right. This creates an inconsistent clubface relationship to the target path and too much variance in the speed of the stroke. In cases where the right hand is so active that it should be in position where it can do little or nothing to break down the left hand and wrist, we recommend overlapping the two fingers of the right. This moves the hand higher and gives it less chance to pressure the clubhead.

The grip in which you overlap the forefinger of the left and the little finger of the right is another way to move the right hand higher and take it more out of play during the stroke. But we would advocate it only for somebody who already has a reasonable amount of left-side control in the stroke. It's more difficult to develop left-side control from scratch with this grip.

Experiment with the grips that are compatible with your putting philosophy. Because the size and configuration of your hands and fingers are also factors, you may have to make slight adjustments until you come up with a grip that is both solid and comfortable.

Perhaps our biggest concern in the putting grip is the position of the palms. We prefer one of two situations: (1) a completely "neutral" grip in which the palms are facing each other and are square or perpendicular to the line of your stroke; or (2) a grip in which the palms are diametrically opposed, that is, however much the left hand is turned under or counterclockwise, the right hand will be turned under or clockwise an equal amount.

In the opposing grip, the position of the right hand insures against the left hand opening or closing the blade going back and the position of the left hand issures against the right hand causing blade deviation on the forward stroke.

In either grip, the thumbs will be placed on top of the shaft. In the neutral grip, they will be more or less straight up and down the shaft, whereas in the opposing grip they will be turned in opposite directions. In both cases, the wrists should be slightly arched to further inhibit hand rotation.

Again, experiment to find the grip that works best for you. In general, the wristier your stroke, the more you should set your hands diametri-

### The putting stroke is a pendulum action

In the top sequence, Bob Toski shows that the putting stroke is a pendulum-like action, the clubhead, hands and arms all being swung back and through as a single unit. The club starts back low, but there is no attempt to keep it low, so it rises naturally as the arms swing back, then returns through the ball on a low, level path. Note that the blade opens naturally because of the natural rotation of the arms

going back, then closes just as naturally in the impact area. There is no breakdown in Toski's left wrist as he swings through. In the bottom sequence, note how the same single-level pendulum action causes the clubhead to move inside the line on the backswing, then back on the line and inside again as Toski strokes through the ball. Pay particular attention to the fact that the stroke is long enough to allow gradual acceleration without the need to add flash speed with the hands.

cally opposed. The quieter your hands are during the stroke, the more you can use a more neutral grip.

*The setup.* Your weight should be slightly toward your right side, which gives you the feeling of staying behind the ball and stroking more toward the hole. Your knees should be slightly flexed, your weight solidly distributed between the balls and heels of your feet. Your arms should hang, your elbows resting close to your body, a position which allows less error during the stroke because your elbows aren't waving around in the air. This position occurs naturally, especially if your hands are at all opposed in the grip.

Bend from the hips so that your eyes are over the target line. A friend can help you with this, or you can hold a club or weighted string and let it hang from between your eyes to determine if they are in the correct position. How much you bend from the hips depends on how far you stand from the ball. Find the position that is best for you, the rule of thumb being that you bend as much as possible while staying in balance.

The ball can be played anywhere from just inside your left heel to the center of your stance. Playing it farther back than center  can create a steeply descending blow that causes the ball to hop. Your hands should be even with or slightly ahead of the ball at address. This makes it easier to keep them firm and leading the clubhead through the stroke.

*Optics.* Aim and alignment of the blade are so important in putting that it's virtually impossible to be consistently successful if your optical alignment is not correct. That's why it is vital to have your eyes over the target line and also set parallel to that line, not cocked askew in one direction or another. Your eyes should also be set slightly behind the ball, which you accomplish by putting your weight to the right. This lets you view the line from behind and through the ball to the target. When you sight the putt from your setup position, do so by rotating your head and eyes down the line of play. Don't lift your head up and around as you take aim, because this destroys the relationship of your stroke to the line.

*The stroke.* We liken the putting stroke to the swinging of a pendulum. The stroke is done with the arms. It's a two-sided action, with the left hand and arm dominating, while the right hand rests lightly on the club and stabilizes the stroke. You should feel you are using a "one-lever" system, stroking through the ball with the left wrist stabilized and the left hand and arm remaining in line. *(See photos, pages 228-229.)*

One of the main causes of poor

putting is deceleration on the forward stroke because the left forearm doesn't keep moving. Stabilizing the left wrist overcomes that problem. The left wrist may be allowed to hinge slightly on the backswing for a longer putt, but it must be firm and "unbroken" swinging forward.

Swing without making any manipulation of the putterhead with your hands. The putterhead will swing inside the target line on the backswing and back inside on the follow-through on all but the shortest putts. The face will appear to fan open on the backswing, returning naturally to square at impact. Remember, it is fanning open only in relation to your target line, not to the path of your stroke. Any attempt to keep the face square to the line throughout the stroke results in a manipulation with the hands. You actually alter the face position by hooding it, which requires a compensating adjustment on the forward stroke. Some great putters—Billy Casper may be the best example—have putted this way, but it requires extreme talent and a lot of practice, with strong emotional control.

Try to contact the ball at the bottom of your swing arc. If anything, feel you are tapping down slightly on the ball. All putts skid for a few inches before beginning to roll across the grass, and any attempt to uppercut the ball to put overspin on it results in a less-solid blow that gives you a poor roll and distorts your feel for distance. Striking a putt solidly, which is extremely important, means contacting the ball squarely with the "sweet spot" of your putter. Heel or toe hits may cause the putt to roll off line.

Your putter's sweet spot, incidentally, can be found easily by holding the putter aloft with two fingers at the grip end and tapping along the face with a pencil. The spot at which the putter rebounds straight back without twisting is the spot on which you want to strike the ball.

Building these mechanics into good feel on the greens begins by properly developing your sense of pace. Basically, this means you *stroke* a putt rather than *strike* it. While acceleration is vital throughout the forward swing, it must be a constant acceleration, as in the action of the pendulum, rather than a sudden thrust which too often is created by giving the stroke "flash" speed with the hands. Allow the putter to swing back far enough so you can accelerate smoothly through the ball toward the target without forcing the action of the stroke.

The striking action comes from the stroke. Most players miss putts because they cut off the backswing and then force the forward action with overactive hands, which changes the speed and alters the club facing. Most players three-putt because they don't have any sense of the pace—the length, speed and rhythm of the stroke—needed to get the ball to the hole. They either accelerate too fast through the ball and strike it too hard or they decelerate on the forward swing and come up short.

Usually this occurs because they are thinking too much about mechanics. Your mechanics should be ingrained on the practice green and you shouldn't have to think about them on the course. Out there your concerns are, first, the direction of the putt and, most important, your motion—how much motion and acceleration you need to get the ball to go the correct distance. The stroke then becomes a reaction to these factors. If you try to *make* the stroke happen, you won't putt very well, because it's tough to think of mechanics and feel at the same time. You may make a perfect stroke that sends the ball right on line, but you'll have lost the feel for the amount of acceleration you need to get the ball to the target.

Develop your sense of pace by starting with a light grip pressure and, as we indicated in the section on mechanics, a little more pressure in the last three fingers of the left hand. Your overall grip pressure should be as light as possible while still allowing you to control the force of the stroke you want to make.

South Africa's Bobby Locke, a member of the World Golf Hall of Fame who won four British Opens and briefly dominated the U.S. tour in the late 1940's, was perhaps the greatest putter we've ever seen, and it's doubtful that anybody has ever held the putter with a lighter grip than he did. Locke never attacked the ball aggressively. He applied just enough pressure to control the force of his stroke. We didn't like his mechanics—he seemed to hook every putt, as he did all his full shots—but he probably got away with this because his sense of feel and pace for all putts was fantastic. He probably made more long putts and left himself more tap-ins than any player ever.

As your stroke becomes longer, you will instinctively apply more pressure to control it. The slower the green, of course, the more pressure you must apply. But no matter how light or how tight your grip pressure, it should remain constant throughout the stroke. Most putts are ruined because the grip pressure changes, often quite violently, during the stroke. This forces the blade out of the square position and off line. Lightness and lack of tension in your hands help you better feel the weight in the head of the putter and get a kinesthetic sense for the stroke you want to make. You also will find it helpful in judging the pace you need for your stroke to feel the firmness and texture of the putting surface in your feet when walking on the green.

Build your feel for motion and pace by starting with short practice putts, no more than 18 inches. Little success patterns build bigger ones. Start with a flat putt on a relatively fast green if possible.

Get the feeling of accelerating the club through the ball just enough to make the ball die around the hole. When you play, you may want to strike the ball more firmly to overcome the flaws in the green, but first learn the feeling of acceleration for the correct distance. As we said, the striking action come from the stroke. As the putt becomes longer, the stroke becomes longer and the putterhead accelerates through the ball farther and farther.

Once you have learned to pace the stroke for the short putt, allowing it to happen without over-controlling it, move gradually backward until you have taught your muscles to feel the pace and force necessary for putts of any length.

After you have developed your sense of pace, you can put it to work on the course by allowing yourself to react *instinctively* to the target. As you prepare to putt, look at the hole, pick out the line on which you want the ball to travel, then visualize the ball rolling along that line and into the cup. An excellent way to relate distance and ball speed to swing pace is to track along the line of the putt with your eyes *at the same speed you visualize the ball rolling.* "Look the ball into the hole," at the speed you want the ball to actually roll there.

This lets the eyes subconsciously feed back the speed and distance you'll need, and your mind will direct your muscles to make a stroke of the proper length and speed, as long as you *let it happen.* But without that target reference, your mind has nowhere to direct the muscles. When you forget the target, you miss the short putts and turn the long ones into three-putts.

The rewards are great for developing a well-paced stroke and relating it to the target. On long putts you will leave the ball close to the hole more often and have only tap-ins instead of those nerve-wracking three- and four-footers. You'll begin to feel that you'll never have to three-putt a green again.

You'll find yourself making more putts, both long and short. You will have less tendency to jerk the putterhead off line and alter its facing. You'll be able to judge breaking putts of any length better when you know your ball will be rolling at a consistent speed every time.

No matter how well you stroke the ball, of course, you are going to miss some putts. Even the professionals miss a lot of six-foot putts and more than half of their 10-footers. The putting green is not a perfect surface and you are not a machine. You can learn only through experience to judge the roll or break in a green, and you'll never be able to read every putt perfectly.

This is where *patience* becomes

233

so vital. If you are stroking your putts well and have the ball around the hole most of the time, don't get discouraged because a couple of six-footers lip out. Don't start trying to force things on the green. We're sure some players feel they can make every putt they hit. Ben Crenshaw, one of the game's finest putters, probably has that attitude often. That's fine, but it's not always realistic. It's more important to get those long putts close. Don't feel you *have* to make every putt of 10 feet or less. Be calm and have the trust and patience to keep making the best stroke you can without over-controlling the club. If you miss, go to the next hole, try to hit a good shot and get within range again, then make a good stroke.

In other words, *strive* for perfection but never *expect* it. The gods of golf will even things out in the long run if you just give them a chance.

And never second-guess yourself when putting. Don't get over a putt and decide that maybe you don't have the correct line after all. All your mental effort in assessing a putt should be made while you are away from the ball, behind it or to the side of it figuring out the proper line and speed. Trust your decision. Once you get to the ball, aim the putter on the line you've picked out, then concentrate on the target and the pace of your stroke. Even if you haven't read the putt properly, you're more apt to sink the putt or

get it close than if you change your mind in mid-stream and swing indecisively.

You now know how to make the scoring shots—the chips, pitches, sand shots and putts—that can get you around the golf course with the lowest possible numbers. But knowing how is not the same as being able to execute. As we said before, only *you* can teach yourself to do that. It takes practice and experience and application on the course to ingrain the mechanics and to learn the feel and the subtleties of how the ball is going to react.

# DRILLS

## Target drill

Set targets out 25, 40 and 55 yards and alternately hit one shot at a time to each. This will help you relate distance to arm motion, rather than tension and effort. It will let you develop judgment, not just technique.

## Hit balls with eyes closed

This drill is designed to show that you don't have to watch the ball fixedly and become ball-bound. It also helps you develop good pace in your arm swing. Just try to make a smooth motion back and forth to the target, and you'll strike a pretty good shot. If, with your eyes closed, you consciously try to hit the ball, you'll miss it.

## Strike short shots at pie plates

Staple or tape paper pie plates onto dowels at varying heights and practice chipping and pitching to these targets. This helps you relate arm swing on the short shots to both trajectory and distance.

## Chip with an extra-long club

To keep your left hand and wrist firm on the short shots around the green, practice with a special club. Cut the grip cap off an old chipping or pitching club, find an old golf shaft and stick it in the shaft of the club. Now grip the club normally and practice your short shots. The extension of the shaft will force you to keep your left wrist firm and your hands ahead of the ball going through the shot. Your ribs will tell you if you don't.

## Anti-shank board drill

This is a by-product of the board drill for the full swing. Place your two-by-four parallel to the target line and set the ball so there is no more than half an inch from the toe of the club to the board. Start hitting little chip shots, then gradually longer pitches. The board prevents the club from going outside the line and thus keeps you from shanking or hitting the ball with the hosel.

## Chip over bag

Put your golf bag 18 inches in front of the ball. Tap down on the ball with no follow through and pop the ball over the bag. This creates a descending blow. If you try to scoop the ball, either your clubhead or the ball or both will hit the bag. The pitfall is that you may tend to throw the club with the right hand and jam it into the ground.

## Slap drill

Open the face of your sand wedge 90 degrees so the leading edge is parallel to your target line. Then make a few swings with a very steep, descending blow. Feel the club slap the sand and bounce out. This develops the sensation of flange or bottom hitting first, instead of the leading edge. Then gradually close the clubface with each succeeding swing until you no longer feel the bounce and are getting drag from the leading edge. This further develops the different shots you must play in the sand.

## Perpendicular club in sand

Place a club or shaft in the sand about three inches outside the ball and perpendicular to the target line. At address, set your left hand and arm in front or on the target side of this perpendicular shaft. Make some swings, trying to return the left hand and arm in front of the shaft before you feel the club hit the sand. As long as you keep the left arm and hand in front at impact, you can effectively use the club's bounce.

## Practice off a board in sand

To better understand the principle that a shot from hard sand or hardpan requires a softer swing, practice striking shots off the broad side of a two-by-four board. Spread a thin layer of sand on the board for effect if you like. If you use the flange or bounce of your club properly, allowing it to slap down behind the ball, it will skid over the hard surface and send the ball flying much farther than you might expect. It's the same effect you'll get from hard sand or dirt. Practice off the board to get an idea of the speed of swing you need for various distances.

## Look at hole

Set up to the ball, then rotate your head and eyes to the hole and keep them there as you stroke the putt. This makes you aware of the target instead of becoming ball-bound. You'll be more apt to stroke through the ball instead of hitting at it. As with the eyes-closed drill, you can putt several balls in succession without taking your eyes off the target. Again, vary the distance.

## Ball curve

Pick a spot on the practice green that gives you a breaking putt of about 20 feet. Visualize the line of that putt, then place 10 or 12 balls along that line, setting the first one an inch from the cup and each successive ball about 18 inches back. Putt the first ball in the cup, then putt each successive ball over the spot where the previous ball lay, giving it the speed that will let it die at the hole. When you get to the last ball, examine where the other balls have ended up, decide whether your line is good or bad, then try to make the final putt. This drill teaches you how to read breaks and helps you judge the right combination of distance and direction you need for breaking putts. It helps you avoid the common error with a putt that has a great deal of curve, that of letting your eyes track directly from the ball to the hole. It makes you realize you must adjust your thinking and your aim and alignment to the direction in which the ball must start. The greater the curve, the more important it is that you do this.

## Three for speed

This is a drill favored by Paul Runyan that provides both mental and physical practice. Take three balls and place them about three feet from the hole for a putt that has some break to it. With the first one, try to stroke it with a speed that lets it drop just over the front lip of the cup. With the second ball, try to stroke it at a speed that lets it hit the liner at the back of the cup. Try to make the third ball hit the back lip, bounce up and drop in the hole. This drill teaches your mind and body to sense the length and speed of your stroke and how that affects the speed of the rolling ball, which in turn influences the amount of curvature you will play.

## Use a board for path

Place a two-by-four parallel to your target line and put the ball next to it so there is no more than half an inch from the toe of your putter to the board. Stroke putts of varying distances. This teaches you the correct inside-to-inside clubhead path, just as it does in the full-swing drill, on page 142.

## Right arm only

As in the full-swing drill, putting with the right hand and arm only helps develop the sensation of what they should be doing in the putting stroke. The pitfall to avoid is getting too wristy during the stroke.

## Putt cross-handed

Instead of using your normal grip, place the left hand below the right. This drill bridges the gap from left-arm-only to having both hands on the club. It helps stabilize the left hand and wrist and promotes the feeling of a one-lever stroke.

## Ladder drill

Place eight or 10 tees in the green one pace apart. Then try to lag balls successively between the tees. Relate the distance the ball goes to the arm motion needed to get it there. When you go to the golf course, you then can pace off your putts and have a frame of reference for the amount of arm motion you must produce.

## Putter-length back drill

Putt around the putting clock on your practice green. Wherever the ball stops, move it back one putter-length on a line from the hole to the ball. This drill is a lot of fun when it's done with two players competing against each other. It keeps you from making mechanical strokes on the practice green and teaches you the essence of putting—getting the ball in the hole in the fewest strokes possible.

## Circle drill

Line up several balls in a circle around the cup, 18 inches away. Putt around the circle, keeping the putter head on the target line as you stroke back and through. Make your putterhead end up over the hole each time. This makes you aware of the left forearm going to the hole in an actual stroke. This drill also can be done with a tennis wristband anchoring the shaft to the arm. To further develop your awareness, do the drill using the left arm only.

## Shaft against arm

Place your left hand several inches down on the grip and anchor the butt end of the putter to the inside of your left arm with a tennis wrist band. Then stroke putts without letting the butt end pull away from your arm. This develops the one-lever putting motion you want.

## Strike-and-hold putt

Strike a 15-foot putt and hold your follow through position. Follow the putt only by rotating your head and eyes. Don't stand up and turn your head. Hold your shoulders parallel to your line and just follow the ball with your eyes until it comes to rest. This teaches you to keep your body still, avoiding body movement that can be disastrous during the putt. It helps keep your body parallel to the line of the putt. You also get a positive optical feedback by following the ball all the way to the finish with your eyes in proper position.

## Putt with eyes closed

Line up your putt, then close your eyes and make your stroke. This forces you to visualize the path you want the ball to take. It also smooths out your stroke. If you try to hit the ball instead of stroking it, you'll probably hit it off line. Line up several balls a couple of inches apart and stroke them in succession without opening your eyes. You'll be amazed at how close you can come to the hole. Vary the distance from short to medium-lengths to long putts.

## Pull ball into hole

Place your putterhead behind a ball 18 inches from the cup. Using only your left hand and making no backswing, pull the ball into the cup. Your putterhead should end up right over the cup. This makes you move the club down the target line with your left forearm. This drill can be done with the wrist band anchoring the shaft against the inside of the arm.

## Mirror drill

Take a mirror 1 ½ x 12 inches and place it behind the ball on your target line. Place your putterhead behind the ball and take your normal setup. If you can see your eyes in the mirror and they are parallel to the line, you are in the correct position. If not, adjust your posture and/or foot position until you get your eyes properly over the line, behind the ball and parallel to the line.

243

# 10

# THE TROUBLE SHOTS

Golf would be a much simpler game if every shot were played from a level lie, off short grass, with no obstacles in the way. Unfortunately, that doesn't always happen. Depending on the nature of the course you play, you may make very few shots during a round that meet all three ideals.

To play golf effectively you must be able to strike shots from uneven lies, to curve shots around trees or bushes and to get your ball out of the rough and sand. Skill in executing these shots depends on practice and experience that develops the necessary feel for the shot. Only you can accomplish this.

To help you, we'll give you con-

cepts that will let you take your knowledge of the golf swing and ball-flight laws and adapt them to each situation you face on the course.

## Uneven lies

When you face a shot from an uphill, downhill or sidehill lie, the first thing to be aware of is the ball-flight tendency from that particular lie. Basically, if the ball is below your feet, your shot will curve to the right; if it is above your feet, it will curve to the left; from an uphill lie, you will tend to pull-hook the ball to the left; from a downhill lie, you will pull-fade it to the right.

An easy way to predict the flight

pattern from a sidehill lie is to remember that the ball will tend to curve in the direction of the slope. If you were to roll a ball along the ground, it would run downhill. Your shot will "run" the same in the air.

A rule we like to use, not only for uneven lies but for intentional curves or any trouble shot, is that you should alter your swing only as a last resort. So your first option in any such situation is aligning yourself to allow for the ball flight you're going to get.

Your second option, if you don't have room to start the ball left or right and must hit a straight shot, is to influence the ball flight by your posture and alignment—of both body and blade—then make your normal golf swing.

An important point to remember—when your stance is precarious because of an uneven lie, you must swing the club at a speed that keeps you in balance. This usually means your pace must be slower and even smoother than normal.

Let's examine some specifics.

*Sidehill lies.* You'll always minimize the effect of the hill if you can sole your club properly on the turf. So choke up or down on the club and play the ball closer to or farther from your feet to accommodate the soling of the club.

Sidehill lies will tend to distort your posture and made you alter your swing, so you must be aware of these effects. For example, if the ball is below your feet, you'll instinctively want to get your weight back on your heels, into the hill, for balance. That will put your legs and spine angle into positions that make your swing become shoulder-oriented and sometimes produce a wild pull-hook just when you're expecting a fade. If the ball is above your feet, your tendency will be to lean your upper body forward too much to stay in balance. This creates a too-upright swing that doesn't fit the slope, causing you to hit behind the ball and spoil the shot.

You can overcome these tendencies and assume the correct posture without having to think about it simply by satisfying three criteria: Make sure your arms are hanging freely as in a normal shot, get your weight toward the balls of your feet for good balance and sole the club properly within the guidelines we just indicated. This will keep your leg position unaltered, which we prefer, and will get your spine tilted at the proper angle. *(See photos, page 247.)*

If the ball is below your feet, for instance, take a longer club than you feel is necessary for the shot, choke down on it and bend more from the hips so your arms will hang. The ball will be played closer to your feet. You'll feel your eye line is almost over the ball. This will automatically give you the more upright swing you need to accommodate the slope.

With the ball above your feet, follow the same rules. Sole the club properly, grip it so your arms are suspended and make sure your weight is toward the balls of your feet. This will make your spine angle a little more upright, but you haven't had to think about it. Your swing plane thus will be flatter and better able to fit the slope.

In aiming the clubface and aligning your body, remember your options. If you can, allow for the curvature of the shot. If the ball is above your feet, you will tend to pull the shot slightly and hook it. So simply aim far enough right to accommodate this curve. With the ball below your feet, you will tend to push the shot and fade it, so aim to the left accordingly.

If there is no room to allow for the curve and the ball is above your feet, align your body slightly to the right and open your clubface a little. Then make your normal swing. The blade adjustment will counteract curvature, your alignment will counteract the pull and you can strike a reasonably straight shot. If the ball is below your feet, aim slightly left and close the blade a bit to counteract the pushing and fading effects.

On all sidehill lies, take more club than normal and make an easier swing for better control. As the lies get more severe, try to pick the ball cleanly, especially if you have to hit it straight. Taking a divot tends to

twist the clubface because you'll probably not be able to get the clubface soled exactly flush with the ground and will have the heel or toe catching first.

When the lie is severe, a fairway wood can be a great savior. It has a curved sole that will minimize the effect of the heel or toe catching first, it has a longer shaft to work with in gripping up or down and you can swing easier for better control.

*Uphill lies.* For this shot, assume your normal setup and let your weight fall naturally back on the right side. Set your shoulders in line with the slope. Remember that the ball will fly higher and, because you will tend to hang back on your right side during the swing, you will likely pull the ball to the left. The first rule is to allow for that high pull if you can, overcoming its effects with alignment and club selection. Align yourself to the right of your target, which will compensate for the pull. The higher ball flight can be taken care of by selecting a longer club, choking down and swinging easier.

You can eliminate the pull by moving your legs and your lead arm more aggressively up the slope on the forward swing. This will keep the club on line longer and enable you to hit a straight shot. But you will have changed your normal swing to do this, so we don't advise it.

Unless the lie is exceptionally severe, don't alter the ball position

## *Sole club properly on sidehill lies*

To play the ball off sidehill lies effectively, you must make sure (1) your club is soled properly, (2) your arms are hanging freely and (3) your weight is toward the balls of your feet for good balance. With the ball above your feet (left), Bob Toski demonstrates that the ball will be played farther from your body, your arms will be slightly extended and your posture more erect. With the ball below your feet (right), the ball and your hands will be closer to your feet and you will have more upper body tilt.

247

in your stance, because that forces a change in your swing. As the slope gets steeper, you *will* have to move the ball forward, more off your left foot. Figure out how much by taking a practice swing and noting where your divot occurs. Then position yourself so the ball is slightly behind that spot. *(See photos, page 247.)*

That same rule, incidentally, holds true on downhill lies when you must move the ball toward your right foot.

*Downhill lies.* This shot is difficult for most golfers because there is a cutoff point, determined by distance, at which you must change your set-up and the type of swing you make.

With the short irons, set yourself with the slope of the hill—your weight will be left, your shoulders will be positioned with the slope and the ball will be back according to the rule we just gave you. From that point, you should feel nothing but your arms swinging the club.

The cutoff point for this shot will be the distance you feel you can negotiate without swinging your arms too hard and fast or creating excessive body action. This can create a reverse pivot. This distance may be 150 yards or less, depending on how strong you are.

Shots longer than that cause two problems: 1) You are using a club with less loft and the slope will de-loft the club even more, so you have trouble getting the ball airborne; 2) The force of the swing required will make most golfers reverse their weight shift and hit the shot fat.

To overcome the first problem, take a more lofted fairway wood, a 5-, 6- or 7-wood rather than a long iron. Hitting any iron less lofted than a 5-iron off a downhill lie is very difficult for all but the best players.

The second problem can be handled by setting your weight on your *right* side. The ball is still played back. Then just swing your arms back and up and let your legs move down the slope of the hill on the forward swing.

Remember that the ball will tend to go to the right. Rather than trying to compensate for this, we suggest you aim more to the left and open the clubface. Magnify the ball's curve to the right. This open clubface will help get the shot airborne.

In all cases, you must get the club moving as parallel as possible to the slope to get the ball in the air. The more descending the blow you make, the lower your ball flight will be. That must be avoided on a downhill lie.

From any distance, take a more lofted club than you normally would need. A 7-iron will react like a 5-iron, for example, so you'll get the distance you need.

## Intentional curves

When you need to hook or slice the ball around an obstacle, there is a simple formula devised by Peter Kostis of the Golf Digest schools

## Set weight, body with slope
## for uphill, downhill lies

As in the sand, your body should be aligned with the slope for uphill and downhill lies. For the uphill lie (left), set your weight back and align your shoulders with the slope, as Bob Toski is doing here. The ball is usually played in its normal position. For the shorter shots from downhill lies, set your weight left and the ball back, your shoulders approximating the slope of the hill as closely as possible.

## How to curve the ball intentionally

To curve the ball intentionally the correct amount to the target, simply set your clubface where you want the ball to finish, then align your body and swing along the path on which you want the ball to start. Allow plenty of clearance around the obstacle in your way. To slice the ball intentionally (above), set your clubface open, aimed at the target, and make your swing path go well to the left of the obstacle. For an intentional hook (right), your clubface will be aiming at the target but closed to your stance line, and your swing path will be well to the right of the obstacle.

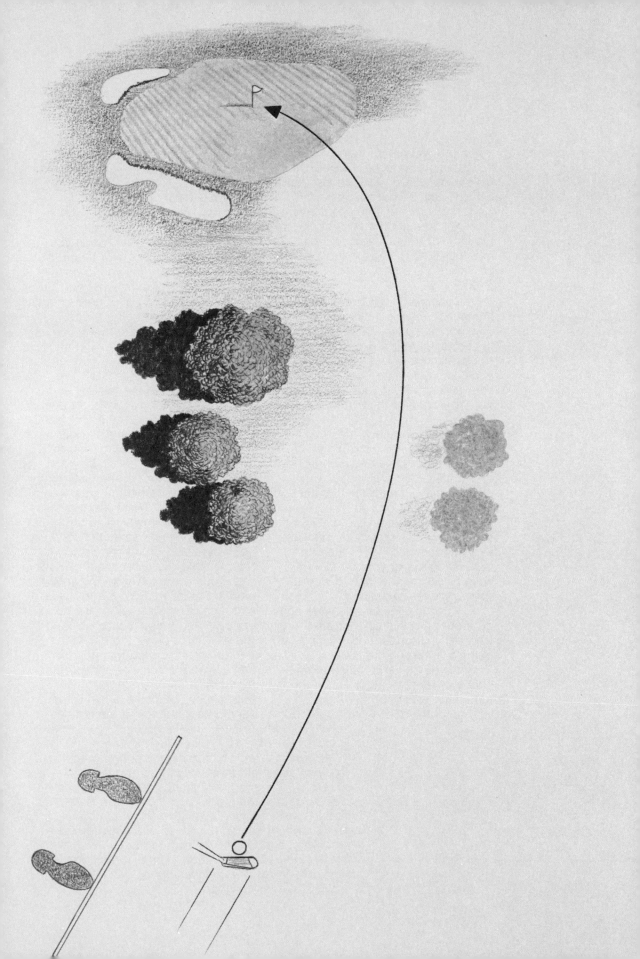

staff for getting the exact amount of curvature you need—set up your body and swing along the path on which you want the ball to start and aim the clubface at the spot you want the ball to end up. Your swing path will produce the correct starting flight of the ball and your clubface position will induce the proper curvature. (See illustrations, pages 250-251.)

To become competent in these shots requires the ability to aim the clubface and align your body properly and to let your arms be the controlling factor in your swing. If your shoulders dominate, they'll change your swing path. If your hands dominate, they'll alter the clubface position.

Before you practice these shots, reflect on whether your bad shots are pushes or pulls or whether they are of the curving variety. If you push or pull, you are too shoulder-oriented. If your bad shots hook or slice, your hands are too active. Instinctively, your shoulders will want to swing the club where the clubface is looking or your hands will want to square the face to where your arms are swinging.

To minimize these problems, concentrate on swinging your arms and keeping your upper body behind the ball while making the shot.

Until you become skilled at these shots, it's best to allow plenty of clearance with your starting path. Your shot might miss its target, but that's better than pulling or pushing the ball into the tree and having to start all over again.

## Playing from rough

The best way to deal with rough is to stay out of it. Assuming that doesn't always happen, when you do get in the rough the first goal is getting out. That may sound obvious, but that's exactly what we mean—worry first about getting out, next about getting to the green.

Everything depends on your lie in the rough. If the grass is high and your lie is poor, choose a club and play the type of shot that will get you out and down the fairway as far as possible. If the rough is not deep and you have a decent lie and feel you have enough strength to get the ball on or near the green, then try it.

Your techniques for rough play will vary with your lie, the distance you need and the type of shot you want to execute. There are two general precepts to follow: The shot from rough should be played with an open clubface, and it should be made with a more descending blow than your normal swing. The open clubface adds needed loft to the club and compensates for the tendency of the grass to wrap around the hosel and close the clubface. The descending blow will pop the ball up more quickly to escape the high grass. (See illustration, right.)

In almost all cases, your weight should be set more to the left than

*How to play from greenside rough*
*If the grass is firm and tough or is growing against you, play the ball off your right toe and with a square clubface, strike a steeply descending blow directly behind the ball to pop it out (top). If the grass is not as tough or is lying in the direction of your swing, open your clubface and play it like a sand shot (bottom). Strike behind the ball with the flange rather than the leading edge, letting the club ride through the grass under the ball and exploding it out on a cushion of grass.*

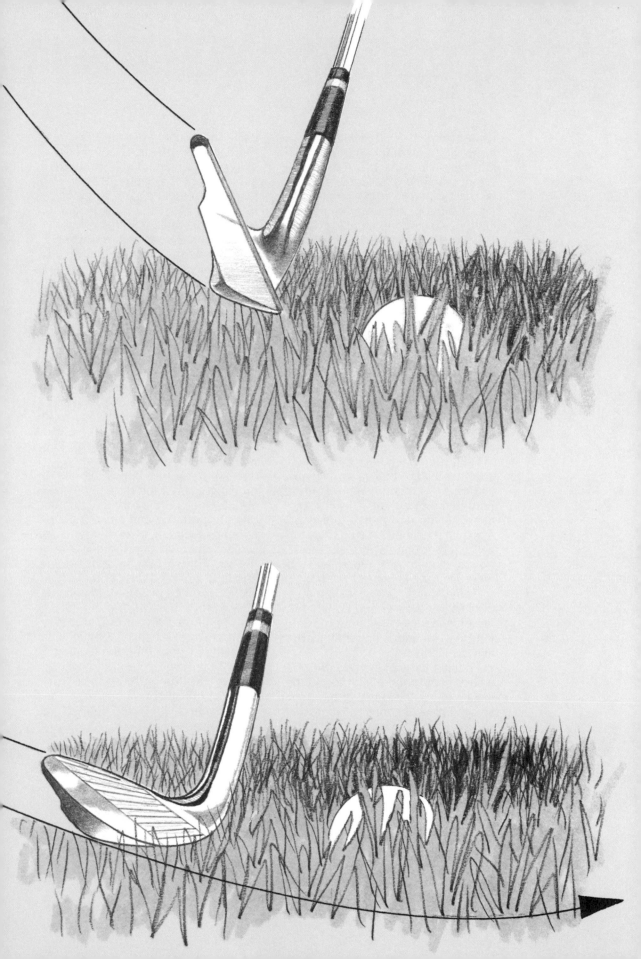

for a normal shot. This will allow you to swing the club up and back on a more vertical path, which creates the descending blow coming forward. The more vertically you take the club back, the less chance you have of slowing the clubface in the grass going and coming forward and the less grass you will get between the clubface and the ball. If you take the club back too low and flat, which is the common fault in rough shots, you'll come back to the ball the same way, get the club entangled in the grass and deaden the blow.

You also must insure that the clubface does not turn over and shut when you swing through the shot. Do that by applying more grip pressure in your left hand and accelerating your left arm through the impact area.

With your weight set left, you can't attack the ball as strongly as you could with your weight starting right and moving left. This is fine, because you really want to swing more smoothly and easily to get the ball out of rough. With a violent swing, you'll tend to close the clubface and may fail to get the ball out.

Remember that by creating a descending blow with an open clubface the ball will come out more to the right, so adjust accordingly by aiming slighty left.

Position the ball in your stance for a shot from rough according to the distance, the thickness of the grass and the type of shot you want to play. The deeper your lie, the more the ball must be struck a descending blow, which means the farther back toward the center of your stance you must play it. Another rule of thumb is that for a long rough shot, when you are using a fairway wood or a long iron, you should play the ball forward, about off the left heel. If your shot requires less than a full swing, you may want to move the ball back toward center. With the pitching clubs around the green, especially, you have the luxury of playing the ball forward or back, depending on your lie and the type of shot you choose.

From thick rough around the green you can play a shot one of two ways, depending on which way the grass is lying, the type of grass and how much green you have to work with. If your ball is nestled down in thick, wiry grass that is growing against the direction of your stroke, you can play the ball almost off your right toe and strike a very steep descending blow with your left forearm that will pop the ball into the air. If the grass is not as tough and is lying in the direction of your swing, you can play it almost like a bunker shot. Position the ball forward, make sure your clubface is open and strike behind the ball with the flange rather than the leading edge of the club. The flange will tend to part the grass and you "explode" the ball out.

In general, we would suggest you

play the bunker-type shot out of bent or bluegrass and the "pop" shot out of Bermuda grass, more predominant in the South and Southwest.

On the longer shots, whenever possible you should use a fairway wood rather than a long iron. The wood, with its curved sole and smoother hosel area, will ride through the grass better, parting the blades instead of cutting through them. Thus, you have less risk of grass getting wrapped around the hosel and closing the face. To cut through the grass with a long iron requires exceptional strength.

All of these shots require a degree of finesse that can be learned only through experience. To make your rough play productive, you must practice. Hit long shots and short shots out of the rough until you learn how you can do it best.

A final warning on playing from the rough: because you normally will get grass between the clubface and the ball on these shots, you will not be able to put as much spin on the ball as usual. This means that it is almost impossible to curve a shot out of the rough, so you are better off not trying it. The relative lack of spin also may cause the ball to fly and roll farther, depending on the thickness of the rough. This is especially true from a decent lie in light rough when you can expect to make good contact with the ball but still get that grass against the clubface. Be aware of these probabilities and allow for them. In a "flyer" situation, take more club and swing easier to compensate for the extra distance you probably will get.

## Playing from fairway bunkers

The first rule for playing from a fairway bunker is the same as for a shot from rough—be sure you get the ball out. The type of shot you play and the club you choose depend on your lie in the sand and the height of the bunker lip. Always select a club with enough loft to clear the lip, no matter how far it is to the green. If your ball is buried or sitting poorly in the sand, take the club with which you can explode the ball safely into the fairway, even if it's only a sand wedge that will leave you far short of the green. Playing your next shot from the fairway is far better than leaving the ball in the bunker.

Assuming that the height of the bunker lip allows it, you can get the ball on or close to the green from a fairway trap if you know the proper technique, which is determined by your lie in the sand. Davis Love, another school staffer, has devised an excellent method for playing fairway bunker shots from good, medium and poor lies.

For any shot from a fairway trap, work your feet into the sand, angling slightly downward toward your toes, until you have a firm stance. Dig the insides of your feet in deeper than the outsides, angling your feet inward. This holds you steady so you won't slip.

When your lie is good, the ball sitting up nicely on top of the sand, try to contact the ball first with your normal swing. Simply choke down on the club by the same amount you have buried your feet in the sand, set up with your weight to the right, position the ball normally off the inside of the left heel and just try to make a good swing. If you do, you can almost get your normal distance with whatever club you have in your hand. *(See illustration, right.)*

If the ball is just slightly buried in the sand, you'll still want to contact the ball first, but this time with a more descending blow to keep from striking the sand first. Choke down by the amount your feet are buried and set your weight left to induce a steeper swing arc. Position the ball farther back toward the center of your stance. The weight-left/ball-back position will induce the steeper swing arc without your having to think about it, so just go ahead and make a good arm swing. The distance you achieve may be 15 or 20 yards less than normal with this shot, so adjust your club selection to compensate for that if the lip height will allow it.

If your ball is buried in the bunker so deeply that you could not expect to get airborne by striking the ball first, but is not so deep that you have to wedge it out, you can use a technique similar to that for greenside bunker shots. Use the flange or bottom of your club the same as you would the flange of your sand wedge. Strike a slightly descending blow into the sand two or three inches behind the ball, letting the club ride through the sand.

This shot is most effective with a lofted fairway wood club, if you are not too close to the green, because the soleplate of the wood will slide more easily through the sand without digging in.

Your weight should also be set left for this shot with the ball played forward off the left heel. But this time don't choke down as much to compensate for your buried feet, because now you're after club-sand contact instead of club-ball contact. Lay your club back or slightly open.

You can't get anywhere near your maximum distance with this shot, but you can get the ball closer to the green than you might expect. Remember that the ball will tend to slice, because the sand inhibits the closing of the face, so allow for it.

We'll warn you that the ball can easily be left in the sand if you don't make a well-executed swing on this shot. Normally, it should be attempted only by an advanced player. Practice it until you feel competent enough to try it on the course.

Your guideline in deciding to make this shot is that you must have a very good chance of saving a stroke. Otherwise, play it safe.

**How to play from fairway bunkers**
*If your ball is sitting up nicely (top), make a normal swing, contacting the ball first. If your ball is sitting slightly down in the sand (middle), you'll still want to contact the ball first, but with a slightly descending swing. If your ball is buried so deeply that you could not expect to get it out by striking the ball first (bottom), lay your clubface back and strike a slightly descending blow two or three inches behind the ball, letting the sole of the club ride through the sand and eject the ball.*

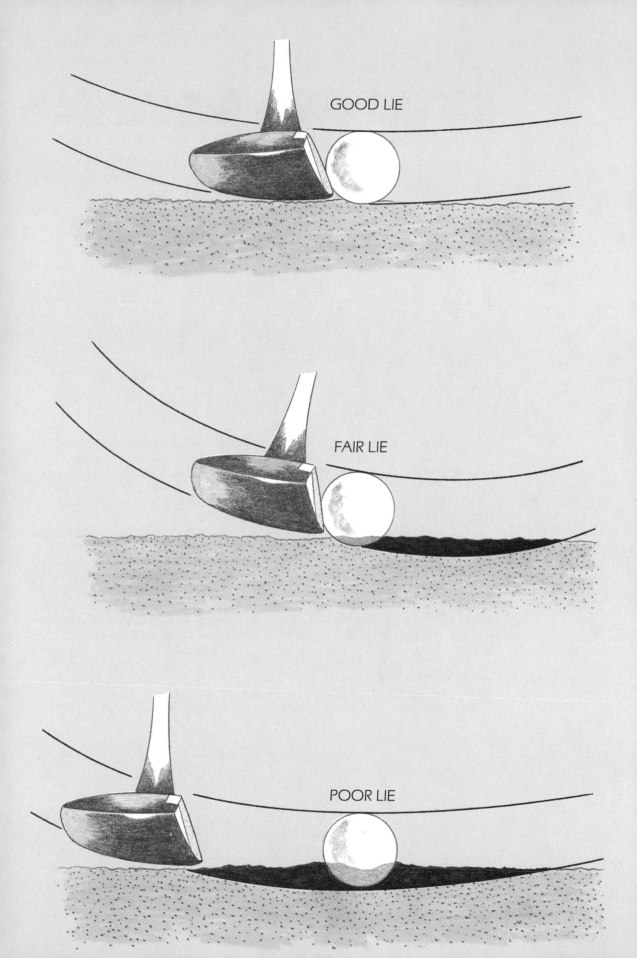

# 11
# LET'S PLAY GOLF

All that has gone before in this book has directed you toward one goal—*playing golf.* If that sounds obvious, consider this quote from Davis Love: "Too many people spend all their time on the golf course practicing instead of playing."

If you are serious about playing better golf, you hopefully will do a lot of practicing to incorporate the swing concepts we've given you. But your goal lies beyond merely the ability to make a pretty swing and hit 5-irons straight on the practice tee.

Quite often we hear one golfer say to another, "What a beautiful swing you have. I wish I could hit the ball like that." But the recipient of that praise may not be the best *player* at the course. We know players with bad-looking swings who score well, but we seldom hear anybody say, "Gee, I wish I could score like you."

Yet the one immutable fact of golf is that the lowest score wins. It's not who makes the most beautiful swing, but who puts the lowest number on the card and collects the trophies or the money at the end of the round. Everything we do in golf should be predicated on that.

Of course, a nice-looking, effective swing is the surest way to better golf. But to become a complete player requires a combination of striking, playing and scoring. And your scoring likely won't reflect your ball-striking ability until you orient yourself toward scoring.

In order to score you've got to get out on the course. That's why a week of beating balls on the practice tee every evening might not pay off for you on Saturday morning. Practice your ball-striking, to be sure, but take a couple of those evenings to play a few holes, too. That will help you switch your mind from the problems of building a golf swing on the practice tee and orient it instead to competing and scoring on the course.

The great player isn't as good from tee to green as the average high handicapper thinks. He simply takes advantage of his good shots and recovers from his poor ones. He maximizes his birdies by following one good shot with another. He minimizes his bogeys by shrugging off a bad shot and getting the ball up and down to save par.

While he's on the course, the good golfer isn't thinking much about his swing. He's thinking about getting the ball in the hole. A golfer can be compared to a mechanic and a race-car driver. The mechanic lifts the hood of the car and works with the parts. He works inside with the guts of the engine. But when all the parts are in working order and the car is ready to go, the driver then gets in the car and is thinking only of accelerating, turning the wheel, directing the car, getting in-volved in the pace and flow of the race. He's looking outward and forward.

You, the golfer, must be both mechanic and driver, but not at the same time. When you are working on your swing to improve your ball-striking ability, you are thinking about the parts of the swing, the creation of that swing and putting the club to the ball, which are in-ward thoughts. When you are playing golf to make a score, you should be thinking about the whole swing, reacting to the target and sending the ball to that target, or outward thoughts. When you're driving the car, you can't be fixing the parts.

If a driver's car is mechanically not the fastest in the race, he might not win. But if he drives skillfully, he *can* finish as high as the speed of his car will allow, and he probably will finish ahead of a lot of faster cars whose drivers aren't as skillful. It's the same with you and your golf swing. Your swing might not be as good now as it will be in the future, but you can get the most out of that swing by intelligent and skillful application on the golf course. You can *play* to the potential of your swing, which is all any of us can hope for. And, like the race driver, in doing so you often can beat better ball-strikers who aren't utilizing their skills as effectively. This is what makes golf fun, because this is something we all can do, no matter what our physical limitations.

Playing golf, as opposed to swinging a golf club, is mental. In its application to golf, *mental* has been a rather nebulous, all-inclusive term. We've tended to take a lot of factors that don't have to do with actually swinging a club, sweep them all under the rug and label them *mental.* But few teachers have sorted out what all this means. We'll try to do just that.

As you progress in your ability to swing the club, most of you need help in playing the game. As Davis Love says, if you want to learn how to swing the club, you see a teacher; if you want to learn how to play the game, you talk to a player; if you want to know how to compete, see a coach. We believe our diverse backgrounds can help you in all these areas.

The mental part of golf isn't only thinking what to do, it's thinking how to do it so you don't lose your target perception and your path. You need a conceptual understanding of situations and how to cope with them, followed by a thought which lets you get the job done without stilting your motion and losing the playability of your swing.

Errors made on the golf course fit into three categories: a *pre-swing mistake,* a *setup mistake* or an *execution mistake.* The first two categories are mental, the third physical.

*Pre-swing mistakes* involve your preparation for the shot. Did you try to play the wrong club? Did you not take into consideration the lie, stance, wind and other factors that will affect your shot? Were you trying to play the ball into a target area that was too small for your ability with the club you chose? Should you have shot for the larger part of the green instead of going for the flag tucked behind a bunker? Should you have gone for the wide part of the fairway instead of trying to nip over the edge of a bunker? Once you make the wrong decision in these areas, your shot is 90 percent of the time destined for failure, because you subconsciously place so much pressure on your swing that you cannot stay within your correct pace and your swing will break down.

*Setup mistake.* When you set up to the ball, did you fail to properly visualize your shot and its flight to the target? Did you align yourself incorrectly? Were you careless with your posture, your weight distribution or your ball position? If you err in any part of your setup routine, again you are likely to cause your swing to malfunction.

*Execution mistake.* Finally, did you do everything else correctly and your physical swing simply broke down? The initial reaction from most players is that 90 percent of their errors are caused simply by poor execution. "I just made a bad swing," you tell yourself.

Yet, we see in most of our students, and in ourselves as well, just the reverse—90 percent of the mistakes made playing golf are in those first two mental categories, thus causing faulty swings. Ony 10 percent of your mistakes come after you have done everything else correctly and then, because you are human and not a robot, make a bad mechanical swing.

That's strong evidence to back up what we said earlier—most golfers prepare themselves for disaster, while the good players prepare themselves for success.

To play golf well, you must develop the three A's and the three C's we mentioned before—ability, ambition and attitude; confidence, composure and competitiveness.

You develop *ability* by working with your swing and improving your physical skills. *Ambition* is an individual thing. Only you know what you want to get out of playing golf and how hard you are willing to work to achieve your goals. Whatever those goals are, the most important factor in achieving them is your *attitude.* You must have an attitude that directs your mind to the things that are important in playing golf well and enhances your ability to accomplish them.

The right attitude develops something that is so important in learning to play golf well, and that is awareness. You must be aware of each situation on the course as it arises.

You must have an awareness of yourself and factors that might keep you from playing to your potential. We had a student in our schools who wrote us that she usually played very well in tournaments and at other times when she really *wanted* to play well, but she had a tendency to get careless. Then, after she had wasted a couple of strokes, her swing got tight and her game deteriorated. That's awareness.

Once you become aware of problems like this, you can do something about them. You must also be aware of your swing, of your alignment tendencies, of your ball-flight pattern. You must be able to handle these tendencies and relate them to making the best score possible.

This awareness helps you achieve control in the three vital areas of playing the game, which are:

*Control of your swing,* accomplished by target projection rather than segmented swing thoughts and by making pace and path your thoughts on the course. This gives you the ability to execute at the level of your swing development.

*Control of yourself,* the ability to stay on an even emotional keel so you can make the right decisions and get the most out of your swing under all circumstances.

*Control of your game,* which means having an awareness of the strengths and weaknesses of each hole and the strategy needed to cope with them, then applying this awareness with a realistic assessment of your own strengths and weaknesses.

Control in these areas will be reflected in your development of the three C's. It will build your *confidence* that you can get the job done and will give you *composure* to do it under the most difficult conditions. This will enhance your *competitiveness,* at the same time giving you the capability to compete under pressure.

Developing control of your swing, yourself and your game is what the rest of this chapter is about.

## Control of your swing

We mentioned earlier that when you are building a golf swing you deal with specific areas of that swing. As long as you continue to build and improve your swing, you must work with specific thoughts on the practice tee. But when you *play,* think in generalities, with *whole-swing thoughts.* Think of the shot, including the target and your strategy to that target, not the stroke.

When you practice, your thoughts are backswing-oriented. Your mind is directed toward segments of your swing, toward controlling the club in various positions. You are consciously trying to make something happen. Your attention is almost always on the ball, not on the target.

On the practice tee, there is no penalty for a poor shot. You can hit it again while the swing picture is vivid in your mind. But on the golf course, there usually is a severe penalty for a poor shot. Every swing counts. There are lengthy delays between shots, making it difficult to keep a good swing picture in mind. You are faced with difficult lies and circumstances, with distractions, with the pressures of competition.

That's why it's vital that your play thoughts be oriented to the forward swing, to picturing the ball-flight to the target and to feeling the motion and flow of the whole swing related to that target. Divorce yourself from technique. The club must swing in proper position—with freedom. You cannot be thinking of specific positions, because if you are you will over-control the club and ruin the swing. If you think about positions, you become a mechanic, not a golfer. *(See illustration, right.)*

When you start mis-hitting shots on the course, it isn't that your swing itself suddenly goes awry. Something happens within you that forces your swing to break down. Your tension level changes. Anxiety over the shot you're facing causes you to grip the club tighter, so the tension in your arms and shoulders increases. You try to force the swing.

Sam Snead's thoughts for controlling his swing on the course are to keep his grip pressure and his arm tension constant throughout his whole swing and to keep it the same

### Visualize your target
*On the course, your thoughts must be oriented to the whole swing related to the target rather than to the parts of your swing. As you prepare to make each shot, it is vital that you picture your intended ball-flight to the target and feel the motion and flow of the swing that will send the ball there.*

from first tee to 18th green. To keep his grip pressure light and his arms as tension-free as possible in a tight spot, Snead says he walks slower, breathes deeper and makes a conscious effort to grip the club more lightly.

These are methods that help reduce anxiety and keep it from overcontrolling your golf swing. Maintaining a pace you can control and making a concentrated effort to play within yourself are also helpful.

When you learn to dance, after you get your steps down, you think only of the rhythm and feel the beat of the music. That's the essence of playing golf well. Teach your mind and your body to become one.

In *Zen in the Art of Archery,* Eugene Herrigel says, "The right shot at the right moment does not come because you do not let go of yourself. You do not wait for fulfillment, but brace yourself for failure."

Champions *allow* the swing to happen, trusting the subconscious, while most players try to *make it* happen with conscious action. That's why the good player looks so natural, so smooth. His swing is almost a ballet-like movement, because his mind is not cluttered with mechanical details but rather is wholly related to good pace and the target.

How many times have you pulled off a difficult trouble shot because you were thinking of where you wanted the ball to go rather than how to make your swing? And we've all had times when we've stood over a putt and visualized the ball dropping into the hole. That's when we make putts—not when we worry about the mechanics of the stroke.

Program your mind before the swing. Relate to your goal and the rhythm of making the ball go there. For example, on wedge shots around the green, program your arm swing to relate to the distance you need. The most common mistake we see is too little arm swing. The player ends up overworking his hands, which is a physical reaction, but the hands were the only agents available to get the ball to the hole.

The feeling of an arm swing that will make the ball fly the distance you want will give you the pace you want. And everybody can live with a swing deficiency to some degree if his pace is correct. If your pace gets quick, it aggravates the deficiency in your swing.

To better marry your swing feel to the target during a round, take a practice swing similar to the real shot you're going to make. If you're 50 or 60 feet from the hole on the green, take a practice stroke with your putter related to that distance. Knocking a long putt 10 feet past or short of the hole is not a result of physical error but of faulty mental programming. If you must hit a shot from an unusual lie or a peculiar stance, take a practice swing from that stance. That's just common sense, but too often golfers lose their common sense on the golf course because their minds are too concentrated on the mechanics of the swing. They are too swing-oriented or ball-oriented, which means their minds are directed to hitting at the ball rather than swinging through it to the target.

That's why awareness of path is so important. It enables you to sustain clubhead speed as you swing it toward the target. You must identify the path of the backswing and forward swing, which means you should always take a preparatory swing toward the target.

Properly preparing so your swing will work on the course requires a certain amount of mental toughness. How many times have you addressed a shot or a putt knowing that your blade was not aligned properly, that you were not quite set, not quite prepared to strike the shot, yet you went ahead and made a swing anyway? Usually the results are unsatisfactory, if not disastrous.

You probably told yourself subconsciously that you could get away with it. Moreover, you were retreating to your comfort zone, because you didn't feel quite comfortable putting the blade or setting up your body the way you knew it should be.

You will find this happening often as you work on correcting bad setup and alignment habits. You must be mentally tough enough to set things up the way they should be, then go ahead and let your swing happen as a reaction to the target. As you continue to work and improve in these areas on the practice tee, you will find it easier and easier to get yourself prepared properly for a shot on the course.

Here's a good way to discover whether you are oriented to scoring on the course rather than to your swing. When you finish a round, does your mind immediately turn to how you struck the ball or to what you shot? If you are concerned about your bad swings rather than the shots you wasted because of improper mental preparation, your mind is oriented in the wrong direction.

The next time you play golf, especially on a strange course, sit down for a moment after the round and try to recall each hole, each shot you played and the conditions under which you played it. If you can't do this, then you weren't out there playing golf. You were just making swings.

As an aid to making your swing work in all circumstances, you also need the ability to recall the perfect shots you hit, the super shots you struck under stress. Then, when you get in a similar situation, you can be confident you can make the shot. The average player has a tendency to recall the bad shots he has played, so he stands over the ball with a negative feeling that is guaranteed to ruin his shot.

Be aware that your swing feel and your swing itself may change from day to day as your body chemistry changes. Bobby Nichols once remarked prior to warming up for a round, "I've got to go to the practice tee and find my swing." It wasn't that a player of his caliber had to "find" a swing—he simply was going to identify the feeling of his swing for the day. You should try to make the same identification prior to a round, also becoming aware of your ball-flight tendencies. If you seem to be slicing the ball a bit during your preround warm-up, accept the fact and play with that swing that day. Be aware of that tendency and allow for it on the course. The time to fix it is afterward, back on the practice tee, not during the round.

Our goal for you is to have you hit the ball reasonably straight. But becoming a master player also requires learning to curve the ball to fit those situations where an intentional slice or hook is called for. You know what makes a ball curve, and once your swing reaches a satisfactory level of development you should work on curving the ball during your practice sessions. Either rotate your forearms more or less as you swing through the shot, or simply pre-set the clubface in a closed or open position to make the ball hook or slice, whichever works best for you.

You'll go through a transition period between practice thoughts and when you try to do this on the course. For awhile you might be thinking of mechanics, but eventually you'll be able to "internalize" the swing feeling that produces an intentional curve. Then, as you study the layout of each hole, mentally fit your ball-flight picture into the target area by imagining your ball curving to that target. If you have a trouble shot that calls for you to fade or draw the ball around trees, visualize the shape of that shot. Your swing can instinctively respond to that picture.

As Sam Snead puts it, "I just think hook or think fade." Snead is letting his subconscious direct his swing motion. None of us may ever be able to do it as well as Snead, but by following that thought we'll be able to accomplish the same thing to the limit of our ability.

## Control of yourself

Golf was invented as a game, a means of relaxation, a way to slow down our pace of life and take time out for enjoyment. It is not a violent game, yet it too often is played violently. Most people approach it in the same hectic fashion they lead the rest of their lives—too aggressively, too fast.

These people don't pace their lifestyles and consequently fail to pace their approach to golf. They don't relax and prepare for each shot calmly, even though relaxation is paramount when it comes to playing golf well.

Bob McGredy of the Dyco Corporation, a psychological testing service, has said that the ingredients and characteristics that make a man successful in business can very well be the same characteristics that destroy him on the golf course—try harder, work harder, get the job done fast. He has his lifestyle oriented to over-controlling everything, pushing here and pushing there. Saturday morning he jumps in his car, probably still thinking about a couple of business deals he has going, speeds to the course and carries that same attitude with him as he goes out and tries to play golf. He has no chance unless he learns to throttle back, relax and play the game at the pace at which it is supposed to be played.

Arnold Palmer probably has done more than any single person to popularize golf, but as McGredy points out he may be the worst possible player for most golfers to identify with. When Arnold hitches up his pants and charges, attacking every shot fiercely, it excites us all. But he has the physical ability—and the mental composure—to do that. You may not, so you'd better cool it and play golf at a calmer pace that will let you control your mind and your skills.

Your emotions, you see, control your ability to perform. We see it at the highest levels as well as the lowest. A perfect example is the low-handicap player who has just won his club championship. Now, a week later, he's going to play in a pro-am event with Jack Nicklaus. Obviously, he's at the peak of his game and is confident of his ability. On pro-am day he meets Nicklaus, walks to the first tee, sees 5,000 people standing there and suddenly panics. He completely loses his composure. All he wants to do is get off the first tee without hurting somebody, so he swings at the ball with no plan or target in mind and muffs it. From there on he's in a negative frame of mind and may play his worst round in 10 years unless he can relax, compose himself and begin to do what he has to to play well.

The point is, this man's physical ability didn't suddenly desert him. His emotions simply overpowered his mind so it could not direct his physical skills effectively. As Bob Toski recalls: "In 1952 I shot 69 in the first round of a West Coast tournament. I was just a youngster on the tour and the newspapers the next morning referred to me as one of the "morning glories" who would soon fade from contention. The next day I birdied the first hole and was four under going to the fourth, where we had a wait on the tee. Just as I was ready to tee it up, Ben Hogan came off the third green and walked through the ropes onto the tee. Of course I'm very aware of his presence, and I'm concerned. I hit an inch behind the ball, and I was practically by it by the time it landed. As I walked quickly away I heard Hogan ask, 'Who in the hell was that?' I looked back and saw him shaking his head. I shot 81 that day. My emotions overcame my abilities."

How do you prevent this from happening? The answer is relax—physically and mentally. We find that deep breathing, as Snead says, is an effective physical relaxation method. The next time you're standing nervously on the first tee, take a deep breath and let it out slowly, right from the pit of your stomach. Do this two or three times, and the slower you exhale, the more relaxed you'll become. Anytime during the round that you feel anxiety overcoming you, try the same technique.

However, no amount of deep breathing will help if you can't rein in your ability to think logically and clearly; you must try to stay on the same emotional level throughout a round. This means not getting too excited over a birdie as well as not getting despondent over a double-bogey. If you make a double-bogey or if you hole a long putt for a birdie to go three under par, you must maintain a certain state of ease and grace, a calm, composed feeling within your mind and body until the round is completed. If you don't, your body mechanisms are going to speed up to the extent that you can't control your swing.

Once, playing with Peter Kostis, Jim Flick made a hole-in-one. Obviously elated, he turned to Kostis, who said, "Don't get excited, Flick, even a stopped clock is right twice a day." Worthy advice indeed.

Naturally, the despondency over a double-bogey is harder to conquer than the elation that comes from making a birdie. This is where a sound philosophical approach becomes so necessary. In every round of golf, some undesirable things will happen to you. It's an old saw but an apt one that "golf was not meant to be a fair game." The golfers who seem to play most consistently are those who can accept the bad breaks and not let it affect their shotmaking. Every time you play you are going to lip out some putts, get some bad bounces and find your ball in some bad lies. You have to develop a philosophy that says, "Okay, this is one of those times. These are the averages, and I'm still going to make the best shot I can. It's all going to even out in the long run."

The best philosophy in the world is of no use, of course, unless you can implement it on the course. For example, when you are playing well, you are in a special state. You are seldom aware of what your body is doing. Your mind is clear, uncluttered with swing mechanics or irrelevant thoughts. You clearly visualize how you want to execute each shot before you strike it. You feel comfortable, neither too relaxed nor too tense. You swing with a controlled abandon, relaxed and confident of the outcome. You seem to be almost in a trance, with nothing on your mind except your enjoyment at seeing the ball fly to the target. Perhaps you can recognize this phenomenon in some of the best rounds you have played.

How do you achieve and maintain this euphoric state? The obvious answer is concentration, but most of us don't really know what that means. The word frightens us a little, because most people think concentration means going out and keeping your attention directed to your goal for four solid hours. You can't force your mind to stay hemmed in that long. Ideally, you want to be able to concentrate for the 20 seconds or so that it takes to approach and make each shot. To us, concentration means the ability to keep in your mind positive pictures of what you want to do.

This gets back to relating to what you've done well in the past. Johnny Miller credits much of his success to the brilliant final-round 63 that won the 1973 U.S. Open for him at Oakmont. Now he says he can see a successful conclusion to every shot. "Before that I didn't think I could handle pressure," he admits. "I wasn't any different than anybody else in this respect, but I thought I was. Now I can relate to success."

Not many of us have a 63 in the U.S. Open to relate to, but we all have hit good shots. As time goes on, you will hit more. These are the shots you want to remember, not the bad ones.

To concentrate effectively, you must stay in the present tense, which simply means you should be concerned about the shot at hand rather than worrying about the tough 16th coming up or that green you just three-putted. It's a cliche, but it can't be emphasized too strongly: The most important shot in golf is the shot you're preparing to play.

Here's a good way to identify whether you're keeping your mind in the present tense. When you finish 18 holes of golf and it seems like you've only been on the course for 20 minutes, you can be sure your mind was clear, alert and in the present and you were using it effectively. On the days when you're not thinking well and your mind's effectiveness has been diluted by worries about outside problems, it will seem as if you've been on the course for a month.

In many cases, the distractions of the golf course itself—other players, the wind, the hazards—will make your mind wander. Or you're thinking about something at home or at your job, which keeps you from directing your attention to the shot at hand. Too often you start thinking about the rewards for winning—or the consequences of losing.

In the 1974 World Open at Pinehurst, Frank Beard was on the verge of breaking a long slump. But he missed an eight-foot birdie putt on the first hole of a playoff with Johnny Miller, Jack Nicklaus and Bob Murphy, then lost to Miller's birdie on the next hole. "I got in my own way," Beard said afterward. "I started thinking about the money and what I was going to say at the presentation ceremony."

How many times have you gotten within three holes of your best score ever and then tried to protect that score? You began to over-control the club and take away the very motion you'd been using successfully for 15 holes. . . .and you probably finished in a state of collapse.

We think this is what happens when players apparently choke during a round. They haven't disciplined their minds to let the subconscious work. When the shot becomes important, they try to be so careful and protective that they don't allow the swing just to happen. They won't trust it, so they consciously try to control it.

The mind is never a void. It contains either positive or negative thoughts. In instances like this, the player stops thinking about the results and starts thinking about the consequences. The negative thoughts crowd out the positive ones.

Hubert Green won the 1977 U.S. Open at Southern Hills in Tulsa. To do it he had to make a four-foot putt for a bogey on the final hole after he bunkered his second shot and ended up well short of the hole on his explosion from the sand. Afterward, he said: "I stood out there before my second shot and told myself not to hit it in the left bunker. So that's exactly where I hit it. When I went into the trap to hit the sand shot, I said, 'Don't chunk it.' So I did."

That happens to the best of players. The mind reacts to the negative thought. The player consciously tries to direct his shots and ruins the fluid pattern of his swing. We don't think players choke. We think they over-try.

Just the opposite kind of story came from Jack Nicklaus after he had won the 1976 World Series of Golf with an exceptional display of putting. "I had it in my mind that I was going to make every putt," Jack said. "I wasn't worrying about which side I was going to miss it on but whether it was going to go in the center or not."

The good player tries to develop a vivid target picture and a preprogrammed feel for the swing that will let him overcome all distractions. His approach to the shot is one in which he simply sets up and hits it. He's not bogged down with details and is secure in the knowledge that his swing can perform.

If you don't have this kind of strong picture, you won't go at the shot with a feeling of control and determination. You'll start wishing the ball around the course, and that never works for very long.

That attitude crops up often in putting. Either you'll develop a negative approach to the putt or you'll take it for granted it's going to go in. In either case, the result is a tentative stroke and usually a missed putt.

You can handle this by telling yourself that with all the hours you've spent working on your putting, it doesn't make sense not to do the best you can with the chance you have right here. *Always follow a good shot with a good shot.* We see too many players make a fantastic recovery shot and then not finish the hole with every bit of concentrated effort they can muster. Bob Murphy once remarked that he tries harder after a super shot than he did before. He doesn't want to get in the careless habit of taking for granted that just because he played a great shot to within four feet of the hole that the ball is automatically going to jump in the cup for him.

You owe it to yourself to develop that same determined attitude. All the great teams in sport—the old New York Yankees, the Green Bay Packers, the Boston Celtics—took advantage of their opponents' mistakes and their own good breaks. They seemed to try harder at that point. The killer instinct, it's called.

In golf, the killer instinct that lets you take advantage of good breaks and good shots doesn't come from

trying hard in the sense that you develop physical tension. It comes from your mind, directing your full attention to the job at hand, coolly reviewing what you must do to get it done and developing that clear target picture that lets it happen.

That's why it's so important in golf to understand the fundamentals. Your mind and body will be that much more ready for the act and be able to perform it more consistently under all circumstances.

That fundamental knowledge also helps you trust that what you're doing is right in the long run. To maintain your confidence and composure when the bad shots occur, as they will, don't be overly critical of yourself. We once saw Jack Nicklaus half-top a short wedge shot from what looked like a perfectly good lie. Asked about it later, he said in all seriousness, "I had a very thin lie." The point is, he was putting the blame somewhere other than on his own swing. Thus he did nothing to tear down the confidence he has built in his skills. That may be a rationalization, but in this case it's a healthy one.

A loser will hit a bad shot and call himself a dummy. A winner will never do that. He will never degrade himself or lower his self-esteem.

The winner is a realist. He knows that every shot won't come off exactly as he had planned. Most of them won't, in fact. He doesn't make the mistake that too many golfers do of trying to make perfect swings instead of playable swings. That puts a pretty heavy burden on you and creates a lot of unwanted tension. Good players really don't care how the ball gets to the target as long as it gets there. They're prouder of their effective misses than most golfers are of their great shots.

Realism also means that when you go out to play, you must take the swing you have and live with it. It it's a "C" swing at the moment, don't expect to make an "A" score with it. You'll be less frustrated and have more fun—and because you can stay relaxed in the face of poor shots, you may even end up scoring a bit better than you know how.

Beware, however, of a peculiar phenomenon. As your swing and your playing ability continue to improve, you'll go through "comfort zones" in your scoring. Your scoring zone might be 105 or 94 or 75, but anytime you get in the area of that score you'll be pleased. And it won't really seem to make any difference what kind of course you're playing.

So while your swing might get better as time goes on, your score may not. If you have your mind focused on a number that you think you should shoot, you'll find a way to make that number. That's why a player so often plays a super front nine holes, then has a poor back nine. As soon as he gets two or three shots ahead of where he nor-

mally plays, he subconsciously feels he can waste two or three shots and still stay within his comfort zone. So he wastes them. Without realizing it, he's striving for that comfort zone.

To overcome this phenomenon—and to overcome a bad start to your round or a bad hole as well—learn to play each stroke for what it is, which is just one stroke to be counted in the total at the end of the round. For example, when you knock your second shot eight feet from the hole on the hardest par 4 on the course, how many times do you make the birdie putt? Probably not very many, because you allow yourself to get excited over the possibility of a birdie. Given that same putt for a par or a bogey, the chances are greater you'll make it. In the first instance, you unconsciously feel you'll be gaining something on the course if you make a birdie, and that thought causes your mind to be diverted. Yet an eight-foot putt for a par or bogey counts exactly the same at the end of a round as an eight-footer for a birdie.

You can never get out of your particular comfort zone until you stop anticipating a total score. There are no bogeys or pars or birdies. There are just strokes, and at the end of the round you add them all together to see what you shot.

*Competitive pressure.* To the three stages of your golf swing—the practice swing, the practice tee swing and the swing on the course—can be added a fourth, you swing under competitive pressure. To be able to compete effectively is really what almost everybody who plays golf is striving for, whether he or she realizes it.

We can teach you to become perhaps a super striker of the ball, but competitiveness is something that comes from within the individual. You either have it or you don't, which is not to say that you can't develop it.

To become competitive, you must place yourself in competitive situations, whether it be a tournament or simply a serious $2 Nassau bet. Find out how you react to competitive. Do you relish it and seem to play better because of it, or do you have the feeling you can't handle it and want to run away? Do you anticipate making a pressure shot on which all the bets are riding, or do you shrink from it? If the latter is your attitude, there are several things you can do to overcome it.

First, of course, forget the consequences of the shot and focus your attention only on the target and what you must do to make the ball go to the target.

Identify the weaknesses in your game and battle them until you feel more competent, which will give you the ability to respond positively in competitive situations. Rather than playing "winter rules," play the ball as it lies in all situations, because

that will give you confidence down the road. Go to the back tees, even though you may feel you're not quite ready to handle the course from back there.

We fight to protect our egos, but your ego can't get any better if you don't keep challenging it. Soon you'll begin to want that challenge and will be able to accept it in a positive way. You'll begin to feel you can handle whatever develops on the course, and you'll look forward to making shots from uncomfortable situations. When you reach this stage, you can be an effective competitor.

Competitiveness must be channeled properly, of course, and competition must always be placed in proper perspective. Unless you're playing it for a living, golf should always be fun. You're out there for exercise and relaxation, to get away from the tensions of business or family problems. The game is not life or death. A golf course is a playing ground, not a battleground. It doesn't care whether you shoot 65 or 105. Compete against the course on that basis. Accept the challenge it poses, which is simply to get around it in the lowest possible score. Don't go to war with it.

Compete against your playing partners on that same basis. Everybody instinctively wants to win, to prove his or her superiority. The fun comes in playing well and in winning, and we would never tell

273

you not to try to do both. But if you place too high a premium on it, if you put so much pressure on yourself that your mind and body can't handle it, all you've done is defeat yourself.

Dr. Cary Middlecoff, one of golf's all-time greats, says that when he faced a pressure situation he would tell himself that if he didn't pull off the shot, his wife would still love him and he'd still have steak for dinner that night. In other words, it wouldn't be the end of the world. If you can adopt that kind of attitude, you will learn to control yourself under pressure and, in the process, become a much better competitor.

## Control of your game

To this point, we have discussed how to make better shots on the golf course. What follows will help you in relation to your goal of getting around the course in the fewest possible strokes.

To become a better course manager, you have to become a better self-manager. The first factor in achieving self-management is a knowledge of yourself, a realistic evaluation of what your swing can do and the shots you can play, of your abilities at the time you are playing—not last week, not next week, but *now*. You must have a knowledge of the strengths and weaknesses of the golf course at the time you are playing it, which takes into account weather conditions, distance, hole layout and hazards. Finally, you must be aware of the situation—whether you are playing the member-guest tournament, the club championship, your regular foursome or are just out there fooling around. All of these factors have an effect on your composure and your physical ability to play a shot.

This knowledge can produce mental relaxation. That breeds confidence and promotes self-management, which allows you to manage the course successfully.

Course management means playing tactical golf by planning each hole. Know where the hole goes and devise a plan for playing it. Be in command of the golf course. The course is just lying there. It won't command you unless you let it. Find a way to get in position to beat each hole. Position golf is practical golf; power golf is poor golf.

Even the top professionals who play power golf get into trouble. Of the 150 or so pros who tee it up in tour events every week, only a small percentage drive the ball consistently enough to put it where they want it. But the professional can survive because of his strength and his ability to play recovery shots that sometimes are unbelievable. If you don't have this strength and recovery ability, you should play for position and stay out of trouble at all cost. You might think you're losing some strokes by not getting all the possible distance and firing at every flag, but you're not losing nearly as many as you would by hitting it into the ninny-bushes on every hole.

The key to playing the game well is to keep the ball in play and minimize the number of penalty strokes. Play a round of golf and see if you can eliminate all penalties. Note how much that lowers your score.

By keeping the ball on the fairway, you give yourself a lie that is more conducive to playing a good shot than any other lie on the course. You don't have to contend with rough, sand, trees or water. Even if you take a longer club to get to the green, you can manage it much better off the short grass.

We have an exercise we use with students that teaches them the value of eliminating penalty shots and shots out of trouble. During a playing lesson, if the player knocks the ball out-of-bounds or in the water or anywhere off the fairway, we have him put the ball back in the fairway and give him a 10-yard penalty. That's the difference of just one club or so, depending on the player. We find that if the player can stay in the fairway, even with that 10-yard distance penalty, he can save about 10 strokes a round.

Staying in the fairway eliminates the double- and triple-bogeys that are usually the result of poor planning rather than poor execution. For instance, if you see two bunkers

guarding a rather tight landing area for your drive, don't take a driver unless you're certain you can control the ball enough to put it between the bunkers. Play a lesser club so you won't reach the bunkers. Depend on a longer club to put your next shot on the green instead of attacking the hole, putting your ball into a bunker and turning a 4 or 5 into a 6 or 7.

By using a 3-wood instead of a driver, you probably lose only a couple of clubs' worth of distance. But most golfers don't use the 3-wood because they haven't learned to trust the fact that they have 14 clubs in the bag. Learn to play with and trust all of your clubs.

Of course you will miss some fairways and greens no matter how well you plan, simply because you are human. But you can plan for that eventuality, too. Play toward the side of the fairway that gives you the most margin for error and penalizes you the least if you miss it. Evaluate the strengths and weaknesses of each hole before you tee your ball.

During a playing lesson in one of our schools, we came to a straightaway par-4 hole with bunkers on each side in the landing area. One student remarked that neither side was weaker than the other. But we pointed out that one was—the bunker on the right was a lot shallower than the one on the left. If you landed in the right-hand bunker, you could get out with a much longer club that would either get you on the green or close enough to it to minimize your chances of error on the third shot. From the left-hand bunker, all you could do was pitch back to the fairway.

When we came to a hole with water on one side and trees on the other, many of our students became so intimidated they failed to think clearly. They just hit and hoped without a plan. But the plan on the that hole really was quite clear. It was better to be in the trees than in the water. You can't play out of water; it's an automatic penalty. And we're trying to eliminate the penalty factor.

The same kind of thinking must go into shots played to the green. For example, if the flag is tucked into the right corner of the green behind a bunker, you can fire right at it if you're a good bunker player, because you know your chances are good of getting down in two shots if you miss the green. But if you're a poor sand player, you'd better plan to stay out of the bunker at all cost. Maybe the green is bunkered on the other side, too, but at least if you pull your shot into that one you have more green to work with getting out.

These are the things you must be aware of on the course. It sounds simple to read it here, but it's surprising how they're overlooked while you're playing.

Course strategy, then, is really a simple thing: *Just choose a path to the target that gives you the most margin for error and offers you the best position from which to make your next shot.* That means putting your ball, if possible, in a place that offers the largest target area into the green, gives you the greatest chance for success and offers the least penalty if you mis-hit it.

The best possible spot for your next shot may not always be the safest spot to aim for, of course. If this is the case and you have some doubts about your ability to put your ball there, then choose the safest route instead, even if it means a harder job on the next shot. In most cases, you'll have some kind of a shot to the green from anywhere on the fairway, but if you get your ball behind some trees you've reduced you chances considerably.

The story is told of an observer who watched Ben Hogan when he won the 1951 U.S. Open at Oakland Hills. After the first round, the witness remarked that Hogan was the luckiest player he had ever seen, because Ben always had a level lie for his second shot while his playing partner was contending with uphill, downhill and sidehill lies on the rolling Oakland Hills course. During the second round, the observer changed his mind, because he noticed Hogan was playing his second shots from exactly the same spots he had played from the day before. Ben had learned the most advantageous positions in which to hit his tee shots and was putting the ball there time after time.

You can do the same sort of planning, but to do it you must evaluate your own abilites realistically. Chances are you can't control your shots as well as Ben Hogan—we don't know of anybody who could— so you must choose a target area that will accommodate your own tendencies. Determine your ball dispersion pattern by hitting, say, 10 shots with a particular club and measuring the size of the area the balls cover. Then find a target area into which you can fit that dispersion pattern.

Stick with that plan throughout the round. Play within your capabilities and don't try to hit shots you know you haven't perfected and can't pull off. Don't try to knock a 5-iron shot at a flag tucked into a 20-foot space behind a bunker if you're not capable of making that shot consistently.

If you know you're not a strong long-iron player and your chances of putting the ball on the green from 180 yards out are poor, your target area should be the front of the green. Take less club, then chip the ball up and try to make your par instead of putting the ball in the bunker and maybe making 6 instead of 5 or 4.

Hank Johnson, head professional at North River in Tuscaloosa, Alabama, and an instructor in our schools, says it so well: "When you're getting ready to play a shot, you should decide where your average shot would end up if you had to hit that shot 10 times."

A disciplined player will reach the point where his mind just won't let him take a poor percentage shot. It will force him instead to hit the shot with the greatest chance of success. That's a shot on which you can swing without excessive tension, just trying to meet the ball solidly. If you do, it will end up somewhere on the fairway or on or around the green. If you miss it, your ball will still wind up somewhere in play.

Always try to match your strengths against the weaknesses of the hole, if possible. As an exercise, mentally review your golf course and rate the landing area on each green from 1 to 4, number 1 being probably the most ideal position but also the most difficult to hit. Number 4 is the weakest part of the hole insofar as it's the easiest area for you to fit your ball pattern into. Your target and the numbers may vary depending on the pin position, of course, but you get the idea. Rate the fairway on each hole the same way, number 1 being ideal (hardest) and number 4 being the easiest.

Now, during the warm-up session before you play, rate yourself honestly, according to your abilities that day. If you're hitting the ball about as well as you can hope to, that's number 1. If you rate yourself

4, maybe you should have stayed home and mowed the lawn, but you still must play because the rest of your group is counting on you.

Say you rate yourself 2 for the day. You're hitting it pretty well but not perfectly. Then you should be able to try for target 2, 3 or 4 on each fairway and green. *(See illustration, right.)*

At this point, you have to be careful in realistically assessing your abilites. Perhaps your number 1 swing is still not good enough to put the ball consistently into the number 1 target area. In that case, no matter how well you are swinging, you might never be able to go for number 1 until you improve.

Also, your ball-striking ability may change after that initial warm-up session, so you must keep re-evaluating it during the round. You may start hitting the ball better—or worse—so you must keep yourself apprised of the changes if you're going to score your best.

In any event, at no time should you shoot for a lower number on the course than the number at which you are currently evaluating your abilities. If you do that, you'll more often than not put a higher number on the scorecard when you finish. *Never let your anxieties exceed your abilities,* no matter how strong the temptation. You might miss out on some of those miracle shots that draw cheers from your fellow players, but you'll probably wind up with a score that draws money from their pockets.

One of the most important factors in planning the play of a hole is correct club selection. Most players seldom choose enough club, simply because they have an inflated idea of how far they can hit an iron shot with control. It's particularly amazing how far people try to hit sand wedges and pitching wedges. We see them trying to hit those clubs 110 and 120 yards. Bob Toski never tries to hit a pitching wedge more than 100 yards. He'll hit a 9-iron 120 yards, an 8-iron 130, a 7-iron 140, a 6-iron 150, a 5-iron 160, a 4-iron 170, a 3-iron 180 and a 2-iron 190 or at the most 200 yards, depending on how much green he has to work with and how well he is swinging. But those are his limitations. And Toski can drive the ball 260-270 yards consistently, as long as most of the players on tour.

It's not important that you hit an iron a long way; it's important that you get it close. What is better, to hit a 7-iron 10 feet from the hole or an 8-iron 30 feet away?

You will always hit a better shot into the target with a three-quarter swing and more club than you will with less club and a full swing. An easier, smoother swing will give you the keen sense of timing and arm speed you need to direct the ball to the target. Any good player who has played for some time no longer beats the hell out of the ball as he

## Rate your ability against the course
*Before you play on any given day, honestly rate your abilities, how well you are striking the ball during your warm-up session. Then realistically match your ability against the strengths and weaknesses of the course. If you feel you are good enough to attack the strongest part of each hole, then go for the No.1 positions. If your ability is less than that, go for No.2 or 3 or 4, whichever you feel you can make with the greatest consistency. Keep re-evaluating your ability level during the round.*

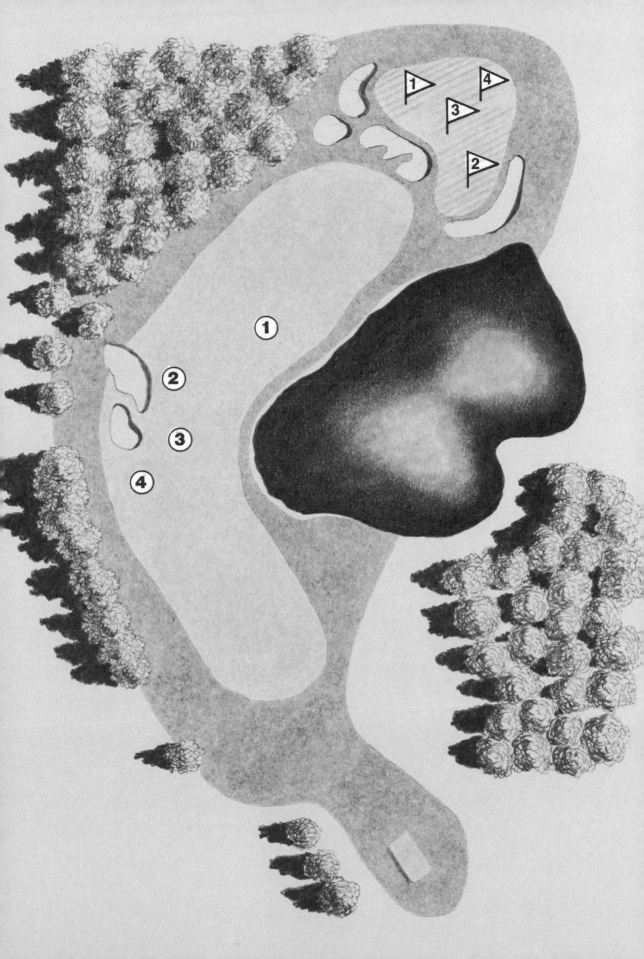

did when he was a kid. He's found by trial and error that he's had to go down a club or two to get more control and strike the ball closer to the flag. He's become wiser and more mature.

Consider the wind. Anybody who has played at all knows that you should take less club it you are playing downwind and more club if the wind is against you. But have you considered that a crosswind also hinders the flight of the ball and requires a longer club to get to the target?

Do you take into account the terrain of a hole? If you are firing uphill at the flag, take one or two longer clubs, depending on the steepness of the grade. If your target is downhill, less club is required.

What do you do when you find your ball in a bad lie, take the same club you would from a good lie and try to force the ball up and out to the target? If so, you'll lose your arm flow, you'll get your body ahead of the shot and you'll lose all your power. You'll either mis-hit the shot completely and advance it only a few yards down the fairway or you'll end up in a bunker or the rough.

Instead, try taking a more lofted club, play the ball back in your stance and swing easily. You might be surprised at what happens. With the more lofted club you'll have more confidence in your ability to get the ball out of a bad lie and you'll make a better swing. By play-

ing the ball back in your stance you have delofted the club and will get more distance out of it than normal. The fact that the ball is coming out of a tight lie will make it run more than usual. You might find yourself in the middle of the green even if you weren't trying to get there. At the very least, you'll be in good position for a pitch and putt that will save your score on the hole.

*Playing a round of golf* can be divided into three areas: *long game, short game and putting.* The long game is everything that requires a full swing. The short game is primarily from 75 yards on in for most players—anything from the edge of the green back to the point they begin making full swings. The putting game is self-explanatory.

As we indicated in the early part of this chapter, mistakes within these areas always fall into three categories: mental preparation, setup and alignment, swing motion.

Let's look at some statistics involving these three categories to see how some people actually play. In a Golf Digest school evaluation session, we watched players of all handicap levels, all former participants at our schools, play nine holes. During that play, 52 percent of the swings we saw were good. Eighty-one percent of the time the setup and alignment were faulty; which means that only 19 percent of the time did the players perform acceptably. If we subscribe to the theory that the swing can only be as consistent as the alignment and posture, then these golfers had only a 19-percent chance of making a good swing that would send the ball to the target.

Mental preparation was satisfactory only 27 percent of the time. That figure is low enough as it is, but remember that we include club selection under mental preparation. Disregarding the obvious club selections—a driver off the tee, a sand wedge from a bunker, a putter on the green, which are almost predetermined choices—the mental preparation factor decreased to 11 percent. That's almost nine out of every 10 shots in which the golfers virtually predetermined a bad shot. Even though their swing motions were more than 50 percent good, they really didn't have a 50 percent chance of getting the ball to the target.

Finally, of all the shots we watched, 65 percent were in the short game and putting categories. Probably not many of those students spend 65 percent of their time working on these two areas of the game. How much time do you spend on them?

During that evaluation session, we saw 29 players play one par-3 hole. Of the 29, four put the ball on the green. Only eight took enough club from the tee to let them get the ball on the green. Just one of the 29 hit it past the flag. Four pars were scored, while there were 29 full shots played and 95 pitches, chips, bunker shots and putts—that's 77 percent of the shots on the hole.

We timed the length of preparation these players took. In every case they spent twice as long preparing for the tee shot as they did in playing the pitch or chip shot to the green. And when that shot was not successfully executed, even less time was taken preparing for the next one. One player took 25 seconds getting ready to hit his 7-iron from the tee. He took 15 seconds getting ready to hit his pitch, which he stubbed and left short of the green. He took 10 seconds preparing to hit the chip shot, which he put seven feet from the hole, and only four seconds getting ready to hit the putt.

It's not that they lacked talent, but their tenacity levels were low. They couldn't handle the slightest bit of adversity.

On the other hand, the four players who hit the green from the tee took as much time preparing to make their first putts as they did to hit the shots that put them on the green. That may sound common enough, but the point is that the difference between 6 and 5 is exactly the same as the difference between 5 and 4 or 4 and 3. At the end of the round, each stroke is but one in your total, and you hurt yourself if you give strokes away by failing to prepare yourself. The golf course will take enough from you during an 18-hole round without you giving *it* any bonus strokes.

In about 60 percent of the returns we get from post-school surveys sent to participants, the student reports he or she is hitting the ball better but not scoring better. The statistics we've given you proved why. Do you recognize yourself in any of those examples?

*Playing an actual hole.* We'd like to walk you through the playing of a hole, with some thoughts which may help you when you go out there yourself.

First, always determine the "real" yardage the hole is going to play. That means more than just looking at the scorecard or the tee stanchion. For example, let's say you're playing a 370-yard par 4, but the tee markers are 10 yards behind the stanchion. It's a chilly day, so your swing isn't quite as loose as it normally is, and there's a brisk wind in your face. Each of those factors may add 20 yards to the effective length of the hole. So instead of playing a 370-yard hole you are now playing a 420-yard hole. Realizing that is important to your mental equilibrium. If you are planning to play the hole with a driver and a 7-iron and suddenly find you need a 3-wood instead on your second shot, it can be disconcerting. At that point, you've reduced your chances

of hitting your second shot successfully.

In that regard make a realistic evaluation of what you plan to score on the hole. If you would have to hit two super shots to get to the green, instead plan to make a 5. That will allow you to be more reasonable and confident in your club selections and the path you take to the flag. You'll probably end up closer to the green with your second shot than if you had tried to slug two mighty blows, and you'll have a good chance to get your 4 with a pitch and a putt. If you don't, you had figured to make 5 anyway and so won't be upset as you head for the next tee.

Study the hole beforehand and find out where its strong and weak areas are. Is there a bunker to avoid? Does water come into play? Are there trees? If there are combinations of these hazards, which there usually are, which offers the least penalty? With this in mind, choose the safest area into which you want to put your tee shot and pick out a spot in that area.

Now pick out an intermediate spot on that line and tee your ball accordingly behind that spot. You may occasionally have trouble finding an intermediate spot in the fairway, but there is always something on the tee which can be seen easily. Remember, the rules allow you to tee up as much as two club lengths behind the markers, so you can always use an old divot or a broken tee as your spot.

Go through your preparatory routine and strike your tee shot. If you successfully land it in your intended area, begin to assess your second shot as you walk up to it. If you're going to try for the green, know the distance to the flag so you can make the proper club selection. Determine the largest and safest area of the green into which you can fit your shot, even if it's not directly at the flag. Study your lie, because it can affect all these factors.

If you have decided that 5 is the score you want to make on the hole, plan to hit your second shot into the area that will leave you the easiest, safest approach to the flag. Don't necessarily try to get as close to the green as possible. You might find a full shot with a 9-iron or pitching wedge easier to pull off than a delicate little pitch, particularly if you happen to hit your second shot off line and must play over a bunker.

If you do hit your tee shot or your second shot into trouble, there is a rule of thumb which should guide your decision on the next shot: *Always play the shot you feel you can accomplish at least seven out of 10 times.* Be realistic. If you feel the percentages aren't that much in your favor, select a club you are confident you can hit and choose a safer route. You might feel you're wasting a stroke, but you'll be better off for it in the long run.

The point is, never follow a bad shot with another bad shot or bad decision. When you do, you get yourself into physical trouble and also into a state of emotional upset which can ruin further play on that hole and subsequent holes. Every poor round starts with one bad shot.

*Preparation and slow play.* Everything we learn in golf or life takes some time. It's going to take you some time to learn to prepare yourself for every shot and to become comfortable in your pre-shot routine. You may play more slowly than normal because of this. In that case, you must be courteous—either choose a time to play that is not crowded or let a group through if it is pushing you.

Soon you will learn to make your decisions more quickly and your play will speed up. The way to start that immediately is to begin planning your next shot as soon as your ball comes to rest from the shot you've just struck. Do some of your thinking as you walk down the fairway instead of worrying about your swing or what went wrong on the previous shot. Examine your lie, consider your options, if possible, and be ready to move into your pre-shot routine as soon as it's your turn.

Yes, you're going to be a slow player if you don't give any thought to your shot until it's time to strike it. But if you keep thinking ahead, there is plenty of time for preparation. And the 20 seconds extra you take preparing yourself for the shot isn't going to be nearly as time-consuming as the five minutes required to hunt for your golf ball in the woods because you didn't prepare.

*Know the rules*. Golf is a game played by a set of rules, rules which may seem complicated at first glance but which really are quite simple when the test of common sense is applied. It is to your advantage to know them and to carry a rule book in your bag. Not only might you save yourself from unknowingly committing a violation that could cost you strokes or a match, but there are many times you can take advantage of the rules to improve your position on the course. Unless you know the rules, you might be playing some kind of game out there, but it may not be golf.

## Umbrella drill

Stick your umbrella or an old cut-off shaft into the ground, down your target line in front of your ball. Then try to hit the umbrella handle with your shot. This forces you to elevate your intermediate target from a spot on the ground to something in the air. It develops an awareness of both trajectory and the correct swing path. This drill can be used with all clubs by varying the height of the umbrella either by slanting it more into the ground or moving it closer or farther away. Trial and error will soon tell you how far away and how high to set it for the trajectories with different clubs.

## Ball into clouds

Pick different spots in the clouds and try to hit balls to those spots. You can also practice hitting balls over trees of different heights and at different distances. This helps you visualize trajectory and gets your mind oriented to flight rather than to the ball.

## Play your worst ball

This is the reverse of the individual scramble (see page 260). Hit two balls off the tee and choose the worst shot. Play two balls from that spot, choose the worst shot and play two more. Continue until you get in the hole. This teaches you the importance of keeping the ball in play and achieving consistency in your shot-making, and it helps identify the parts of your game that need the most help.

### Take one more club

Play a round, carefully determine
the club you want for each shot,
then take one more club each time.
You may be surprised how close to
your target you get. This is an important drill in teaching you not to
over-estimate your abilities in making club selections.

### No woods off tee

Play a round without hitting any
woods off the tee. This teaches you
to make different shots with different clubs that you might not get
during a normal round. It also is a
good way to adapt your game to a
longer course you might be planning
to play.

### Target fixation drill

You need a helper for this one. It
can be done either indoors or out.
Pick out a target on the wall or at
some point in the distance, fix that
target in your mind and address the
ball as if you were going to strike it
there. Instead, have your friend pick
up the ball. While you are still looking at the spot where the ball was,
direct him to move the ball along a
line that would get it to the target.
You'll be able to see the ball out of
the corner of your eye, but you can't
see your target. Directing him to
carry the ball on the correct path
and trajectory keeps the image of
the target fixed in your mind. This
drill will help you develop the same
kind of target fixation and ball-flight
projection you should have when
you stand over an actual shot.

## Play with only odd
## or even clubs

This teaches you to hit some less-than-full shots that you might not ordinarily use and makes you aware that there is more than one way to get the ball to the target.

## Shaft aslant in ground

Stick an old shaft in the ground about three or four feet in front of your ball. Set it at an angle that approximately matches the angle of ascent you want with the shot you're going to practice. As you address the ball and eye your target, the shaft keeps you from becoming ball-bound and gets you ball-flight oriented. You'll feel like you are trying to make your lead arm and the clubhead swing on the path indicated by the shaft.

# 12
# HOW TO IMPROVE

If you are going to play golf for the rest of your life, it should be fun. And golf becomes more fun with improvement. That's one reason the game is as frustrating as it is—most people don't improve as much or as rapidly as they would like and, indeed, some get worse instead of better.

People who are successful in their fields tend to forget how long it took them to develop the capabilities that earned that success. They expect golf to be easy. Well, it isn't, even if you have a clear understanding of the game, simply because your muscles won't do what your mind wants until you teach them to do it—and then keep after them so

they don't forget.

Too many amateurs take for granted that once they have learned a shot, it will stay with them; consequently, they don't practice it. The professionals aren't this complacent. Most of you can't practice as much as those who play the game for a living, but your game will get better in direct proportion to how much time you do spend practicing.

Be aware, though, that practice does not necessarily make perfect. *Perfect* practice makes perfect. Don't confuse ball-beating with effective practice that will let you play better. Some people fail to improve, or perhaps get worse, even if they do practice, because they don't use their practice time wisely. They practice the wrong things. They spend time practicing a shot they already hit well, rather than working on something that needs help. Or they concentrate solely on the mechanics of the swing rather than using their minds and time to learn to play better.

In this chapter we will direct you toward a method of constructive practice that will develop the muscles you need in the golf swing, as well as your concept of playing the game more efficiently to shoot lower scores. You'll become aware of the necessity for testing your ball-striking capabilities and evaluating your playing characteristics, both physical and mental. This will steer your practice to the areas where you need it most, at the same time maintaining the strengths you already have in your game.

## Testing and evaluation

The first step in your physical testing program is to find out what your ball-striking capabilities are *right now*. Determine just how consistently you can hit a given club to a given target at a given distance.

The best way to do this, if possible, is to set up target areas on your practice range similar to the diagram on page 261. Mark off boundaries within which you should hit certain clubs at certain distances. For example, set a 10-yard area for the pitching wedge at 100 yards, a 12-yard area for the 9-iron at 120 yards, a 14-yard area for the 8-iron at 130 yards and so on up to a 26-yard area for the 2-iron at 190 yards. Set a 30-yard boundary for your 5-wood at 200 yards, a 32-yard boundary for your 3-wood at 210 yards and a 35-yard area, the width of a normal fairway, for your driver at 230. The distances may have to be adjusted according to your strength factor, but whatever your yardages might be, you should try to see how many shots you can land within those boundaries with each club. If it's not possible for you to mark off your practice range, at least go out some evening when there is nobody around and pace off the area, sighting some landmarks so you have a general idea of the distances and boundaries you're shooting for.

Then take a certain number of practice shots, say 10 or 20 with each club, depending on your stamina, and see how many you can land within the prescribed area. This will tell you clearly what your capabilities are. Obviously, if you can't strike eight to ten 9-iron shots within a 12-yard area and carry them all about the same distance, you need a lot of work with that club. You can similarly evaluate each club right through the bag.

This testing program will point out your deficiencies and tell you where you need to begin your practice program. It will also help you score better immediately, because it will tell what you realistically can and cannot do on the course. It will tell you when you can attempt a shot and when you cannot try one that your testing has shown you can't pull off consistently.

*Expectation always exceeds the realism of execution.* If the latent ego factor which all of us have tells you you can hit this club a certain distance, cut a corner of the dogleg or fly the ball over the lake when your mind and body aren't really prepared for it, you're inviting disaster. If you heed the results of your testing, you'll be able to realistically program your expectations in line with your playing ability. Thus, you can play to get the ball to the green in the best possible manner with the percentages in your favor.

The same procedure can be used to test your short-game skills. See if you can make 10 straight putts from three feet, seven of 10 from six feet, five of 10 from 10 feet. See how many putts you get within tap-in distance from 20, 30 and 40 feet away. See how many chip shots you can stop within a six-foot circle from various distances. Do the same with pitch shots from farther away. See how many shots out of 10 you can hit out of a bunker. See how many of them you can get within six feet, where you have a reasonable chance of making the putt. This type of testing will show you where your weaknesses lie and motivate you to work on them.

Once you have this realistic fix on your ability to strike the ball, evaluate it within the context of your playing ability. Sit down at the end of a round, after the bets are paid and the drinks are drunk, and reflect on how you played both physically and mentally.

From the physical standpoint, evaluate this:

—How many fairways did you hit?

—When you missed a fairway, by how much did you miss it? On which side did you miss it?

—Were you driving the ball farther than normal? Shorter?

—How many greens did you hit with your long irons, and if you missed the green, how close did you come?

—How many greens did you hit with your medium and short irons and how close did you come to your target?

—If you missed the green, how many times did you get down in two shots? How many chip shots from close to the green did you get close enough for a makable putt? How many short pitch shots? How many sand shots?

—How well did you putt? How many three-putt greens did you have? How many short putts did you miss that you felt you should have made? Don't just count the number of putts, because that usually depends on how close you were to the hole to begin with.

## Tighten your dispersion pattern
*Set up a grid similar to this on your practice area, then practice until you can fit your shots into the boundaries for each particular distance.*

290

| WIDTH OF DISPERSION (YARDS) | DISTANCE OF DRIVE (YARDS) |
|---|---|
| 35 | 230 |
| 32 | 210 |
| 30 | 200 |
| 26 | 190 |
| 24 | 180 |
| 22 | 170 |
| 20 | 160 |
| 18 | 150 |
| 16 | 140 |
| 14 | 130 |
| 12 | 120 |
| 10 | 100 |
| | 0 |

Once you pinpoint the areas in which you played well and those you played badly, go a step further and evaluate just why you missed the shots you did. Here you can go right back to the Five P's of preparation, position, posture, path and pace. The mental preparation you make in visualizing your target, aligning your clubface and body and setting up to the ball is almost always reflected in your swing motion.

Did you mis-hit your shots in a consistent pattern? Did your bad shots mostly slice to the right? Did you pull them left? Did you feel yourself swinging too fast, having trouble controlling your pace? Once you have catalogued your errors, you can use your knowledge of the ball-flight influences and the effects of setup and alignment to effectively figure out what you were doing wrong.

First, consider your clubface alignment. Were you aiming on line? Then reflect on your posture and position. Were you set up properly with your body aligned parallel left? Look back on your shot patterns to determine whether your path was correct. If not, perhaps your path was influenced by your pace. When the path is lost, it's usually because the pace of the swing was changed with the right hand and arm. Were you trying to hit the shot too hard? Was your swing pace too quick?

All of this might have been influenced by your picture of the target and ball flight and by how you were trying to play the shot, and with which club. If you can realistically evaluate all these factors, you will lay the foundation for an efficient practice session. Instead of just figuring you were swinging badly and wondering why, you'll be able to go to the basics and solve your problems more quickly.

The reason most players score badly is that they prepare badly, both for executing each shot and in planning their rounds. So your next step is to evaluate how you thought your way around the golf course. Did you assess the strengths and weaknesses of each hole? Count your penalty strokes, often an indication of how intelligently you played within your capabilities. Consider why you played the shot you did into each target area, why you chose the club you did. Did you fail to get on the green because you mis-hit the shot or because you had the wrong club in your hands? Did you select a club on the basis of your average shot or perfect shot?

You'll find over a period of time that a pattern to your club selection will emerge. It may be because of the golf course you play, or it may be that you don't like your 4-iron or some other club. Keep track of what clubs you use and how many times you use them over several rounds. Is there a club you purposely avoid or a club you purposely go to even when it might not be the right one?

These statistics are important. They let you know which clubs to work on in practice so you can gain confidence with them and make a realistic club selection on the course.

From all this information you accumulate in your post-round evaluations, you can chart your strengths and weaknesses realistically, so that in practice you can work on the things that will help you improve and practice with a purpose rather than just beating balls.

## The value of drills

If you ever played any kind of competitive sport, ask yourself how much time you spent actually performing your still in competition and how much time you spent doing drills to improve that skill. The answer, as you reflect on it, might surprise you.

Stan Mikita, former coach and player of the Chicago Black Hawks, once told us his team spends 70 to 80 percent of its practice time doing drills. These are professional athletes, the best hockey players in the world, yet they still spend that much time doing drills.

We see in many of our students a great reluctance to do drills. They seem to feel they have no purpose. They don't understand just how significant drills can be in the development of the ability to play better golf. And, as we check on the students who attend our schools, we see that those who make the most

progress are those who continue to do their drills after they've gone home.

The purpose of drills is four-fold:
—to break down bad habits as quickly as possible.
—to identify the correct pattern of movement in the swing.
—to build correct movement and become familiar with the feeling.
—to maintain good habits once you have formed them and keep your muscles in tone.

Specifically, drills are used to develop motion in which the arms swing freely without tension, to pace and direct that motion, to develop proper body action in relation to the arm swing and, finally, to create the maximum amount of motion for the greatest clubhead speed while maintaining those other ingredients. Drills also develop strength that helps you do all this better. Let's look at a few of the drills we've given you in the preceding chapters and see how they work in that regard for a typical student.

In the first stage of development use the *feet-together* drill, described on page 97. That promotes the basic motion you want, which is arms swinging and body following.

The second stage is to develop enough of that motion to get you behind the ball. At the same time, you also have to interject some left-side control. So, to get the feeling of the left arm making the backswing, *swing with the left arm alone (page*

*143).* To get the feeling of what the right arm does in the swing and how little tension there should be, you can *swing with the right arm alone (page 144).*

Once you get the feeling of the left arm pacing the backswing, you want to make that backswing long enough to pull the left side of the body around in front of the right side to get behind the ball. That can be facilitated by *hitting balls from an uphill lie (page 94).*

You probably still will need more strength in your left arm, so work with the *overlap* drill, in which you swing with the right hand placed entirely over the left *(page 142).* This helps you feel that the left arm is doing almost everything in the swing, although it really isn't.

Once you get to the top of the backswing and initiate the forward swing, the first thing that will probably go wrong is the overworking of the hands, specifically the overworking of the right thumb and forefinger. Here's where the *claw* drill *(page 92),* in which the right thumb and forefinger are laid over the top of the shaft, can help. It aids in pacing the change of direction by quieting the right thumb and forefinger so the left hand and arm and the right arm can swing the club forward.

After that you teach the left arm to pace the right arm by taking the *right hand off the club after impact (page 93).*

Finally, if you lose the feeling of

your arms swinging in the forward swing, go the the *right foot-left toe* drill *(page 175).* This prevents you from moving past the ball with your upper body and forces you to swing your arms.

That, in a nutshell, is what drills can do for your swing development. As you've seen, there are many other drills that can cure specific problems and develop specific areas of your game. The chart at the end of this chapter shows you what those drills are and what they can do. Properly incorporated into your practice sessions, they can greatly speed your improvement, because they can help you use your time productively without supervision.

Drills are especially important when you are tired or are swinging poorly. They absolutely force you to use the correct muscles in the swing instead of just standing there beating balls and perfecting your mistakes.

Every drill can be done with every club in your bag. How long you must do a drill as a developmental aid depends on how much you can practice and how hard you work at it. When the time comes that you can do a drill as well with your driver as with your 9-iron, you can stop doing it as a creative tool and begin doing it less frequently for maintenance.

The drills can also be done in combination—use the overlap or claw grip and take the right hand off after impact, or take the right hand off after impact while using the right foot-left toe drill. This can further increase the proficiency of the movement you are trying to develop.

You'll probably find that the drill you do least effectively is the one you need to do the most. And don't be concerned if you don't strike the ball well when you begin doing the drills. As you'll recall, to consistently strike the ball to the target you need a correct setup position combined with a correct motion. In many of your drills you'll be working to improve your motion from a poor setup position. So understand that even though the ball might not be going where you want it to, the drill is improving the particular motion you need help with. Try to make solid contact, but don't worry much about direction until you become skilled in doing the drill.

We can't emphasize too strongly that once you are able to do your drills effectively, keep working with them on a regular, if less frequent, basis to maintain your skills. We find that most players will discontinue the drills that give them the greatest success. As soon as they begin to strike the ball well their tendency will be to forget the drills and merely practice their swings. They then slide back into their old habits, their swings deteriorate and they can't understand why.

That happened once to Jane Blalock, one of the top stars on the LPGA tour. She told us she was doing her drills regularly, but she got to playing so well that she felt she could quit doing them. Then her game deteriorated. Now she understands the importance of doing her drills every day. No matter who you are, a portion of your practice time should always be allotted to doing the drills that relate to your swing problems.

You will even find it helpful to use drills while you are actually playing if you fall into a stretch of faulty swinging. Use a particular drill that relates to your problems in a rehearsal swing. It will quickly re-identify the correct feel and ease your mind. Then simply let your subconscious recreate that feel on your next shot. This can help you get back on the track before the round becomes a total distaster.

Drills, of course, are used not only for swing improvement, but to develop your short game and improve your playing concept. The conceptual drills we've given you can be done off the course without a golf club, to heighten both the mental and physical awareness of what you want to do. Don't neglect your drills in any of these areas if you want to become a well-rounded player who can go out and score a low number on the course, not just hit nice-looking practice shots.

Be careful in doing the drills, though, because there is a possibility of injury if you go at some of them too hard at the start. For example, taking the right hand off after impact may cause you to hurt your left arm if you make a full, forceful swing without having first identified how freely that left arm will swing on the follow-through. Familiarize yourself with each drill by first doing it with a short club in a mini-swing. Get the feel of it and build your strength gradually until you can do it comfortably with a full motion and with every club in the bag.

There are three other things to guard against in doing drills. First, you may develop a tendency to get careless with your setup and alignment. Second, you may tend to neglect your pre-shot routine, which causes it to begin breaking down. Third, you are likely to become too swing-oriented rather than directing your attention to the target.

Knowing this, however, you can overcome the problems. In the drills that call for a normal setup, which most of them do, be precise with your setup and alignment each time you do the drill. For maximum efficiency go through your routine each time you make a swing during a drill, to insure proper blade alignment if nothing else. And always tie your swing together in relation to the target at the end of each practice session. More comments on that in the next section.

We recommend that you don't do drills extensively just before you go out to play. You might do a few,

such as the overlap or the claw, to identify the correct swing feel. But it's more important to maintain your whole-swing thought and your target orientation.

## How to practice

There are four basic kinds of practice:

1. The warm-up session, in which you prepare to play a round of golf.

2. Practice that improves your technique, the parts of your swing.

3. Competitive practice that directs you mentally toward playing the game.

4. Mental practice without a club, which ingrains into your subconscious the feel of the swing and a positive reaction to play situations.

The last three types can be done independently or, preferably, in some sort of combination. It's important that you work on all to develop your game more fully and more quickly.

*Warm-up.* During your warm-up session just before playing, you should not segment your golf swing by thinking of its parts. It's all right to begin your warm-up with a couple of drills, such as feet toghether, the overlap or the claw, to establish the correct feel of the swing. But after that, work strictly with the feel and pace of your motion related to the flight path and the target. Think nothing but forward-swing thoughts, no backswing thoughts whatsoever. Sticking a shaft in the ground down your flight path will help orient you toward trajectory and target.

*Technique.* The practice session on technique differs because you are trying to repair or improve the parts of your swing that are not in satisfactory working condition. In this kind of practice, you should spend about one-third of your time on drills, one-third working on your routine while making shots to the target and one-third improving your short game. Within these boundaries, you can vary the practice to fit specific needs.

There is an axiom in golf that should be your guide: *You play as you practice and you practice as you play.* Your practice habits carry over to the golf course, so if you want to have the best possible playing habits, you had better develop them on the practice tee. Approach each practice shot as if you were playing it on the course. Visualize your target, go through your routine and make the shot as if it meant something. Don't just rake over one ball after another and hit carelessly without any preparatory thought. That's totally unrelated to what you must do on the course and is the surest way to ingrain bad habits. As Bobby Jones once said: "On the golf course you have to hit the first shot, not the eighth." So make every shot on the practice tee your first and most important shot.

As we said earlier, it is often a good idea to go through your pre-shot routine even while doing drills to relate them as closely as possible to your play on the course.

Here are some further guidelines:

—Practice by yourself. Don't make your practice session a social hour. Get off by yourself, if possible, where you can concentrate without distraction.

—Begin your practice session with the short clubs and progress to the longer clubs. Just as you build success patterns from the hole back, beginning with the shorter, easier swing will help you quickly identify the correct swing feel.

—Never practice without first laying a board or couple of clubs on the ground to maintain your alignment and keep your swing on the proper path. You can't use these aids while playing, of course, but the more shots you hit from a proper alignment and the more you keep your swing on path, the easier it is to do when it counts. Without guides in practice, you're apt to fall into sloppy habits that will carry over to the course.

As you practice, don't work on just one thing for an extended period of time. You can lose interest and get careless, which will undo all that you're trying to accomplish. To keep your mind stimulated and your interest high, vary your session by working on several things. For example, hit five balls using the overlap drill and try to feel the left arm swinging you back to the top. Then hit five balls with a different approach, letting the left arm and left knee tie together your forward swing. Hit five more trying to accelerate the club with the left arm, and then five balls which you're trying strictly to strike to the target.

It's important to remember that no matter what parts of the swing you are working on, what drills you are doing, you must always put the parts together before you finish. Always wind up a practice session by hitting several shots in which you try to capture the feeling of the whole swing and your motion and pace related to the target. Even if the parts aren't working quite to your satisfaction, you may have to play the next day, so tie those parts into the best swing you can muster at the moment.

How long you should practice at one time depends on your strength and stamina. In general, we feel you will get more out of your practice if you do it for shorter periods of time with more regularity. We see many people go to the practice tee and stay there for hours. Eventually, the mind lose its stimulus, concentration disappears and the body tires. This is especially true with drills, which often sap your energy more than a normal swing.

If you sense this happening to you during a practice session and you still wish to continue, take a rest from your full swings and go chip and putt for awhile. This will give you a different mental approach and is less tiring. Then you can return refreshed to your full-swing workout.

You should practice your short game just as you do your full-swing shots. Assess your strengths and weaknesses, what kind of errors you are making. Is your club-ball contact good? Are you playing the right type of shot? Do your mistakes come from poor shot decisions, from setup and alignment or from faulty motion? What causes the motion to go wrong? Do you have enough arm swing so your hands don't have to overwork?

Use the short-game drills we've given you just as diligently as you use the full-swing drills. But always wind up making whole swings, hitting shots to a target and relating your motion to the distance you need to get there.

Putting is perhaps the most mispracticed area of the game, simply because people don't take time to identify the real pattern to their misses. Are your putts missed short, long, left, or right? Do the misses come from misreading the break or from misjudging the speed?

We see too many golfers spending time working only on their strokes rather than working on getting the ball into the hole. They throw down a bunch of balls and hit one after another from the same spot trying to develop their mechanics. Stroke execution is important, of course, but the mental decisions you make, the judgment and touch you develop on the greens are equally important.

Take one or two balls and putt them around the practice clock. Work on your procedure, on reading the green, on uphill, downhill and sidehill putts. Most emphatically, work on the speed of your putts, a factor that is sadly neglected by most players and that costs them more strokes than anything else on the greens.

This is an example of practice that *directs you mentally toward playing golf.* A good portion of the time you spend practicing all aspects of your game should be devoted to this.

*Competitive practice.* Paul Runyan, our colleague on the Golf Digest Professional Instructional Staff and one of the country's outstanding teachers, recommends what he calls *competitive practice.* When you're practicing sand shots, for example, don't just work on your swing. Work on getting the ball close to the hole. Try to get so many shots—two or four or six, depending on your skill level—within four feet of the hole. Try to get so many chip shots within tap-in range. Try to get so many pitch shots within six feet. Try to make so many putts out of 10 from six feet, from 12 feet. Try to putt around the practice clock in so many strokes. Set some standards and try to exceed them, and keep

adjusting those standards higher as your skill increases.

An excellent way to work on your mental direction is to play your course from the practice tee. Imagine the first hole, hit your tee shot and, depending on how well you hit the drive, select the club you think you might need for the second shot. Play that shot to your imaginary green. If you think you would have missed the green with that shot, imagine yourself in a recovery situation, where you must pitch or chip the ball. Once you hit that shot, go on to the next imaginary tee and play that hole. Play all 18 holes in that manner, working on the pace and motion of your swing directed to the target on each shot.

Competitive practice and playing an imaginary round in this manner can help bridge the transition from practice tee to golf course. To complete this transition, spend time actually practicing on the course. Go out in the evening when nobody is around and play three balls for a few holes. Play different shots from the same position but from different lies. Drop half a dozen balls in a bunker and play them out. Practice from the rough, which is something we seldom see anybody do. Try to draw or fade the ball around obstacles. Find our your best shots under playing conditions. Try to make shots you probably wouldn't attempt during a round that means something, because only by doing it

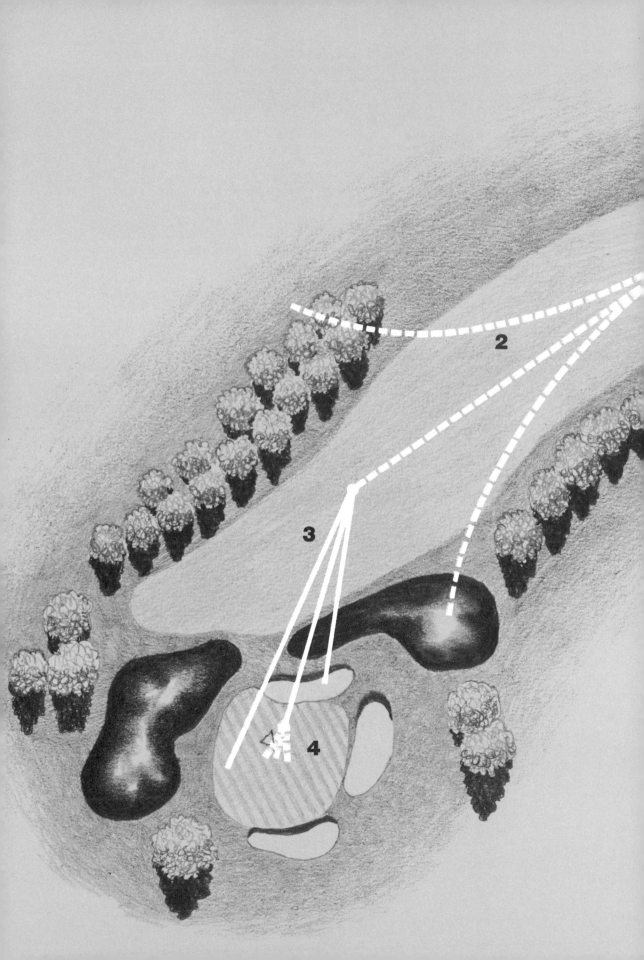

1

## Play your own scramble
To determine your true potential, practice on the course by playing your own scramble. Play two, three or four balls, according to your handicap. Pick your best shot each time and hit all the balls again from that spot, continuing right on into the cup. At the end of the round, your score will give you a realistic indication of your ability. Also, if your first shot is in good position, it will give you a chance to try different shots under actual play conditions with the other balls.

on the course can you develop the skill and confidence to execute these shots when it counts.

Peter Kostis has devised a method that will help build your confidence by showing you your true potential. He calls it playing your own scramble. If your handicap is 0-9, you're allowed two balls; if it's 10-19, you get three balls; if it's 20 or more, play four balls. Hit all the balls from the tee, pick the best shot and play all the balls again from that spot. Continue this way right into the cup. At the end of the round, add up your score and you'll have a pretty realistic estimate of your ability. The more consistently you can hit your best shots, the closer you can come to this potential.

All of this practice involves physical procedure, of course, but that procedure requires mental direction. So it relates more closely to your ultimate goal, which is getting around in the fewest strokes possible, than if you were just working on your swing on the practice tee.

Finally, _mental practice,_ done without a club in your hands, can be performed anywhere—in your easy chair, at night in bed, in your car while driving to the course. Rehearse in your mind the feel of your swing and the keys you need to achieve that feel. Johnny Miller once remarked that while he did not hit a lot of balls on the practice tee, he did spend a lot of time at home just thinking about his swing and his game. You probably will need more physical work than Miller, but you can benefit from mental imagery as well.

Rehearse play situations in your mind. Imagine yourself hitting shots under all conditions. Just before you drop off to sleep at night, go over the round you intend to play the next day. Play each shot in your mind, from first tee to 18th cup. In all of these mental endeavors, of course, imagine a successful conclusion to every shot. You don't build subconscious confidence by rehearsing your duck-hooks and shanks.

Sam Snead once told us that before he was to tee off in the Masters he would play the Augusta National course in his mind, shooting scores like 63 and 62 and 59. "I'd never make a bogey," Sam says, "I'd always have the ball in there close."

If this seems a fruitless exercise, just consider that the mind controls the body. Any success patterns you can program into your mind before you play are bound to be reflected in your physical performance on the course.

## Attitude

Attitude is all-important in establishing your learning curve, your ability to progress and improve your swing and your skill in playing golf. Every student learns in a different manner and at a different pace. Don't be discouraged if your practice sessions don't seem as productive as you think they ought to be, if your progress isn't as quick and steady as you expect. There will always be plateaus in your learning curve, periods in which you seem to go for some time without improvement. But stay at it, because with proper application you soon will climb to a higher peak.

You don't get better by forcing improvement. You get better by letting it happen, by building on your knowledge through the use of drills and other well-directed practice. Keep coming back to the things you know you should be doing. Do them a little bit better the next time, a little better the time after that, until you ingrain the correct swing habits and thought processes. Avoid frustration by realizing that it's going to take some time, and be prepared to spend that time.

## Overall conditioning

A final word on improvement—don't limit your exercise to golf drills. There are those who contend that golfers are not athletes. To that we can only reply that, in our opinion, golf requires more physical coordination and more mental control to play well than any other sport. Strength and endurance are important, because once fatigue sets in, both your physical ability to execute and your ability to control the mind deteriorate.

So anything you can do to improve your overall physical condition will benefit your play. Squeeze a rubber ball to build up strength in your left hand and forearm. Do exercises that strengthen your back and abdominal muscles. Jog or ride a bicycle. If possible, walk instead of riding in a golf car when you play—it keeps you in better touch with the game and the course, it develops leg strength, and over an 18-hole round you will burn up as many calories as you would by running two miles.

Have your physician set up such an exercise program that meets your needs, then stick to it. The payoff will come in your ability to perform at your best over an entire round. You'll also have the strength and stamina to practice more productively for longer periods and more quickly get the improvement you're after.

# DRILL CHECKLIST

## The purposes of drills

1. Develop maximum motion, arms swinging freely without tension.
2. Develop speed
3. Develop proper pace
4. Develop proper path
5. Develop proper angle of approach
6. Develop proper body motion
7. Develop proper leg action
8. Develop strength
9. Develop proper setup, alignment and optics
10. Develop proper concepts

## Swing improvements

Claw, p. 92
Constant light grip pressure, p. 92
Keep a coin between your thumbs, p. 92
Align with a two-by-four, p. 93
Right hand off after impact, p. 93
Don't ground club, p. 94
Swing from uphill lie, p. 94
Visualization drill, p. 95
Use clubs for alignment, p. 95
Swing with heels off ground, p. 96
Use a mirror for optic line, p. 96
Feet-together drill, p. 97
Swing left arm down inside the backswing path, p. 142
Use a board for proper swing path, p. 142
Overlap right hand for left-side control, p. 142
Closed-stance drill, p. 143
Swing with left arm alone, p. 143
Swing with right arm alone, p. 144
Rotation with overlap grip, p. 144
Extended arm rotation, p. 145
Set and swing, p. 145
Strike and hold, p. 146
Back-to-target drill, p. 147
Inside-stripe drill, p. 147
Extra ball drill, p. 148
Inside-loop drill, p. 148
Hit balls off your knees, p. 149
Hit balls from a chair, p. 149
Hit balls off each leg, p. 149
Preset impact drill, p. 150
Toe-up to toe-up drill, p. 150
Tee to re-tee drill, p. 151
Right foot—left toe, p. 175
Right foot behind left, p. 175
Use a whippy shaft, p. 176
Baseball drill, p. 176
Tee ball high, p. 176
Swish drill, p. 177
Swing a weighted club, p. 177
Flip drill, p. 178
Full motion—half speed, p. 178
Left foot off ground at top, p. 178
Split grip, p. 179
Walk-through or machine-gun drill, p. 179
Arm swing—knee fling, p. 193
Stop at the top, p. 194

## Drills to improve pitching and chipping

Claw, p. 92
Right hand off after impact, p. 92
Overlap right hand for left-side control, p. 142
Swing with left arm alone, p. 143
Swing with right arm alone, p. 144
Inside-stripe drill, p. 147
Inside-loop drill, p. 148
Toe-up to toe-up drill, p. 150
Preset impact drill, p. 150
Right foot behind left, p. 175
Chip with an extra-long club, p. 235
Hit balls with eyes closed, p. 235
Strike short shots at pie plates, p. 235
Target drill, p. 235
Anti-shank board drill, p. 236
Chip over bag, p. 236

## Drills to improve sand play

Claw, p. 92
Right hand off after impact, p. 93
Feet-together drill, p. 97
Overlap right hand for left-side control, p. 142
Slap drill, p. 236
Perpendicular club in sand, p. 236
Practice off a board in sand, p. 237

## Drills to improve putting

Look at hole, p. 237
Ball-curve drill, p. 238
Use a board for path, p. 239
Putt cross-handed, p. 239
Right arm only, p. 239
Ladder drill, p. 240
Putter-length back drill, p. 240
Circle drill, p. 241
Shaft against arm, p. 241
Strike-and-hold putt, p. 242
Putt with eyes closed, p. 242
Mirror drill, p. 243
Pull ball into hole, p. 243

## Drills for on-course and play orientation

Visualization drill, p. 95
Make a dry run, p. 193
Ball into clouds, p. 285
Umbrella drill, p. 285
Play your worst ball, p. 285
No woods off tee, p. 286
Take one more club, p. 286
Target fixation drill, p. 286
Play with only odd or even clubs, p. 287
Shaft aslant in ground, p. 287

# EPILOGUE

If you have read this book carefully, and if you continue to study it and absorb the thoughts it contains, you will have a better understanding of how the golf swing is executed and how you can apply that knowledge to strike the ball correctly and make lower scores.

This should heighten your motivation, inspire you to greater goals as a player and increase your interest in learning the finer points of the game.

This book gives you a method, a plan that will help you play better golf in the years ahead. It stresses long-range development rather than a quick cure for your problems. History tells us that anything built too quickly crumbles quickly, and golf is no exception. There are thoughts you may be able to use to get immediate but temporary success that will restrict how well you play over the long haul.

So we hope you will give yourself time to learn this method. It took us 25 years to learn what we have put down here. It will take you a lot less time than that if you read, re-read and diligently apply the principles you have read.

How much time it actually takes you to improve, and eventually to reach your full potential, depends on your basic physical skills, your mental awareness and the time you devote to developing these factors. You must realize that often you must regress before you can improve fur-

ther, that temporary setbacks can lead to permanent progress. You must trust your method and stay with your plan long enough to perfect it. If you jump from thought to thought, you'll be unable to translate any thought into swing feel because you never experience it long enough to develop an awareness of what it should feel like, why it works and how you should relate to that thought under playing conditions.

We have fallen in love with golf, and we hope you will, too. We suspect that you already have. But as great as any love is, it has its period of adjustments and frustrations, of tears as well as joy. Golf will bring you many more joys than tears, but you must cope with the lows as well as the highs. We hope this book will create in you an attitude that will let you cope, a willingness to work and persevere that will strengthen you through disappointment and dejection.

Experience in our schools and in the thousands of individual lessons we have given tells us that the students who succeed are those who take a realistic look at their strengths and shortcomings, then develop realistic goals that relate to their practice habits and the amount of time they are willing to spend.

They realize that having a sound plan and staying with it is the best way to reach their true potential. They know you play better golf by forming better mental and physical habits.

The wise golfer knows that he can build a more lasting game and come closer to perfection, but he can never achieve perfection. This approach helps him maintain his emotional equilibrium.

Be realistic about measuring your success and proficiency against the great professional stars. They play golf for a living and must devote more time to it than you probably can ever spare. You should play golf for yourself, not for what others may think, measuring your success not against what Jack Nicklaus has done, but against what you can do. The challenge lies not in conquering golf. The challenge lies in conquering yourself so you can have more fun by playing the game as well as you possibly can.

If you accept that challenge, it can be the beginning of a lifetime of pleasure.